"A masterpiece of language and gender research, and a powerful political intervention in current times. Covering a broad geopolitical spectrum, and employing different theoretical and methodological approaches, this book is an indispensable read for everyone who wants to challenge sexism through intellectual and activist practices."

Tommaso M. Milani, University of Gothenburg
and University of the Witwatersrand, Johannesburg

"Persuasive arguments for revisiting and reinterrogating the central questions for feminists in the 1960s, in relation to linguistically mediated violence, evaluating where progress has been made and where more nuanced contextualised work still needs to be done."

Sara Mills, Emeritus Research Professor in Linguistics
at Sheffield Hallam University

"This collection focuses our attention on the continued verbal and structural violence that shapes and restricts women's experience in the world. The chapters reflect critically on the political, social and interpersonal impact of sexism; they are eloquent in outlining ways in which the world could be different – and in articulating the factors that impede those changes."

Miriam Meyerhoff, Victoria University of Wellington

INNOVATIONS AND CHALLENGES: WOMEN, LANGUAGE AND SEXISM

Innovations and Challenges: Women, Language and Sexism brings together an outstanding collection of internationally recognised researchers to recontextualise some of the questions raised by feminist thinkers 40 years ago. By taking linguistically mediated violence as a central topic, this collection's main objective is to explore the different and subtle ways sexism and violence are materialised in discursive practices. In doing so, this book:

- Takes a multi-stranded investigation into the linguistic and semiotic representations of sexism in societies from an applied linguistic and semiotic perspective;
- Combines critical discourse analysis, multimodality, interactional sociolinguistics and corpus methodologies to look at language, visuals and semiotic resources in the context of consumerist culture;
- Examines the conflicted position of women and the discourses of discrimination that still exist in every strand of modern societies;
- Contextualises pervasive gender issues and reviews key gender and language topics that changed the ways we interpret interaction from the early 1970s until the present;
- Focuses on institutional discourses and the questions of how women are excluded or discriminated against in the workplace, the law and educational contexts.

Innovations and Challenges: Women, Language and Sexism revisits the initial questions posed by the first feminist linguists – where, when and how are women discriminated against and why, in postmodern societies, is there so much sexism in all realms of social life? This book is essential reading for those studying and researching gender across a wide range of disciplines.

Carmen Rosa Caldas-Coulthard is Professor of English Language and Applied Linguistics at the Federal University of Santa Catarina, Brazil. She is also Senior Research Fellow in the English Department at the University of Birmingham, UK, where she taught and researched for many years. She has published widely in the areas of Critical Discourse, Media and Gender Studies.

INNOVATIONS AND CHALLENGES IN APPLIED LINGUISTICS

Series Editor:

Ken Hyland is Professor of Applied Linguistics in Education at the University of East Anglia and Visiting Professor in the School of Foreign Language Education, Jilin University, China.

Innovations and Challenges in Applied Linguistics offers readers an understanding of some of the core areas of Applied Linguistics. Each book in the series is written by a specially commissioned expert who discusses a current and controversial issue surrounding contemporary language use. The books offer a cutting-edge focus that carries the authority of an expert in the field, blending a clearly written and accessible outline of what we know about a topic and the direction in which it should be moving.

The books in this series are essential reading for those researching, teaching and studying in applied linguistics.

Titles in the series:

Innovations and Challenges in Applied Linguistics from the Global South
Alastair Pennycook and Sinfree Makoni

Innovations and Challenges in Language Learning Motivation
Zoltán Dörnyei

Innovations and Challenges: Women, Language and Sexism
Edited by Carmen Rosa Caldas-Coulthard

www.routledge.com/Innovations-and-Challenges-in-Applied-Linguistics/book-series/ICAL

INNOVATIONS AND CHALLENGES: WOMEN, LANGUAGE AND SEXISM

Edited by Carmen Rosa Caldas-Coulthard

LONDON AND NEW YORK

First published 2020
by Routledge
2 Park Square, Milton Park, Abingdon, Oxon OX14 4RN

and by Routledge
52 Vanderbilt Avenue, New York, NY 10017

Routledge is an imprint of the Taylor & Francis Group, an informa business

© 2020 selection and editorial matter, Carmen Rosa Caldas-Coulthard; individual chapters, the contributors

The right of Carmen Rosa Caldas-Coulthard to be identified as the author of the editorial material, and of the authors for their individual chapters, has been asserted in accordance with sections 77 and 78 of the Copyright, Designs and Patents Act 1988.

All rights reserved. No part of this book may be reprinted or reproduced or utilised in any form or by any electronic, mechanical, or other means, now known or hereafter invented, including photocopying and recording, or in any information storage or retrieval system, without permission in writing from the publishers.

Trademark notice: Product or corporate names may be trademarks or registered trademarks, and are used only for identification and explanation without intent to infringe.

British Library Cataloguing-in-Publication Data
A catalogue record for this book is available from the British Library

Library of Congress Cataloging-in-Publication Data
Names: Caldas-Coulthard, Carmen Rosa, author.
Title: Innovations and challenges: women, language and sexism /
edited by Carmen Rosa Caldas-Coulthard.
Description: London; New York: Routledge, 2020. |
Series: Innovations and challenges in applied linguistics |
Includes bibliographical references and index.
Identifiers: LCCN 2019051093 (print) | LCCN 2019051094 (ebook) |
ISBN 9780367133719 (hardback) | ISBN 9780367133726 (paperback) |
ISBN 9780429026140 (ebook)
Subjects: LCSH: Sexism in language. | Language and languages–Sex differences. |
Language and sex. | Women–Language.
Classification: LCC P120.S48 I47 2020 (print) |
LCC P120.S48 (ebook) | DDC 408.1–dc23
LC record available at https://lccn.loc.gov/2019051093
LC ebook record available at https://lccn.loc.gov/2019051094

ISBN: 978-0-367-13371-9 (hbk)
ISBN: 978-0-367-13372-6 (pbk)
ISBN: 978-0-429-02614-0 (ebk)

Typeset in Bembo
by Newgen Publishing UK

I inscribe this work to Malcolm,
English, innumerable.
I offer him that kernel of myself
that I have saved somehow
the central heart that deals
not in words, traffics not with dreams
and is untouched by time, by joy
by adversities.

(after Jorge Luis Borges (1972) "Two English Poems", in
Di Giovanni, N.T. (ed.), *Jorge Luis Borges selected poems, 1923–1967*.
London: Allen Lane The Penguin Press, p. 87)

CONTENTS

List of illustrations xi
Notes on contributors xii
Acknowledgements xvii
Preface – Carmen Rosa Caldas-Coulthard xix

PART I
Language, discourse and gender violence 1

1 Women, language and public discourse: five decades of sexism and scrutiny 3
   Alice F. Freed

2 The gender respect gap 19
   Deborah Cameron

3 The transgressive, the traditional: sexist discourses of grandmothering and ageing 34
   Carmen Rosa Caldas-Coulthard and Rosamund Moon

4 Disco divas and heroic knights: a critical multimodal analysis of gender roles in "create the world" LEGO cards 60
   Jai Mackenzie, Laura Coffey-Glover, Sophie Payne and Mark McGlashan

5 Sexual harassment as reported by the Brazilian press: ambivalent and contradictory framings 77
Branca Telles Ribeiro and Liliana Cabral Bastos

PART II
Sexism and institutional discourses 93

6 "Until I got a man in, he wouldn't listen": evidence for the gender order in New Zealand workplaces 95
Janet Holmes

7 Sexism and mediatised recontextualisations: the case of a battered woman who killed 113
Sibley Slinkard and Susan Ehrlich

8 The discourse of (re)exploitation: female victims in the legal system 131
Nicci MacLeod

9 Language-based discrimination in schools: intersections of gender and sexuality 144
Helen Sauntson

Index *159*

ILLUSTRATIONS

Figures

3.1	Beautiful grandma	41
3.2	Grandma with child in kitchen	42
3.3	Grandma knitting	43
3.4	Transgressive grandmother	44
3.5	Gangsta Granny illustration by Josh Roberts	47
3.6	"Naughty" granny	48
4.1	Composition of a LEGO "create the world" card	64
4.2	Card 011: BOXER	65
7.1	Photograph of Teresa Craig, *Times Colonist*, 19 April 2008	124

Tables

4.1	Minifigure card titles by classification	68
4.2	Gender classification types in minifigure card titles	69
4.3	Functionalisation in card titles, organised by theme	72
9.1	Data-set information	147

CONTRIBUTORS

Liliana Cabral Bastos is Associate Professor in the Letters Department of the Pontifical Catholic University of Rio de Janeiro, Brazil. She received her Ph.D. in Linguistics from the Pontifical Catholic University of Rio de Janeiro. She has been a research fellow at Georgetown University, during her doctoral studies, and at Harvard University, as a postdoctoral student. Her research interests include the study of interaction in institutional contexts, identity/gender construction and narrative analysis. Her recent publications are involved with narrative studies, focusing on the construction of violence, identity/gender, exclusion and stigma in different social movements and urban contexts, such as hospitals, prisons, schools and police departments.

Carmen Rosa Caldas-Coulthard is Professor of English Language and Applied Linguistics at the Federal University of Santa Catarina, Brazil. She is also Senior Research Fellow in the English Department at the University of Birmingham, UK where she taught and researched for many years. She has published widely in the areas of Critical Discourse, Media and Gender Studies. Her current interests are in Social Semiotics and Gender Representation, Visual Communication, Identity Politics and Social Semiotics. She is the author of: *Language and sex* (Brazil: Atica, 1991), *News as social practice* (Brazil: UFSC, 1997) and co-editor with Malcolm Coulthard, of *Texts and practices: reading in critical discourse analysis* (London: Routledge, 1996) and *Translation: Theory and Practice* (Brazil: UFSC, 1991). She is also the co-editor with Michael Toolan of *The writer's craft, the cultures' technology* (Amsterdam: Rodopi, 2005) and with Rick Iedema, *Identity trouble: critical discourse and contested identities* (London: Palgrave, 2008). She was the editor, with Tommaso Milani of the journal *Gender and Language*, Equinox (2014–19).

Deborah Cameron holds the Rupert Murdoch Professorship in Language and Communication at Worcester College, Oxford University since 2004. She also worked at Roehampton University in London, Strathclyde University in Glasgow, the Institute of Education in London and the College of William and Mary in Virginia, USA. Her research interests are in the areas of language, gender and sexuality; language attitudes/ideologies and "verbal hygiene"; discourse analysis; language and globalisation. She has published widely and is internationally known particularly for her books *Working with spoken discourse* (2001), *On language and sexual politics* (2006), *The myth of Mars and Venus: do men and women really speak different languages?* (2007) and *Verbal hygiene* (2012). Her blog "Language: a feminist guide" is an important tool through which she communicates with a wider audience about language and linguistic research.

Laura Coffey-Glover is Lecturer in Linguistics at Nottingham Trent University. She teaches on the BA Joint Honours Linguistics and MA Linguistics programmes. As a feminist linguist she is primarily interested in the study of gender and sexual discrimination in mediated contexts, using a range of methods and approaches in discourse analysis and corpus linguistics. She has published a number of journal articles in these areas, including on representations of same-sex marriage, sexism in popular music and women's magazines. She is the author of *Men in women's worlds* (Palgrave). She sits on the editorial board for the Journal of Language and Discrimination and the executive committee for the British Association of Applied Linguistics Language, Gender and Sexuality Special Interest Group.

Susan Ehrlich is Professor of Linguistics in the Department of Languages, Literatures and Linguistics at York University, Toronto, Canada. She has written extensively on language, sexual violence and the law and is currently working on a project that investigates intertextual practices in the legal system, demonstrating how such an investigation can shed light on broader patterns of social inequalities. Recent books include *The handbook of language, gender and sexuality* (co-edited with Miriam Meyerhoff and Janet Holmes) and *Discursive constructions of consent in the legal process* (co-edited with Diana Eades and Janet Ainsworth).

Alice F. Freed is Professor Emeritus, Linguistics Department, Montclair State University. She received her BA, MA and Ph.D. in Linguistics at the University of Pennsylvania. Her areas of specialisation are sociolinguistics and discourse analysis with a focus on language and gender, question use in English, institutional discourse and language of food. At Montclair State she taught in Linguistics, Women's Studies, the Honours Programme and the General Education programme. She also taught at the University of New Mexico (as part of the LSA 1995 Summer Linguistic Institute), at New York University as a visiting adjunct professor and as part of Montclair's Global Education Programme at Beijing Jiaotong University, China (2010, 2011), at Shanghai University (2013) and Graz University of Technology (2014). She served as Chair of the Linguistics Department at Montclair State from 1986 to 1993 and in 1995. She was a member of the LSA Committee on the Status of Women in Linguistics (COSWL) from 1992 to 1995. She worked as a consultant in discourse analysis at AT&T Labs, Research Department (Florham Park, NJ) from 2002 to 2004. She is the author of *The semantics of English aspectual complementation* (Reidel, 1979), co-editor with Victoria Bergvall and Janet Bing of *Rethinking language and gender research: theory and practice* (Longman, 1996) and co-editor with Susan Ehrlich of *"Why do you ask?": the function of questions in institutional discourse* (Oxford University Press, 2010). She has published numerous chapters in anthologies and articles in peer-reviewed journals.

Janet Holmes is Professor Emeritus of Linguistics, Victoria University of Wellington, New Zealand. She is a Fellow of the Royal Society of New Zealand and an Officer of the New Zealand Order of Merit (2016). She is Associate Director of the Wellington Language in the Workplace project, an ongoing study of communication in the workplace which has described small talk, humour, management strategies, directives and leadership in a wide range of New Zealand workplaces. She was also Director of the project which produced the Wellington Corpus of Spoken New Zealand English which is available on CD-ROM. In the early 1990s, with Allan Bell and Mary Boyce, she conducted the first social dialect survey of New Zealand English in the Wellington area. Her publications include a textbook, *An introduction to sociolinguistics*, now in its fifth edition, the first book of articles in sociolinguistics, *Sociolinguistics*, co-edited with John Pride, a book on sociolinguistic methodology co-edited with Kirk Hazen *Research methods in sociolinguistics*, the first book of sociolinguistic and pragmatic articles on New Zealand English, *New Zealand ways of speaking English*, co-edited with Allan Bell, several books on language and gender, including *Gendered talk at work: women, men and politeness*, *The Blackwell handbook of language, gender and sexuality*, co-edited with Susan Ehrlich and Miriam Meyerhoff, and an edited collection of papers *Gendered speech in social context*. She has also published on a range of sociolinguistic and pragmatics topics, including New Zealand English, New Zealand women's language usage, sexist language, pragmatic particles and hedges, compliments, apologies, disagreement, humour and small talk, and many other aspects of workplace discourse.

Jai Mackenzie is a British Academy Postdoctoral Fellow at the University of Nottingham. Her primary research expertise lies in explorations of language, gender, sexuality and parenthood, especially in new media contexts. She is the Principle Investigator for the Marginalised Families Online project, which explores the role of digital media for single and same-sex parent families in the UK. She also teaches on the BA English programme in the areas of language, society, gender and feminism. She has written a number of chapters and journal articles, and recently published her first monograph: *Language, gender and parenthood online*. She is on the executive committee for two of the British Association of Applied Linguistics' Special Interest Groups: Language, Gender and Sexuality, and Language and New Media.

Nicci MacLeod works at Northumbria University, Newcastle upon Tyne, UK. She gained her Ph.D. in Forensic Linguistics from Aston University in Birmingham, UK, in 2010, on the topic of the language of police interviews with women reporting rape. Since then she has been employed on various research projects, focusing on seventeenth-century legal discourse, authorship analysis of tweets and assuming identities online in the context of undercover online operations against grooming and child sexual exploitation. She is now a Senior Lecturer in English Language and Linguistics at Northumbria University and a freelance forensic linguist. www.forensiclinguist.co.uk

Mark McGlashan is Lecturer in English Language at Birmingham City University's School of English where he teaches undergraduate and postgraduate programmes in English Language and Linguistics. His research interests predominantly centre on social issues relating to nationalism, racism, sexism and homophobia; and how methods from Corpus-based (Critical) Discourse Studies, Social Semiotics and Multimodality may facilitate their study. His recent work has focused on data from online sources such as newspaper websites, forums and social media to analyse the language of rape threats, far-right nationalism and antisemitism.

Rosamund Moon is an honorary research fellow in the Department of English Language and Linguistics at the University of Birmingham, where, until her retirement, she was a senior lecturer. Before joining the Department, she had worked for 20 years in publishing as a lexicographer. Her main research areas have been lexis and phraseology, figurative language, lexicography and corpus linguistics, and she has published widely on these areas: her publications include *Fixed expressions and idioms in English: a corpus-based approach* (Oxford University Press, 1998) and, with Murray Knowles, *Introducing metaphor* (Routledge, 2006).

Sophie Payne is a course tutor in German in the Department of Languages and Cultures at the University of Reading where she teaches German language on the institution-wide language programme. She also teaches undergraduate programmes in German linguistics and German post-war history. Her research interests focus on linguistic representations of conflict, particularly of feminism and women's issues. Her recent work has dealt with online discourses around contemporary feminist protest groups in Germany and the UK. She co-founded the Gender and Sexuality Research Network at the University of Reading and in the AHRC's South West and Wales doctoral training partnership, and has been an editor for the Language Studies Working Papers.

Branca Telles Ribeiro is Distinguished Professor, Lesley University (Cambridge, USA) and Researcher, Federal University (Rio de Janeiro, Brazil). Ribeiro has developed research in Language and Health Communication; Language, Health and Immigration; Mediated Intercultural Communication: difference and adaptability. She is a presenter at Harvard Medical School; Georgetown Round Table of Language and Linguistics; International Association of Applied Linguistics, among others. Her most recent publications are "Positioning Self and Other: how psychiatric patients, psychiatric inmates, and mental health care professionals construct discursively their relationship to total institutions" (co-authored with Diana Pinto); "Mental healthcare professionals' role performance: challenges in the institutional order of a psychiatric hospital" (co-authored with D. Pinto and C.G. Mann). Ribeiro received her Ph.D. and MS in Linguistics from Georgetown University, and her MA in Portuguese Linguistics from the Catholic University in Rio de Janeiro. She lives in Washington, DC and Rio de Janeiro.

Helen Sauntson is Professor of English Language and Linguistics at York St John University. She teaches on the BA English Language and Linguistics and the MA Postgraduate Linguistics programmes. Her main teaching and research interests are in the areas of classroom discourse analysis; language, gender and sexuality; language in education; gender and sexuality in education. As a former teacher, she maintains an interest in classroom interaction and her research in this area focuses on how gender and sexuality identities are constructed through linguistic interaction in classroom settings. She has published a number of authored and edited books and journal articles in the research areas listed above. She is co-editor of the Palgrave Studies in Language, Gender and Sexuality book series

Sibley Slinkard received her Ph.D. in Linguistics and Applied Linguistics from York University (Toronto) in 2019. Her dissertation utilised critical sociolinguistics to examine the language of a murder trial for a woman who killed and claimed self-defence. Her research interests include discourse analytic approaches to language in legal settings, particularly the intersection of law, intimate partner violence and language, as well as media representations of gender and law. She is currently an instructor in the College of Professional Studies at Northeastern University.

Editor's personal information
Prof. Carmen Rosa Caldas-Coulthard
Federal University of Santa Catarina (UFSC) Brazil
Senior Research Fellow, University of Birmingham
Email: carmenrosacaldas@gmail.com
Address: Avenida Irineu Bornhausen, 3148/901
Ed. Carina, Florianópolis, Santa Catarina, Brazil
CEP 88 025 200
Telephone: 55 48 32077585

ACKNOWLEDGEMENTS

I am grateful to the following copyright holders for permission to reproduce material in Chapter 3: Figures 3.1, 3.2, 3.3, 3.4 and 3.5 (courtesy of iSTock/Getty Images); and Chapter 7: Figure 7.1, Postmediada Network Inc.

The authors have attempted to clear the use of all copyright material reproduced in this volume. In the event that any copyright holder has inadvertently been overlooked, the publisher will make amends at the earliest opportunity.

This collection of chapters was inspired by extremely stimulating discussions during the "Invited symposium innovations and challenges in gender, language, and society" at the 2017 AILA meeting in Rio.

I would like to thank, first of all, Ken Hyland, the general editor of the series *Innovations and Challenges in Applied Linguistics* for inviting me to edit this volume. I am also indebted to Adam Woods, my Editorial Assistant, who took this project on and guided me patiently and very efficiently through the final stages of the production process.

My heartfelt thanks also go:

To all the contributors to this volume, many of whom also participated in the AILA Symposium, dear friends and fighters for a more equal world.

To Susana Funk, Brazilian colleague and very dear friend who introduced me to Gender theories in the 1980s and has been a part of my academic life ever since.

To Tommaso Milani, who co-edited with me for five years, 2014–19, the journal *Gender and Language*. I am very grateful for the opportunities to discuss and debate with him so many topics on gender issues.

To my close friend, Rosamund Moon, who has exchanged ideas about Gender and Language with me for many years. This project was first born from our discussions.

Of course, my deepest thanks go to my students who researched a variety of topics in the area of *Gender and Language* with me, many of whom are now experts in the field.

And finally, many, many thanks go to Malcolm Coulthard, who reviewed and evaluated with incredible care all the drafts of all the chapters.

Carmen Rosa Caldas-Coulthard
Florianópolis, October 2019

PREFACE

This book, which brings together an outstanding collection of truly internationally recognised researchers from four continents, aims to recontextualise some of the initial questions posed by the first feminist linguists some 40 years ago – where, when and how are women discursively discriminated against.

Gender and Language, as an area of applied discourse studies, has evolved tremendously in the last decades and our research has contributed in many ways to the growth of awareness and innovation about gender and discourse issues, focusing especially on the discursive constructions of the social.

It is undeniable that significant advances have been made through the work of many different social movements and agents and linguistic practices have been modified in response to feminist pressure. The use of "they" in English, as a singular non-binary pronoun is a classic example, as Freed demonstrates in the introductory chapter of this collection. In fact, the famous British pop singer Sam Smith has very recently announced in the press a desire to be referred to as "they" from now on. And a very recent petition, signed by 30,000 people, asked Oxford University Press to change "sexist" definitions of the word "woman" in their dictionaries. This petition proposes to "eliminate all phrases and definitions that discriminate against and patronise women and/or connote men's ownership of women, to enlarge the dictionary's entry for woman and to include examples representative of minorities, for example, a transgender woman, a lesbian woman" (Behrmann, 2019).

Many of the issues discussed in discursive circles during the second half of the twentieth century, however, continue to be a problem and sexism, racism and ageism have not disappeared from private and institutional discourses and contexts but rather remain a constant to the present day. In many parts of the world, there is a considerable backlash in terms of conservative views on gender issues, materialised in different ways for meaning-making. For us, as linguists and social semioticians, linguistic derogation is a central topic that needs constant attention and research since it continues to co-exist with other social asymmetries.

In my own country Brazil, in its present moment of social turbulence, examples of plain verbal violence appear daily in the media, in social interactions and representations. There is a growing political movement which aims to strengthen the military presence and increase restrictions on abortion, gay marriage and even secular education. There are proposals in the Brazilian Congress, for example, to abolish discussions of gender topics in schools and even to modify educational curricula because the teaching of "theories of gender" is seen as a threat to the general public, children being the main target.

The current president, Jair Bolsonaro, for example, metaphorised in sexual terms his criticism of the perceived interference of international powers in the preservation of the Amazon Rain Forest as: "Brazil is a 'virgin' that all foreign perverts lust after" (G1. O Globo, 2019). On another occasion he used the official presidential Twitter account to make fun of the president of France, Emmanuel Macron, by endorsing a post which visually invites the reader/viewer to compare unfavourably a picture of Macron's much older wife with Bolsonaro's third and younger trophy wife by saying "Don't humiliate the guy" (Mundo ao Minuto, 2019). The implication is that the value of a woman is directly and uniquely related to youth and beauty not educational and professional achievements.

These examples show Brazil's president exercising verbal violence and abuse by describing, undermining, name calling and trivialising women by his use of the linguistic code. Raymond Williams, back in the 1970s, labelled these "critical descriptions of attitudes and practices discriminatory against women" as *verbal sexism* (Williams, 1976: 285), a label currently so relevant in the obscure days of right-wing politics.

Brazil, of course, is just one of many social contexts where the same phenomena are displayed. A representative of the so-called "first world", the current Prime Minister of Britain, Boris Johnson, labelled one of his male predecessors, David Cameron, "a girly swot". He also provocatively called Jeremy Corbyn, the leader of the opposition, "a great big girl's blouse" (*The Guardian*, 08/09/2019).

A final and telling example of the constant repetition and persistence of verbal sexism comes not from politics but, amusingly, from the world of weather reporting. The British Met Office failed to predict a tempest in August 2018. This storm was named, as many others, by a female label – *Doris*. Because of its name, the press and social media were inundated with verbal abuse of the storm, and "Doris", then morphed into a real woman, was called "lewed, a crazy little old lady with insanely strong lungs, causing havoc, running around knocking things over with her bag" (*Sunday Times*, 19 August 2018). Moving from naming to personifying a storm as an old, rejected, crazy old lady with a destructive bag beggars belief. But again, the same semiotic resources are used once again to denigrate women.

These linguistic derogations by feminisation reaffirm the findings of the early feminists who pointed to the fact that texts reproduce sexist positions because the world represented encodes cultural beliefs and stereotypical views about the place of women in society. It is the ways of representing culture that "define the nature of femininity and masculinity" (Cameron, 1985: 69).

The present concerns of the great majority of gender research projects are on sexuality and differing gender identities, and justifiably so. However, women, who were the prime focus at the beginning of linguistic and discourse-oriented applied research into *Gender and Language* seem to have been side-lined, although gender inequalities still persist and verbal and semiotic violence against women occur on a daily basis as my few very recent examples and the discussions of the different chapters in this collection show.

This book has, therefore, as its main objectives, to readdress the different and subtle ways sexism and linguistic violence against WOMEN are materialised in discursive practices and to highlight what Freed, Cameron and Holmes (in this volume) call "the persistent and banal sexism in the gender order" in both private and professional/workplace settings.

The individual chapters discuss both practical and theoretical topics, focusing on specific issues related to gendered discursive constructions of social practices through macro and micro analyses of different public and private situations and settings. Their innovative approaches contribute to the understanding of not only questions linked to human diversity, but also of how to challenge the continuing discrimination realised in discourses.

The chapters report on multi-stranded investigations into the linguistic and semiotic representations of sexism in societies from an applied linguistic and semiotic perspective. Combining the latest theoretical tools of critical applied discourse analysis, multimodality, interactional sociolinguistics and corpus methodologies, we look at language, visuals and semiotic resources, in the context of consumerist culture, to examine the conflicted position of women in texts. In presenting key findings from the different strands, we show how our approaches complement one another and illuminate the phenomena observed, including the kinds of social stereotypes imposed on women.

Part I, *Language, discourse and gender violence* begins by contextualising pervasive gender issues and reviewing key gender and language topics that changed the ways we interpret interaction. A series of research-based chapters follow, starting with "words" and the ways in which women are named or represented (or not) lexically. We then explore the pressing questions of a more private nature: the representation of ageing in both old and new media, the child's world through the examination of toys, sexual abuse and sexual harassment. Ageing (problematised for women, less stigmatised for men), and childhood, for example are still fundamentally undiscussed gendered issues and we contend that in our complex social environment, the construction of self-identity is more problematic for females than for men.

In "Women, language, and public discourse: five decades of sexism and scrutiny" *Alice Freed* opens the book by tracing the pattern of negative sexist commentary that persists despite the otherwise positive effect that feminism has had on women's lives. The chapter provides examples of successful modifications and reforms that have taken place in America and contrasts these with examples of the sort of prejudicial language that still occurs. The chapter illustrates that while efforts to reform language at the lexical level have been somewhat effective, language practices that comprise anti-female comments and sexist beliefs, offensive communicative styles and attitudes of contempt towards women are still a common aspect of public discourse in twenty-first-century America.

Deborah Cameron, in "The gender respect gap", examines patterns of language use which fulfil the shared function of enacting and normalising a "banal" form of everyday sexism – the assumption that women are not entitled to the same level of respect that is routinely shown to men of comparable status in the same social setting, which produces what she calls "the gender respect gap". Her discussion focuses on two main settings: professional/workplace settings, where women's status may be downgraded through silencing, interruption and the withholding of professional titles and address forms; and encounters between strangers in public spaces, where the norm of non-intrusion on unacquainted others is persistently violated by men addressing women. Her conclusion calls for more research examining this important but until recently neglected form of sexist linguistic practice across a wider range of contexts and languages.

In the chapter "The transgressive, the traditional: sexist discourses of grandmothering and ageing", *Carmen Rosa Caldas-Coulthard* and *Rosamund Moon* discuss how "Age", as an important gendered dimension, has been comparatively neglected within gender studies. They investigate the semiotic representation of a role performed in the main by older women: that of "grandmother", a social category particularly associated with ageing. They find that grandmothers are contextualised in two ways: sharing semiotic resources of childhood or domestic contexts, or presented as transgressive actors, located in incongruous situations or performing behaviours inappropriate for their "age". Their conclusions point to processes of social devaluation: ageism and sexism are the pervasive and underlining ideologies in the representations examined.

Jai Mackenzie, *Laura Coffey-Glover*, *Sophie Payne* and *Mark McGlashan* in "Disco divas and heroic knights: a critical multimodal analysis of gender roles in 'create the world' LEGO cards" investigate how gendered identities are constructed in the world of represented toys. They focus on the representation of LEGO minifigures (small human-like toy figurines), presenting a systematic analysis of the way these figures are named, visually depicted and linguistically described on the cards. Their findings highlight some of the ways in which restrictive norms and sexist ideologies can be perpetuated through products targeting young children. They also demonstrate the importance of an in-depth analysis and critique of such products, as a resource for resisting and challenging harmful and limiting gendered norms.

Branca Telles Ribeiro and *Liliana Cabral Bastos* in "Sexual harassment as reported by the Brazilian press: ambivalent and contradictory framings" examine a discussion of sexual harassment in the Brazilian printed press, addressing a public event that had significant public attention worldwide: the #Metoo movement in the international film industry. Using frame analysis, the text discusses inconsistencies, conflicts and paradoxes that emerged in this debate. Much ambiguity is captured in labels, definitions and interviewees' positions. The discussion illustrates that written media matter, and that it is still relevant to examine how a specific sector of society (celebrities and intellectuals) expresses itself in the press, with robust resonance in the digital world.

In Part II, *Sexism and institutional discourses*, the chapters focus on sexism at the institutional level, and on the question of how women are excluded or discriminated against in the workplace, the media, the law, the criminal justice system and educational contexts. "Rape" is a pervasive issue.

Janet Holmes in "'Until I got a man in he wouldn't listen': evidence for the gender order in New Zealand workplaces" discusses the roles available for women in the New Zealand workplace which have steadily expanded over the last two decades, Senior positions in government and government departments have increasingly been secured by women. Nevertheless, working women typically find themselves constrained by gender ideologies or "the gender order" (Connell, 1987), often based on outmoded stereotypes. Drawing on the database of the Language in the Workplace Project, this chapter analyses a range of evidence for how the gender order continues to influence workplace interaction in New Zealand, noting that similar evidence has been identified in many other countries. Some small indications of positive change are identified in the conclusion.

Sibley Slinkard and *Susan Ehrlich* in "Sexism and mediatised recontextualisations: the case of a battered woman who killed" investigate the media coverage of a woman who killed her abusive partner. They show that the media's portrayal fails to capture the complexities of intimate partner violence and the fact that many battered women kill their abusive partners in self-defence. As an example of linguistically oriented discourse analysis, this chapter offers a new perspective – the ability, given the authors' access to the transcripts of the police interviews, to probe the *veracity* of the media's recontextualisations of the defendant's police interview and to demonstrate clearly how such recontextualisations can differ from their original interactions.

In "The discourse of (re)exploitation: female victims in the legal system", *Nicci MacLeod*, drawing on investigative interviews with female rape victims, explores the ways in which victims' accounts of rape are constrained by the discursive resources available to the narrators. She examines the linguistic structures through which the criminal justice system works against women, demonstrating the subtle ways in which sexist discourses are manifested in these interactions.

Helen Sauntson in "Language-based discrimination in schools: intersections of gender and sexuality" investigates intersections between sexism and homophobia in educational settings. Schools have been identified as places where girls, who identify as gender variant and lesbian, gay, bisexual, transgender and related communities (LGBT+) report routinely experiencing discrimination through discursive practices in schools. Sauntson explores these issues by drawing on a recent research project which conducted a detailed and systematic examination of the diverse ways that language can play a role in constructions of gender and sexual identity in school contexts. The analysis focuses on how language works as a form of social practice which can include and exclude certain gender and sexual identities in classroom settings.

Concluding remarks

The chapters in this collection, in presenting innovative applied linguistics research, challenge patriarchal views as expressed through linguistic and semiotic choices. The conclusions reached by the individual authors not only contribute to the understanding of epistemological questions linked to the place of women in society, but also add innovative insights to the question of the silencing of oppressed women.

Systems of power are never isolated, nevertheless, but intersect and simultaneously operate at interpersonal, organisational, societal and cultural levels. The challenges we face as women living in male-dominated societies are immense. At every social level we encounter sexism and discrimination.

Only through the work of building awareness at all discursive levels, can we begin to uncover, interrogate and stop inequalities and difference. Since Discourse is a major instrument of power and control, we, as critical discourse analysts and applied linguists feel that our role is to clarify how power and discriminatory values are inscribed and mediated through semiotic and linguistic systems. However, the big challenge remains: how to subvert the gender order. We need much more research to make visible the issues of gender and sexual diversity, in private settings, in the workplace, in the media and in education, in order to support the needs of many women.

Women, Language and Sexism as an area of Applied Linguistics, continues to be an important locus for the exposing of linguistic aspects of gender violence against women and structural inequalities. If we reveal the linguistic means by which exclusion and discrimination against women is achieved, we can act upon the world in order to transform it and make possible re-education for a better progressive world.

Carmen Rosa Caldas-Coulthard
Florianópolis, October 2019

References

BBC (2019) "Macron tem que retirar os insultos". At: www.bbc.com/portuguese/internacional-49483220 (accessed 27 August 2019).

Behrmann, A. (2019) "War of words over 'sexist' definitions by Oxford University Press", *The Times*, 18 September. At: www.thetimes.co.uk/article/war-of-words-over-sexist-definitions-by-oxford-university-press-jt59xgvvf (accessed 18 September 2019).

Bell, T. (2019) "Insights... 'big girl's blouse', 'girly swot'? The prime minister should choose his insults more carefully", *Guardian*, 8 September. At: www.theguardian.com/commentisfree/2019/sep/08/insights-big-girls-blouse-girly-swot-prime-minister-should-choose-insults-more-carefully (accessed 8 September 2019).

Cameron, D. (1985) *Feminism and linguistic theory*. London: Macmillan.

Connell, Robert(a) W. (1987) *Gender and power: society, the person and sexual politics*. Stanford, CA: Stanford University Press.
G1. O Globo (2019) http://g1.globo.com/globo-news/jornal-das-dez/videos/v/brasil-e-virgem-que-todo-tarado-quer-diz-bolsonaro-ao-falar-sobre-amazonia/7746416/ (accessed 7 July 2019).
Mundo ao Minuto (2019) "'Não humilha, cara': Bolsonaro reage a comentário sobre mulher de Macron". At: www.noticiasaominuto.com/mundo/1310372/nao-humilha-cara-bolsonaro-reage-a-comentario-sobre-mulher-de-macron (accessed 26 August 2019).

PART I
Language, discourse and gender violence

1
WOMEN, LANGUAGE AND PUBLIC DISCOURSE
Five decades of sexism and scrutiny

Alice F. Freed
MONTCLAIR STATE UNIVERSITY, USA

Introduction

In 1973, the year that Robin Lakoff (1973) published "Language and woman's place", the United States was coming to terms with the tumultuous civil rights movement of the 1960s, was facing the final years of intense anti-war activity related to the unpopular war in Vietnam, and was confronting the demands of second wave feminism, or "women's lib" as it was mockingly called. This combination of events produced a level of social upheaval not seen in the United States since before the Second World War. The Watergate scandal of the same years led to the momentous 1974 resignation of Richard Nixon (37th President of the United States). CBS's *All in the Family* was the number one prime-time television programme (Top-rated United States television programs of 1973–74, 2017), a show that broached topics until then rarely heard on network television, "racism, …, homosexuality, women's liberation, rape, …, abortion, …, the Vietnam War, menopause, and impotence" (All in the Family, 2019). It was in this social and historical context that Lakoff's article emerged – a publication credited with forging a new field then known as "Women and Language".

Early Women and Language research relied on introspection or limited speech samples collected from homogeneous groups of speakers; details about the speakers' lives were seldom investigated and little interest was paid to the context in which the speech occurred. Narrow findings were repeatedly generalised to the broader population of "women" and "men" and particular attention was directed at superficial speech differences found when comparing women's use of language to men's; these differences were then said to confirm that these two unexamined groups of people, women and men, used language differently. Theories of male–female difference and male dominance ruled the field (Lakoff, 1975; Thorne and Henley, 1975).

By contrast, in the twenty-first century, researchers no longer view women or men as homogeneous groups but instead investigate speakers according to their relationship to class, race, ethnicity, gender, sexuality, sexual orientation, and community of practice. Language is examined in the specific social/institutional/geographic context in which it occurs. The focus on "sex difference" and "male dominance" has receded, the use of empirical data has replaced linguistic introspection, context and participant interaction are deemed critical (especially to qualitative research), and the study of discourse increasingly takes precedence over lexical analysis (see Holmes and Meyerhoff, 2003; Ehrlich, 2008; Ehrlich et al., 2014).

What has remained fairly constant is the consideration of how women are individually and collectively represented – how people talk to and about women – whether in face-to-face encounters, in print or broadcast media, in courtrooms and in boardrooms, on blogs, in tweets, and in Facebook posts. In a word, what continues to plague us is the persistence of sexism in language. In the 1970s and 1980s, feminists (and feminist linguists) filled volumes with discussions and suggestions for "fixing" sexist language (see, among others, Bodine, 1975; Miller and Swift, 1976; Spender, 1980; Kramarae et al., 1985; Frank and Treichler, 1989; Cameron, 1992). While some progress was made, the efforts were uneven. "How ... sexist and androcentric ideas [are] encoded in language and how ... such encodings produce and reproduce gendered inequalities" (Ehrlich, 2008: 14) remains a critical question (see Pauwels, 2003; Ehrlich, 2008: 14–27; Mills, 2008).

In this chapter I trace the pattern of negative sexist commentary that persists despite the otherwise positive effect that feminism has had on our lives. The chapter provides examples of successful modifications and reforms that have taken place and contrasts these with examples of prejudicial language practices that endure and continue to negatively affect women. The topics are organised to highlight examples of "success" in terms of progress towards non-biased language use juxtaposed with language that shows relatively little relief from the influence of androcentrism. Two general areas of language are examined:

1. Sexism and specific lexical or morphological form:
   a. New words and occupational terms.
   b. Pronominal usage: generic *he* and singular *they*.
   c. Titles: *Miss, Mrs and Ms*.
2. Sexism and discursive practice:
   a. Topic/content.
   b. Interrupting and silencing.
   c. Monitoring women's speech.

"Sexism in language" thus encompasses both (1) lexical (and morphological) forms of sexism, sometimes known as overt, direct (Mills, 2008), or word-based codified sexist language (Ehrlich, 2008); and (2) language use that exemplifies covert or indirect sexist language (Mills, 2008) manifested through discursive practices and rooted in male-dominated belief systems (see Cameron's conclusion in Chapter 2.) As I used to explain to my students, sometimes language is sexist and we can suggest changes: e.g. "She's the best man for the job" → "She's the best person for the job". Sometimes language traditions and practices are sexist and we can offer improvements: e.g. "I now pronounce you man and wife" → "I now pronounce you husband and wife" → "I now pronounce you married". But sometimes it is the ideas and attitudes that are sexist and for that we need considerably more than linguistic reform: e.g. women talk too much; women are bad drivers; women are not suited for combat. As Deborah Cameron (1992: 125) wrote, "we cannot root out prejudice ... nor make sexism disappear just by exposing it ... In the mouths of sexists, language [will] still be sexist."

What is presented below illustrates that while lexical level reform has been somewhat successful, language use that contains anti-female comments and sexist beliefs (e.g. "Look at that face! Would anybody vote for that?"), offensive communicative styles (e.g. persistent interruption of women by men), and various attitudes of contempt (e.g. discounting women's claims about sexual violence) are a common aspect of public discourse in twenty-first-century America.[1]

Sexism and specific lexical or morphological form: new words and occupational terms

There have been some meaningful innovations in the area of lexical change and non-sexist language reform, many of which are modifications that feminists suggested early on. Notable among these changes are: (a) the introduction of words for "phenomena that have previously gone unnamed" (Ehrlich and King, 1994: 61); and (b) terminological reforms used for occupational roles. Some of the new terms – words that reflect a feminist perspective – are now well established in English. Prominent among these, with approximate dates of when they were coined, are: *sexism* (1965), *rape-culture* (1970s), *date-(acquaintance) rape* (1975), *sexual harassment* (1993), #Metoo (2006, 2017), and *mansplaining* (2010). The extent to which each of these has preserved its intended meaning has not been taken up in this chapter. (For a discussion of the earlier terms see Ehrlich and King, 1992, 1994.)

Words that name and rename professions encompass terms of several kinds: (1) male-marked terms that were used generically for men or women, designated as generic by self-appointed language authorities who claimed that *man* included both men or women; thus *mailman, policeman, weatherman, chairman* were said to refer "appropriately" to either men or women who held these positions; (2) terms that were grammatically marked for gender but where the male form of a pair carried greater prestige: *actor: actress; waiter: waitress; poet: poetess; hero: heroine;*[2] (3) terms which, while grammatically gender-neutral, were nonetheless treated as signalling "maleness" (or "femaleness") ostensibly because of the traditional scarcity of either women (or men) in these positions: *doctor, lawyer, soldier, president* (or *nurse, secretary, receptionist, school teacher*).

Most of the proposed solutions focused on the use of "inclusive language". Deborah Cameron (2016) points out that while inclusive language is "a reasonable strategy for countering sexism" it "tends to obscure the structural inequalities that were foregrounded in feminist analysis". For example, the phrase "gender-based violence" wrongly suggests that men are as likely to be victims of sexual violence as women (Cameron, 2016). Nonetheless, the movement that advocated for inclusive terminology and contested the "male" reading of gender-neutral terms gained ground. The examples below highlight the successful change of at least some lexical forms. Again, whether these newer terms have entirely replaced the earlier forms is not known; in some cases, the newer and the older words appear to coexist:

policeman → *police officer*
fireman → *fire fighter*
chairman → *chair*[3]
waiter, waitress → *server*
airline stewardess → *flight attendant*
seamstress → *tailor, dress maker*

For the words in category (2), many women simply embrace the formerly male-marked term and call themselves *actor, poet, hero*, etc. For words in category (3), however, where grammatically gender-neutral terms were traditionally used to refer to men, semantic disparity between women and men (to say nothing of social and pay disparity) continues. For these words, there is no obvious lexical reform. People (and institutions) often add the word *woman*, used as an adjective, creating what to many is a less prestigious sub-category of the profession, thus *woman doctor, woman writer, Women's Soccer, woman scientist*.[4] The derogation is achieved through the addition of *woman*, where *woman* becomes a label of primary potency (Allport, 1954) detracting from the professional category by bringing unnecessary attention to the sex/gender of the individual(s). For this set of gender-neutral terms, when the word is only used for men, maleness remains the norm; this usage thereby simultaneously reflects and reproduces gendered stereotypes. Only a few equivalent examples exist in reverse, the most conspicuous of which may be *male nurse*. The resistance to using words such as *doctor, scientist*, etc. without gender designation appears to be related to the prestige of the position. For the most part, the terms most successfully reformed name relatively lower status positions.

Sexism and linguistic/lexical form: pronominal usage

Another significant shift away from sexist reference, also at the level of lexical form, is the change in the use of the third person generic pronoun *he* to the third person pronoun *they*. (Some people initially preferred *he or she* as a replacement for *he*.) The problem of generic *he*, traditionally prescribed as the appropriate referential pronoun for agreement with singular unidentified antecedents whether male or female, was raised by feminist linguists at least as far back as 1973 (see Bodine, 1975). Although speakers of English often ignored the prescription, the topic remained one of academic debate. In 1973, Lakoff expressed pessimism about our ability to bring about change in pronominal usage:

> My feeling is that this area of pronominal neutralization is both less in need of changing and less open to change than many of the other disparities that have been discussed ... and we should perhaps concentrate our efforts where they will be most fruitful. (1975: 45)

Later, in 2004, noting the shift that was in progress, Lakoff revisited her comments and admitted that she was "wrong in thinking that speakers of English would find it impossible to substitute one extant form for another. We are apparently more flexible and more well-intentioned than I believed back then" (Lakoff in Bucholtz, 2004: 102, n. 2).

A number of factors seem to account for the rapidity and triumph of this particular change: the fact that reform efforts focused on written English (Curzan, 2014: 118); that language reform was a priority for feminist linguists; the historical precedence in English of a plural pronoun (i.e. *you*) replacing singular pronouns (*thee* and *thou*); the documented use of singular indefinite *they* as far back as 1375 (Barron, 2018); and finally, the fact that singular indefinite *they* was already commonly used in spoken English when this modern reform activity began. Abundant evidence from online corpora (Curzan, 2014: 127–128; LaScotte, 2016) and everyday speech samples verifies the greater occurrence of singular *they* and the decline of singular generic *he* in contemporary American English. Singular generic *he* is now relatively uncommon in spoken English and significantly less common in writing than it was in 1973. In her chapter on "Nonsexist language reform" Curzan (2014: 114–136) emphasises how remarkable this particular change of *he* to singular indefinite *they* is because of how quickly the change took place.

The evolution of *they* from a plural to a singular third person gender-neutral pronoun is but part of the change that English speakers have brought to this pronoun. It is the more recent meaning of *they* as a singular form used to refer to a known person that is most striking; it is this usage that is entirely new in the English-speaking world. In 2015, the American Dialect Society voted singular gender-neutral *they* the Word of the Year (2015 Word of the Year is singular *they*, 2016), recognising the uniqueness of its new use to refer to a known person "who may identify as 'non-binary' in gender terms".[5]

An excellent example of singular non-binary *they* as a referent for a known person occurs in the American television series *Billions* (Hibberd, 2017):

> it's *Billions*' hyper-masculine perspective that makes [the] ... introduction of Taylor so mesmerizing. As played by Asia Kate Dillon (who, like the character, also does not identify as either gender), Taylor is a hyper-smart rising star intern at Axe Capital who disrupts hedge fund world with their unique

presence (and yes, "they" is the pronoun – as Taylor crisply informs a nonplussed Axelrod when they first meet).

More recent still is an opinion piece in the *New York Times*, where columnist Farhad Manjoo (2019) offers reasons why all English speakers should adopt singular gender-neutral *they*. He cites both cultural shifts away from a gender-rigid society and linguistic arguments (i.e. the third person singular pronouns *she* and *he* are the only English pronouns that mark sex or gender). Among his examples is the use of gender-specific *they/them* by the ride-sharing services Lyft and Uber: "when Uber or Lyft wants to tell you that your driver has arrived, they send you a notification that says something like: 'Juan is almost here. Meet them outside.'"

It appears that feminist activism allowed for (or perhaps produced the conditions for) speakers to confront traditional pronoun usage as it pertained to broader concerns of gender and sexual identity. These challenges have extended to the trans community. Lal Zimman (2017), in a discussion about transgender language reform, articulates a perspective that could have been written about women 50 years ago. He argues that language has always been a site for political and cultural change as "it is language that serves as the most pervasive ground on which trans [and women's] identities are delegitimised and transphobic [sexist]" (2017: 102).

Sexism conveyed by specific lexical or morphological form: titles: *Ms* (*Mrs* and *Miss*)

Other language reforms that twentieth-century feminists introduced have been less successfully established. Notable is the problematic trajectory of the English language title *Ms* originally envisioned as a companion title to *Mr*, both neutral forms that signal nothing about marital status. In many contemporary settings, however, instead of replacing *Mrs* or *Miss*, *Ms* is used alongside of them, as if to offer it, albeit begrudgingly, as an option for those unhappy with *Mrs* or *Miss*. Ehrlich and King (see also McConnell-Ginet, 1989; Sunderland, 1991) remind us,

> Linguistic meanings are, to a large extent, determined by the dominant culture's social values and attitudes – … terms initially introduced to be nonsexist, nonracist, or even feminist may … lose their intended meanings in the mouths and ears of a sexist, racist speech community and culture.
>
> *Ehrlich and King (1994: 60)*

Lexicographer Ben Zimmer (2009) traces the surprisingly long history of *Ms* in a *New York Times* article that appeared in 2009. He reports that the first introduction of *Ms* was in 1901, in the *Sunday Republican* (Springfield, MA) by an unnamed writer who offered that:

> Everyone has been put in an embarrassing position by ignorance of the status of some woman. To call a maiden Mrs. is only a shade worse than to insult a matron with the inferior title Miss. Yet it is not always easy to know the facts.

With that the writer suggests *Ms.*, which he called "a tactfully ambiguous compromise between *Miss* and *Mrs.*"

According to Zimmer, while there were a few other appearances of *Ms* in the 1930s and 1940s, it was not until 1969 that feminist Sheila Michaels reintroduced it. The term was then more widely adopted by second wave feminists in the summer of 1970. *Ms. Magazine* was founded in 1972. "The New York Times waited until 1986 to announce that it would embrace the use of *Ms.* as an honorific alongside *Miss* and *Mr.*" (Zimmer, 2009).

Using a written survey developed by Donna Lillian (1993), Janet Fuller (2005) examined the use of *Ms* by 291 students, 74 faculty members, and 61 staff members at Southern Illinois University. She found that the faculty used *Ms* more than either the students or administrative staff, selecting *Ms* 83.8% of the time while students chose *Ms* only 61.4% of the time, and staff approximately 53.4% (186). Overall, the staff and the female students showed the most traditional usage patterns (202).

Fuller (2005) describes three competing meanings for *Ms*:

> a transitional meaning, used for women who are too old to be *Miss* but not (yet) married; the default meaning, for use when marital status is ambiguous or nontraditional; and the neutral meaning, where *Ms.* is used … instead of *Miss* and *Mrs.*
>
> *Fuller (2005: 202)*

She suggests that *Ms* is most often used for women "who do not have clearly defined heterosexual marriages" (202) and that for the staff and female students in her sample, "*Ms.* means young and single instead of being a neutral term for all women" (202).

These data confirm that *Ms* has indeed become well established in English but that a variety of meanings in addition to the one intended have taken hold. We are again reminded, "what persists is the linguistic encoding of social distinctions that are … of ideological importance to the speech community" (Ehrlich and King, 1994: 64). As radio host James Valentine (2017) posted, "*Ms.* can only be neutral if its use is universal". In other words, there is no variation in the meaning of the title *Mr* precisely because it is used for and by all men.

Sexism conveyed by discursive practice: content/topic

Other areas of language use paint an even more disturbing picture of the persistence of offensive portrayals of women. The examples in the second half of this chapter make clear the limitations of feminist reform activity that focused primarily on the lexicon. Those early efforts to eliminate sexist language did not remove the spectre of male-dominated language practice. Abundant data are available from contemporary broadcast, print, and social media that verify that women continue to be trivialised, disparaged, and legally undermined in the United States. Public figures routinely offer judgemental and patronising assertions about how women talk, how women behave, how women look, and how they sound. While this trend began well before the 2016 American presidential election, it is difficult not to contemplate this phenomenon in the context of the presidency of Donald Trump and the politically toxic verbal environment that he has created. Circumstances such as these underscore the relationship between socio-political events and public discourse.

Matters have materially deteriorated for women in the United States since Trump took office as an all-out war on women seems to be unfolding. The Violence Against Women Act (2019), first established in 1994, expired on 15 February 2019; although the House of Representatives passed a bill re-establishing it in April 2019, the bill has been ignored by the US Senate. Bans and restrictions on abortion have increased dramatically. According to Planned Parenthood and other news tracking services, as of May 2019, 43 (of 50) states have adopted restrictions intended to outlaw abortion or to make it almost impossible to obtain an abortion beyond a certain point in pregnancy. In addition, the so-called "global gag rule" was reinstated in January 2017 – a policy that blocks funding for any non-governmental agency that advises about or provides abortion services. Finally, the US Supreme Court has shifted dramatically to the right under Donald Trump. Conservative Judge Neil Gorsuch was Trump's first appointment to the court in April 2017. Then in October 2018 the Senate confirmed an even more conservative Supreme Court nominee, Judge Brett Kavanaugh, this despite sexual assault allegations against him dating back to his high school years.[6]

Relevant examples of Donald Trump's sexist comments require little explanation, blatant as they are in their misogynist and caustic portrayal of women, and focused, as so many are, on women's appearance and sexuality. It is the content rather than the specific words that he uses that devalue and trivialise women. Trump's language serves as a useful exemplar of what is currently tolerated in public discourse in the USA. Two of the following examples are from before Trump became president, one is from the 2016 campaign, and one was uttered as president.

1. "Rosie O'Donnell is disgusting – both inside and out. If you take a look at her, she's a slob. How does she even get on television? If I were running The View, I'd fire Rosie. I'd look her right in that fat, ugly face of hers and say, 'Rosie, you're fired.' We're all a little chubby but Rosie's just worse than most of us." (Johnson, 2006)
2. "@ariannahuff is unattractive both inside and out. I fully understand why her former husband left her for a man – he made a good decision." (Trump, 2012)
3. "Look at that face! Would anybody vote for that? Can you imagine that, the face of our next president? I mean, she is a woman, and I'm not supposed to say bad things, but really folks, come on. Are we serious?" (Comments about presidential candidate Carly Fiorina. Rappeport, 2015)
4. "You know, you're in such good shape. Beautiful." (Comment to Brigitte Macron First Lady of France as he gestured towards her body. Moon, 2017)

In each example, Trump expresses his disdain (or in #4, his approval) for the particular woman referred to by commenting on her physical appearance. Trump's remarks constitute insults (even the complimentary one) precisely because there is a cultural assumption that women care more than men about their appearance, want to be considered physically appealing – and that the more eye-catching a woman, the greater her "value". Therefore, to accuse a woman of not being attractive, especially a woman who is a public figure, is a means of disparaging her. Equivalently, to focus positive attention on a woman's looks is a means of downplaying any other qualities. We see Trump building a case, example by example, for his own masculine superiority, using his brashness to establish a discourse of dominance for any man willing to take an aggressive verbal position against women.

Sexism conveyed by discursive practice: interrupting and silencing

In a well-known chapter called "The woman", Otto Jespersen (1922) declared that, in general, women talk too much. Almost a century later, the belief in female verbosity retains considerable strength despite comprehensive empirical studies that provide solid counter evidence (Liberman, 2006; Mehl et al., 2007). In June 2017, David Bonderman, billionaire businessman with a law degree from Harvard Law School, was forced to resign from the board of the ride-sharing company Uber due to his disparaging remark about women's talkativeness. The Uber board was reportedly reviewing the company's culture – a culture that had a reputation for sexist policies and practices. Another board member, Arianna Huffington, journalist and businesswoman, commented on the importance of having more women on the board. "There's a lot of data", she said, "that shows when there's one woman on the board, it's much more likely that there will be a second woman on the board." Bonderman countered: "Actually what it shows is that it's much more likely to be more talking" (Chira, 2017).

It is fairly shocking that a highly educated and well-respected man would contradict another board member, a woman, with such a sexist declaration at a 2017 meeting of an American technology company. And while the damaging publicity that Bonderman received forced his subsequent resignation – a consequence that might not have occurred several decades before – the apparent ease with which he uttered this belittling stereotype substantiates the existence of a culture that tolerates such attitudes. There is no shortage of examples of interactional bullying of women by men in a variety of public settings. As seen in the cases below, men frequently cut women off, explaining as they do what the rationale is for their behaviour. In February 2017, US Senate Majority Leader Mitch McConnell, during Senate confirmation hearings for the Attorney General nominee, told Elizabeth Warren, one of only 20 women in the 100 member US Senate, to stop speaking because she had broken Senate rules by reading past statements against the nominee. McConnell's comments following the confrontation suggest that he believed that his "warning" to Warren should have been all she needed to "obey" his instructions to be silent. Hawkins (2017) reports McConnell to have said, "Sen. Warren was giving a lengthy speech ... She had appeared to violate the rule. She was warned. She was given an explanation. Nevertheless, she persisted."

Then, in June 2017, at public hearings of another Senate committee investigating Russian intrusion into the 2016 presidential campaign, two different senior white male senators interrupted junior senator Kamala Harris. Harris, of Indian and Jamaican descent, was the only minority woman on the committee. She was accused of lacking the courtesy of giving a witness the chance to answer her question – or not answer it – as he saw fit (see also Zimmerman and West (1975)):

> Senator Harris, a former prosecutor, assertively questioned Attorney General Jeff Sessions during his testimony before the Senate Intelligence Committee. Senator John McCain, ... interrupted and chided her to let Mr. Sessions answer her questions. Soon after that, Senator Richard Burr, ... the committee chairman, cut her off, saying her time had elapsed.
>
> *Chira (2017)*

A public outcry about this behaviour did not deter other senators from similar behaviour at future hearings. Senator Chuck Grassley, then Chair of the Senate Judiciary Committee, repeatedly interrupted four of the five women at the 2018 hearing held to investigate Christine Blasey Ford's accusation that Supreme Court nominee Brett Kavanaugh had sexually assaulted her in high school. Grassley interrupted Democratic Senators Diane Feinstein, Kamala Harris, and Amy Klobuchar – and he even interrupted Rachel Mitchell, the prosecutor that Senate Judiciary Committee Republicans hired to question Blasey Ford for them.

These examples illustrate how men use verbal behaviour to try to silence women, to embarrass individual women, or to devalue women in general. They demonstrate how language serves as a conduit for men who want to maintain a sense of dominance by demeaning women. Each case suggests that in the eyes of the male speaker, it would be better if the woman did not talk at all. When the desired outcome – silence – is not achieved, the men in these examples move to negative characterisations of these otherwise powerful women. For example, Elizabeth Warren is called persistent; Kamala Harris is said to lack courtesy. The continued occurrence of such incidents in the twenty-first century confirms the tenacity of the social and institutionalised power inequities between women and men. And because none of these examples contains specific language forms that can be contested, each is, again, an illustration of covert rather than overt discursive sexism (Mills, 2008).

Sexism conveyed by discursive practice: monitoring women's speech

The monitoring of women's speech is yet another measure of the intractability of sexist attitudes towards women. Commentaries about how women "sound" – whether collectively or targeted at individual women – include remarks about women's words (unnecessary or childish), the pitch of women's voices (too high), the way women laugh (annoyingly or distastefully), their communicative style (aggressive or insecure), and their "tone of voice" (shrill or abrasive). In other words, in addition to the insulting content of remarks hurled at women who dare assert themselves in public – people often feel free to offer opinions that belittle how women talk. From ridiculing "Valley girl" speech some years ago, to the disdainful comments about young women's use of the word *like* or their ending sentences with "uptalk" (final high rise), and the supposed peculiarity of "vocal fry" or creaky voice (Wolk et al., 2012), teenage girls and women are repeatedly criticised and scorned for the way they speak (see Quenqua, 2012).

Every few years a new speech characteristic catches the attention of a blogger or journalist and a discussion of the topic goes "viral". In a 2015 *New York Times* opinion piece "Why women apologise and should stop", Sloane Crosley (2015) maintains that women say *sorry* too often as a result of their idea of politeness. She characterises this use of *sorry* as "an assertive apology" (e.g. "I'm sorry but …") and argues that it needs to be avoided. Crosley provides no data, gives no details about which (or how many) women apologise this way, or under what circumstances. Nor is any information available about the occurrence of *sorry* in the speech of men from the same cohort. Next, Google invented an "app" to help with this problem. "Extension Just Not Sorry – the Gmail Plug-in" "that warns you when you write emails using words which undermine your message. We're Just NOT Sorry!" (https://chrome.google.com/webstore/detail/just-not-sorry-the-gmail/fmegmibednnlgojepmidhlhpjbppmlci?hl=en-US).

A more dangerous example of how women's speech is scrutinised is the decades long negative portrayal of Hillary Clinton, Democratic presidential candidate in 2008 and 2016. A particular sort of sexist rhetoric used against Clinton during the 2007–2008 campaign for president, examined by Tanya Romaniuk (2016), relates to the nature of her laugh. "Clinton's laughter became the subject of intense scrutiny by journalists, media commentators, and pundits in the mainstream media and was dubbed 'The Clinton Cackle'" (Romaniuk, 2016: 536). Romaniuk's careful analysis and comparison with male politicians revealed that Clinton's laughter was "a generic interactional practice – one employed by other male politicians in broadcast news interviews" (2016: 547); nonetheless, Clinton's laughter was used to portray her as "witchlike" and undesirable:

> In terms of the "Cackle" coverage, Clinton's laughter was evaluated in terms of a dominant, cultural script for powerful, competent women vying for leadership positions steeped in masculine hegemony – a script in which women are damned no matter what they do. By way of characterizing Clinton's laughter as "inappropriate", the media re-presentations helped to reinforce the ideological belief that Clinton's bid for the White House was also inappropriate. The implication of such a re-presentation is that a powerful woman (i.e. a witch) is more fitting in a fairy tale than in the real world of American presidential politics.
>
> *Romaniuk (2016: 547)*

That is, we learn from Romaniuk's analysis that the press's characterisation of Clinton's laughter as "inappropriate" was both a reflection of and a way of reproducing the cultural belief that a woman's striving to be president of the United States was inappropriate.

We had still another occasion to witness the different treatment of women's and men's verbal behaviour during the October 2018 US Senate hearings held to investigate Christine Blasey Ford's accusation that Supreme Court nominee Brett Kavanaugh had sexually assaulted her in high school. Blasey Ford, a tenured professor of Psychology at Palo Alto University in California, delivered her personal statement clearly, intelligently, and with some displays of nervousness. She spoke in a quiet voice that could be described as acoustically in a high pitch range, putting her at something of a disadvantage (see also McConnell-Ginet (1978)):

> High pitch is associated not only with femaleness, but also with other characteristics which imply a lack of authority, such as immaturity (children have high-pitched voices) and emotional arousal (we "squeal" with joy or fear, "shriek" with excitement, "screech" angrily).
> *Cameron (2018)*

Kavanaugh, on the other hand, delivered his testimony in a loud forceful voice and expressed unrestrained anger – portraying himself as a wronged powerful man in the national spotlight as a nominee to the US Supreme Court. Following a day of testimonies, the media exploded with discussions of the "female" quality of Ford's way of speaking. By contrast, little was said about Kavanaugh's language characteristics. (Some observed only that if a woman, or a man of colour, had delivered a comparable performance and displayed the same bluster and fury, the person would have been summarily disqualified.)

Cameron (2018) reflects on this made-for-TV spectacle in her October 2018 Feminist Language blog: "Language and the brotherhood of men". She reports that a few journalists contacted her to ask about the way Blasey Ford spoke. (I, too, was contacted by a journalist who asked how typical Ford's speech was for a woman.) As far as we both know, no linguist was asked whether Kavanaugh's speaking behaviour typified how men talk:

> People don't tend to treat a male speaker as a generic representative of his sex: they're more likely to ask what his speech patterns say about him as an individual. Women's linguistic performances, by contrast, are routinely treated as performances of gender – and this is true whether the commentator is feminist or anti-feminist, sympathetic or hostile to the woman concerned.
> *Cameron (2018)*

Why, we may ask, is there so much focus on how women sound? Why the attention to the physical quality of speech? Is this similar to sexist remarks about women's appearance? Women are measured, more than men, "by their perceived physical/sexual attractiveness. Judgments on a woman's voice – the most directly embodied, physical aspect of linguistic performance – are part of the same phenomenon" (Cameron, 2018). We know that superficial physical characteristics of humans, quickly assessed by the senses (hearing, sight, and touch), are foundational cultural cues especially used when people are evaluating strangers. We should not be surprised that these markers also contain well-established, culturally determined gendered stereotypes.

Conclusion

Many women's lives have changed dramatically since 1973 when the "women's movement" was in full force and the path of American social history was being irreversibly transformed. Yet evidence confirms that people in powerful places and more generally, the English language media, continue to treat women as a special category of humans. Women are routinely ridiculed and negatively stereotyped. Women's speech continues to be scrutinised and monitored. Institutional sexism is still thriving. The unequal treatment and biased representation of women, while different in detail from the 1970s, has not changed as much as workplace, government, and business practices and populations would have us believe.

This chapter has chronicled the gloomy reality that women, women's behaviour, and women's language are still under attack. In the United States, successful men, regardless of their gender, sexuality, or ethnicity, continue to be granted more autonomy and respect than their female counterparts (see Cameron, Chapter 2 in this volume). I have argued elsewhere that trends such as these may be in response to:

> unexpressed fears that the distinction between the sexes is breaking down, and that social changes taking place are arousing public resistance to variability in patterns of gendered behavior. ... People are increasingly aware that we are able to create and recreate ourselves in part through the enormous flexibility of human language.
>
> *Freed (2014: 640)*

Perhaps as women hold more and higher positions of authority, the need to trivialise and diminish that power is stronger than ever.

When we contemplate why sexism has persisted, and what we might do about it, it is useful to consider Cameron's (2016) reflections about this combination of "successes as well as setbacks". She urges us not to think that the issues of "sexism in language is yesterday's problem: that we no longer need to think about it, or do anything about it, because it was all settled decades ago". Instead she encourages us to remember that: "Every generation of feminists will need both to revisit old arguments and to engage with new debates – and of course, to develop their own ideas about why and how language matters." The need to continue documenting deeply rooted sexism against women and to highlight how intricately it remains embedded in language use remains strong.

Notes

1. All examples in this chapter are based on American English and are primarily from events that took place in the USA. I invite readers from other cultural and national backgrounds to compare the details in this chapter to patterns in their own languages and communities.
2. In some cases, the difference between "equivalent" male and female terms became so extreme that the female term for the same meaning has mostly fallen out of use: e.g. *governor: governess*; *master: mistress*.
3. *Chair*, as a substitute for *chairman*, seems to have more status than the other terms listed but *chair* has not been universally adopted. Its use is common in universities in North America, but in business and government, the term *chairman* is more widely used.
4. For a sense of how sexist the phrase *woman doctor* is, compare it to *woman person*; *person*, like *doctor*, is grammatically gender neutral.
5. There is some evidence from Swedish that introducing a new gender-neutral pronoun is an effective path to eliminating a male bias in language (Lindqvist, et al., 2019; Tavits and Pérez, 2019). As this has not yet had success in English, no detailed discussion is provided of the suggested third person gender-neutral pronouns *ze*, *hir*, and *hirs*.
6. The nomination of Kavanaugh had a certain irony as Trump himself has been accused of "sexual misconduct" by 24 different women. Trump simply dismisses charges and calls his accusers "liars".

References

All in the Family (2019) https://en.wikipedia.org/wiki/All_in_the_Family

Allport, Gordon (1954) *The nature of prejudice*. Cambridge, MA: Addison-Wesley.

American Dialect Society (2016) "2015 Word of the Year is singular *they*" www.americandialect.org/2015-word-of-the-year-is-singular-they

Baron, Dennis (2018) "A brief history of singular 'they'", *Oxford English Dictionary Blog*, 4 September. At: https://public.oed.com/blog/a-brief-history-of-singular-they/

Bodine, Ann (1975) "Androcentrism in prescriptive grammar: singular 'they' sex-indefinite 'he' and 'he or she'", *Language in Society*, 4(2), pp. 129–146.

Bucholtz, Mary (ed.) (2004) *Language and woman's place: text and commentaries*. Oxford: Oxford University Press.

Cameron, Deborah (1992) *Feminism and linguistic theory*, 2nd ed. New York: St Martin's Press.

Cameron, Deborah (2016) "Sexism in language: a problem that hasn't gone away", *Discover Society*, 1 March, p. 30. At: https://discoversociety.org/2016/03/01/sexism-in-language-a-problem-that-hasnt-gone-away/

Cameron, Deborah (2018) "Language: a feminist guide: language and the brotherhood of men". At: https://debuk.wordpress.com/2018/10/11/language-and-the-brotherhood-of-men/

Cameron, Deborah and Kulick, Don (2003) *Language and sexuality*. Cambridge: Cambridge University Press.

Chira, Susan (2017) "The universal phenomenon of men interrupting women", *New York Times*, 14 June. At: www.nytimes.com/2017/06/14/business/women-sexism-work-huffington-kamala-harris.html?smprod=nyt.com

Crosley, Sloane (2015) "Why women apologize and should stop", *New York Times*, 23 June. At: www.nytimes.com/2015/06/23/opinion/when-an-apology-is-anything-but.html?_r=0

Curzan, Anne (2014) *Fixing English*. Cambridge: Cambridge University Press.

Ehrlich, Susan (ed.) (2008) *Language and gender: major themes in English studies*. London: Routledge.

Ehrlich, Susan and King, Ruth (1992) "Gender-based language reform and the social construction of meaning", *Discourse & Society*, 3(2), pp. 151–166.

Ehrlich, Susan and King, Ruth (1994) "Feminist meanings and the (de)politicization of the lexicon", *Language and Society*, 23(1), pp. 59–76.

Ehrlich Susan, Meyerhoff, Miriam and Holmes, Janet (eds) (2014) *The handbook of language, gender, and sexuality*, 2nd ed. Malden, MA: Blackwell.

Frank, Francine Wattman and Treichler, Paula A. (1989) *Language, gender, and professional writing*. New York: Modern Language Association.

Freed, Alice F. (2014) "The public view of language and gender", in Meyerhoff, Miriam, Ehrlich, Susan and Holmes, Janet (eds) *The handbook of language and gender*, 2nd ed. Malden, MA: Wiley-Blackwell, pp. 625–645.

Fuller, Janet (2005) "The uses and meanings of the female title 'Ms.'", *American Speech*, 80(2) pp. 180–206.

Hawkins, Derek (2017) "The silencing of Elizabeth Warren and an old Senate rule prompted by a fistfight", 8 February, *Washington Post*. At: www.washingtonpost.com/news/morning-mix/wp/2017/02/08/the-silencing-of-elizabeth-warren-and-an-old-senate-rule-prompted-by-a-fistfight/?tid=a_inl&utm_term=.9e97d9adf9de

Hibberd, James (2017) "TV's first gender non-binary character introduced in *Billions* premiere", *Entertainment On-line*, 19 February. At: http://ew.com/tv/2017/02/19/billions-non-binary-asia-kate-dillon/

Holmes, Janet and Meyerhoff, Miriam (eds) (2003) *The handbook of language and gender*. Maiden, MA: Blackwell Publishing.

Jespersen, Otto (1922) "The woman", in *Language: its nature, development, and origin*. London: Allen and Unwin, pp. 237–254.

Johnson, Caitlin (2006) "Trump vs. Rosie: the war continues", *CBS News*, 21 December. At: www.cbsnews.com/news/trump-vs-rosie-the-war-continues/2/

Kramarae, Cheris, Russo, Ann and Tredichler, Paula A. (1985) *A feminist dictionary*. London: Pandora Press.

Lakoff, Robin (1973) "Language and woman's place", *Language in Society*, 2(1), pp. 45–80.

Lakoff, Robin (1975) *Language and woman's place*. New York: Harper & Row.

LaScotte, Darren K. (2016) "Singular they: an empirical study of generic pronoun use", *American Speech*, 91(1), pp. 62–80.

Liberman, Mark (2006) "Gabby guys: the effect size", *Language Log*, 23 September. At: http://itre.cis.upenn.edu/~myl/languagelog/archives/003607.html

Lillian, Donna L (1993) "Ms. revisited: she's still a bitch, only now she's older!" Papers of the Annual Meeting of the Atlantic Provinces Linguistic Association, 19, pp. 49–61.

Lindqvist, Anna, Renström, Emma Aurora and Sendén, Marie Gustafsson (2019) "Reducing a male bias in language? Establishing the efficiency of three different gender-fair language strategies", *Sex Roles*, 81(1–2), pp. 109–117.

McConnell-Ginet, Sally (1978) "Intonation in a man's world", *Signs*, 3(3), pp. 541–559.

McConnell-Ginet, Sally (1989) "The sexual (re)production of meaning: a discourse-based theory", in Frank, Francine and Treichler, Paula A. (eds) *Language, gender, and professional writing*. New York: Modern Language Association of America, pp. 35–50.

Manjoo, Farhad (2019) "It's time for 'they'", *New York Times*, 10 July. At: www.nytimes.com/2019/07/10/opinion/pronoun-they-gender.html

Mehl, Matthias R., Vazire, Simine, Ramírez-Esparza, Nairán, Slatcher, Richard B. and Pennebaker, James W. (2007) "Are women really more talkative than men?", *Science*, 317(5834), p. 82.

Miller, Casey and Swift, Kate (1976) *Words and women*. New York: Knopf.

Mills, Sara (2008) *Language and sexism*. Cambridge: Cambridge University Press.

Moon, Angela (2017) "President Trump says French First Lady is in 'Such good shape'", *World News*, 13 July. At: www.reuters.com/article/us-france-usa-trump-brigitte-macron/president-trump-says-french-first-lady-is-in-such-good-shape-idUSKBN19Y2XT

Pauwels, Anne (2003) "Linguistic sexism and feminist linguistic activism", in Holmes, Janet and Meyerhoff, Miriam (eds) *The handbook of language and gender*. Oxford: Blackwell Publishing, pp. 550–570.

Quenqua, Douglas (2012) "They're, like, way ahead of the linguistic currrrve", *New York Times*, 27 February. At: www.nytimes.com/2012/02/28/science/young-women-often-trendsetters-in-vocal-patterns.html?pagewanted=all

Rappeport, Alan (2015) "Donald Trump's uncomplimentary comments about Carly Fiorina", *New York Times*, 10 September. At: www.nytimes.com/politics/first-draft/2015/09/10/donald-trumps-uncomplimentary-comments-about-carly-fiorina/

Romaniuk, Tanya (2016) "On the relevance of gender in the analysis of discourse: a case study from Hillary Rodham Clinton's presidential bid in 2007–2008", *Discourse & Society*, 27(5), pp. 533–553.

Spender, Dale (1980) *Man made language*. London: Routledge & Kegan Paul.

Sunderland, Jane (1991) "The decline of man", *Journal of Pragmatics*, 16, pp. 505–522.

Tavits, Margit and Pérez, Efrén O. (2019) "Language influences mass opinion toward gender and LGBT equality", *Proceedings of the National Academy of Sciences*, August, 156.

Thorne, Barrie, and Henley, Nancy (eds) (1975) *Language and sex: difference and dominance*. Rowley, MA: Newbury House.

Thorne, Barrie, Kramarae, Cheris and Henley, Nancy (eds) (1983) *Language, gender and society*. Rowley, MA: Newbury House.

Top-rated United States television programs of 1973–74, 2017. At: https://en.wikipidia.org/wiki

Valentine, James (2017) "Ms.: the honorific with unintended meaning", ABC Radio Sydney, September. At: www.abc.net.au/news/2017-09-09/james-valentine-ms-meaning-unintended/8886412

Violence Against Women Act (2019) https://en.wikipedia.org/wiki/Violence_Against_Women_Act#Programs_and_services

Wolk, Lesley, Abdelli-Beruh, Nassima B. and Slavin, Dianne (2012) "Habitual use of vocal fry in young adult female speakers", *Journal of Voice*, 26(3), pp.111–116.

Zimman, Lal (2017) "Transgender language reform: some challenges and strategies for promoting trans-affirming, gender-inclusive language", *Journal of Language and Discrimination*, 1(1), pp. 84–105.

Zimmer, Ben (2009) "Ms.: on language", *New York Times Magazine*, 23 October. At: www.nytimes.com/2009/10/25/magazine/25FOB-onlanguage-t.html

Zimmerman, Don and West, Candace (1975) "Sex roles, interruptions and silences in conversation", in Thorne, Barrie and Henley, Nancy (eds) *Language and sex: difference and dominance*. Rowley, MA: Newbury House, pp. 105–129.

2
THE GENDER RESPECT GAP

Deborah Cameron
OXFORD UNIVERSITY, UK

Introduction

In her contribution to the first edition of the *Handbook of language and gender*, Susan U. Phillips (2003: 260) reflected on the recent history of language and gender research, commenting that:

> While a great deal was gained by the new feminist conceptualizing of women as intersections of various aspects of social identity, a great deal was lost too. The rhetorical force of the focus on the universal key problem of a very broad male power over women ... was obscured, and really has not regained center stage in feminist writing since.

As I read it, this statement alludes to two related developments of the 1990s: the turn to identity as the central problematic for feminist theory, and the rejection of global generalisations about gender in favour of "looking locally" at its construction in particular communities of practice (Eckert and McConnell-Ginet, 1992). Research focused increasingly on investigating the diversity of ways in which gendered and sexual identities were performed across cultures and contexts – often with an emphasis on the agency of the performers and the potential of their performances to subvert conventional gender norms. The adoption of new theoretical approaches had, as Phillips notes, many positive effects. But as she also points out, it tended to marginalise older feminist questions about gender as a hierarchical social system in which men are dominant and women subordinate.

In retrospect it could be argued that this de-centring of power reflected the political mood of the 1990s, the decade of "the backlash" (Faludi, 1992) and the advent of "post-feminism" (McRobbie, 2009). But today the mood has changed. Around the world – from Brazil to Turkey, and from Hungary to the Philippines – we have seen the rise of authoritarian, populist, and/or nationalist political movements which seek, among other things, to roll back the civil and reproductive rights women won during the twentieth century (Wodak, 2015; Beinart, 2019). Meanwhile, rights women never succeeded in securing (such as the right to be free from sexual harassment and assault) continue to be violated with impunity (Campbell, 2014), and new forms of anti-feminist extremism, such as the secular misogyny promoted by "incels" and other denizens of the online "manosphere" (Nagle, 2017), have become increasingly visible. These developments have prompted a global resurgence of feminist activism (the transnational spread of the #Metoo movement is a particularly visible recent example), and they also challenge feminist researchers, including researchers of language and gender, to revisit older questions about power and inequality.

This volume is one response to that challenge. Several contributions engage directly with the issues whose prevalence and significance have been highlighted by recent feminist campaigns – including rape, sexual assault, harassment, and online misogyny. In this chapter, however, I want to highlight some more mundane linguistic practices that enact and help to normalise male dominance as an everyday, taken-for-granted reality. The core element of these practices is captured by the name I have given to the inequality they both mark and reproduce: the "gender respect gap" (a term that deliberately echoes the more familiar "gender pay gap", making the point that money is not the only currency in which women are paid less than men). This gap is the result of withholding from women tokens of respect which are routinely granted to men of a comparable social status. Its existence underlines the limitations of an approach which centres on the idea of gender as performed self-identity, and places most emphasis on the agency of the performer. Rather it compels us to attend to the fundamentally intersubjective nature of human social interaction – the way the perceptions and behaviour of the other persons with whom an individual interacts contribute to defining who that individual can be and what place s/he can occupy in the world.

The sexist attitudes and practices that produce the gender respect gap are "banal" in the sense in which that term is used by Michael Billig in his influential work on "banal nationalism" (Billig, 1995). Just as Billig distinguishes what he labels "hot" nationalism (meaning nationalism as an explicit ideology prompting overt conflict) from the "banal" variety (manifested in the taken-for-granted presence of nationalist symbols and discourses in all kinds of everyday contexts), so we might distinguish the "hot" sexism of, for instance, the rape and death threats sent to women online (Hardaker and McGlashan, 2016; Jane, 2017) from the banal sexism manifested in the examples discussed below. Precisely because they are not "hot", they can often remain, in the terms used by ethnomethodologists, "seen but unnoticed"; when they are noticed and complained about, they can easily be dismissed as the trivial, imaginary, or illegitimate concerns of individuals who are either "playing the victim" or else asserting their superiority to others in a manner which is itself disrespectful.

In the following discussion I will consider several linguistic patterns that illustrate the workings of this banal sexism. Since some of these patterns have not been the subject of much recent, systematic research by linguists, my discussion will not centre on the presentation of empirical findings about their prevalence (though where relevant research evidence exists I will draw attention to it). Rather I will make use of naturally occurring metadiscourse about them to probe what they mean and how they are understood – and in some cases, contested – in contemporary conditions. I will also consider how the same or similar issues were approached by feminist researchers in the past, asking whether and how things have changed over the last 50 years, and to what extent earlier analyses remain useful for researchers today. In addition to suggesting that more research is needed (particularly research on naturally occurring interaction in a range of settings and languages), I will suggest that it is important to make connections among what are often treated as discrete or disparate phenomena.

Titles, address forms, and the downgrading of women's status

On Twitter in March 2019, a woman tweeted a screenshot of an online credit card application form that she had just attempted to complete. The form began by asking for a title: the screenshot indicated that the woman had selected "Dr" from the options on the menu. In the next three boxes she had typed, as requested, her first, middle, and last names. Finally, the form asked her to indicate her gender, and she had chosen the "female" option. At the bottom of her screenshot was a message in red explaining that the system had detected an error which she would need to correct before it would allow her to continue. "Your gender", it informed her, "does not match the title you provided. Please check and try again."

The replies this tweet attracted displayed a pattern. Some responses assumed that the woman had encountered a problem because she had made an error (e.g. hitting the back button, or not completing the items in the prescribed order). Most of these comments came from men. Women who commented were more inclined to think the problem was in the system; many of their replies recounted similar experiences. One woman recalled an occasion when her husband had booked a flight for her using the title "Professor": "the system assumed I'm male and I had trouble getting on the plane". Another woman whose cable TV service was registered in the name of "Dr Brown" reported a phone interaction with a cable company employee who told her to get her husband to "call when he gets home from work". Eventually it became clear that the woman who started the thread had received the error message because she had gone back and changed her original title-choice: men who did the same thing got the same message. This was not, in short, a case where the system had been set up to treat men and women differently. But since such cases do exist (for instance, in 2015 many newspapers reported on the experience of a Cambridge paediatrician who could not access the women's changing room with her gym smartcard because the computer automatically recorded anyone using the title "Dr" as male (Fleig, 2015)), it is unsurprising that women judged sexism to be a possible explanation. What is more surprising is the vehemence with which some men insisted that this explanation was impossible and ridiculous, an example of women's tendency to allege bias or discrimination when in fact the fault was all their own.

This anecdotal example illustrates two key points about the gender respect gap. First, it exemplifies the basic mechanism which produces the gap, whereby tokens of respect that are routinely granted to men of a certain status may be withheld from women who share that status. It is a matter of common knowledge that both men and women may earn qualifications or occupy institutional positions that confer the right to use a professional title such as "Dr" or "Professor"; but whereas men's use of those titles is normally treated as unproblematic, women's use of them is frequently treated as "marked" or somehow questionable. Second, the Twitter thread illustrates a common response to women's complaints about being treated with less respect than a comparable man would receive in the same situation. Such complaints are frequently met with denial ("you're imagining it"), defensive explanations ("it's just a bug in the system/a slip of the tongue/X's way of being friendly") and attempts to blame the victim ("you must have made a mistake/you'd get more respect if you spoke with more authority/what kind of self-regarding snob insists on everyone calling them 'Dr'?"). These responses exemplify another way in which respect may be denied to women – through a refusal to acknowledge the reality of their experiences, the validity of their interpretations of experience and/or the legitimacy of their claim to equal/respectful treatment.

Some research has confirmed that women are not imagining the pattern reported in the Twitter thread. Files et al. (2017) investigated the use made of the medical title "Dr" by speakers introducing presenters at "Grand Rounds", a regular event at US teaching hospitals where doctors present recent cases to an audience of their colleagues and students. The researchers analysed more than 300 introductions, using data sourced from two hospitals in Arizona and Minnesota which maintained a video archive of the event for educational purposes. This sample included all possible gender combinations (male introducer/male presenter; male introducer/female presenter; female introducer/female presenter; female introducer/male presenter); in all cases the speaker being introduced was presenting in her/his capacity as a physician, and was therefore eligible to be referred to as "Dr X". The analysis focused on whether in practice speakers were introduced as "Dr X" or whether they were introduced by name only (either "John/Jane X" or just "John/Jane"). They found that women performing introductions almost invariably (in 102 out of 106 cases) used the title "Dr". Male introducers used titles less frequently, suggesting a tendency for men to prefer a less formal style of introduction. However, that preference in itself does not explain the correlation this study also found between the male introducers' choices and the sex of the presenter they were introducing. Whereas men introducing male presenters referred to almost three-quarters of them (72%) as "Dr", men introducing women used a title for just under half of them (49%). This study did not consider potentially relevant interacting variables such as age, seniority and race/ethnicity, but it seems unlikely that these would explain more than a fraction of the reported sex-difference (at this stage of the history of the medical profession there is no reason to assume that the male presenters introduced by men were older and more senior than the women introduced by men). The researchers themselves consider their findings to be evidence of sexism, and suggest that "differential formality in speaker introductions may amplify isolation, marginalization, and professional discomfiture expressed by women faculty in academic medicine" (Files et al., 2017: 413).

This reference to "differential formality" raises a more general issue about the forms of sexism contemporary women experience in the public sphere. Both linguists (e.g. Fairclough, 1996; Goodman, 1996; Leech et al., 2010) and other social scientists (e.g. Wouters, 2007) have argued that one of the major social trends of the past century has been "informalisation", a progressive shift towards less formal, impersonal, and status-marked ways of relating and speaking to others. At the beginning of the twentieth century formality was the rule in all but the most intimate relationships: the writer Harold Nicolson recalled in the 1950s that his father "would never have used the Christian name of any man or woman who was not a relation or whom he had not known for at least thirty years" (quoted in Wouters, 2007: 75). When Nicolson wrote this behaviour already seemed archaic in the context of private life, but formality remained the norm between non-intimates in public contexts. Today, by contrast, even where the parties are unacquainted and/or unequal in status, there has been a weakening of the previously strong presumption that professional exchanges must necessarily involve forms of address and reference that mark deference and social distance (e.g. titles and surnames rather than given names, or in some language communities, the use of a polite rather than a familiar second person pronoun).

This shift in public etiquette is linked to an ideology of egalitarianism, or at least meritocratic opposition to traditional caste and class distinctions, which is now the orthodox wisdom of the modern West. It might be glossed as "individuals should be respected for what they do, not just who they are or what position they occupy in the social/professional hierarchy". The use of professional and other respect titles can be represented, from this point of view, as unwarranted or meaningless knee-jerk deference ("you should care about whether you're respected as an individual, not whether people defer to you by giving you some fancy title"). But for women the result is a classic double bind: they cannot object to what they perceive – not without reason – as the unequal and disrespectful treatment of their sex without prompting accusations of inegalitarianism, snobbery, oversensitivity, and excessive self-regard.

During the past few years this problem has surfaced particularly clearly in disputes about the use of the academic titles "Dr" and "Professor". Though systematic empirical research on this question is in short supply, numerous women have complained that students habitually address them as "Ms" or "Mrs", or by their first names, while the men who teach them are "Dr" or "Professor". In 2014, the Australian academic Katrina Gulliver sparked an online debate when she complained not only about this academic version of the respect gap, but also about the failure of men to understand and support their female colleagues' demand for equal treatment. Far from standing in solidarity with women, some men, Gulliver suggested, were actively undermining them by maintaining that it was authoritarian for any academic to insist on the use of titles. "In most departments", she wrote,

> there is the species of (white) male professor, who wants to be seen as "cool" … who invites all the youngsters to "call me Dave," resting safely in the comfort of assumed male authority. If you're one of these guys: you are not helping the rest of us.
>
> *Gulliver (2014)*

Gulliver's piece prompted many critical responses along the lines of this comment from a male academic: "I worry about making sure I deserve the respect of my students rather than expecting my title or position to simply demand it." This, in turn, provoked angry reactions from women who found it self-righteous and condescending. "It takes a particularly privileged individual", wrote Rebecca Schuman (2014), "to insist, though he commands unearned respect when he walks into a room (even in jeans), that respect must be earned". What both Gulliver and supporters like Schuman were arguing was that white men are differently positioned from everyone else in relation to the egalitarian, "titles don't matter" ethos: they can afford to forgo formal tokens of respect (indeed, some students will give them extra credit for the gesture) because their professional credentials are not in question. For women and members of minority groups these tokens are bound to matter more, because their absence signifies something different: not respect for them as individuals, but a perception of them as interlopers and inferiors.

The debate on academic titles resurfaced in 2018, after the British historian Fern Riddell objected to a new policy adopted by the Toronto *Globe & Mail*: the newspaper had announced that in future it would reserve the title "Dr" for medical doctors, and stop using it for experts who had earned doctoral degrees in other fields. Riddell, who is frequently quoted as an expert by the media, protested on Twitter that:

> My title is Dr Fern Riddell, not Ms or Miss Riddell. I have it because I am an expert, and my life and career consist of being that expert in as many different ways as possible. I worked hard to earn my authority, and I will not give it up to anyone.

This tweet was not making a point about the treatment of women specifically: its target was a decision that would affect everyone who had a Ph.D. But the responses it attracted made it into a feminist issue. Riddell was quickly caught up in a storm of criticism (much of it, she would note in a later interview (Evans, 2018), from men) which accused her of arrogance and conceit. "If you need to tell people you're an expert, you probably aren't", tweeted one. "Humility, Dr Riddell!" urged another: "there's no Ph.D for that!" The problem, it appeared, was not that she had a Ph.D., but that she expected it to be explicitly acknowledged – a demand which, for her critics, made her guilty of the cardinal female sin of immodesty. She responded by creating a hashtag, #ImmodestWomen, which was taken up enthusiastically by her supporters: a significant number of other women who had Ph.D.s also showed their support by adding the title "Dr" to their Twitter handles.

Not all feminists, however, were willing to do this, and even some who did do it said they felt uncomfortable with the gesture, pointing out that the set of women who had earned Ph.D.s coincided to a large extent with the set of women who had benefited from the unearned privileges of being white, middle class and supported in their pursuit of academic qualifications. They did not want to give the impression that they considered themselves superior to people who had not been granted the same opportunities, nor did they wish to suggest that academic knowledge was the only kind that deserved respect. What Phoebe Maltz Bovy (2017) calls "the privilege turn" in politically progressive circles has arguably exacerbated the double bind for professional women, making it more difficult for them to challenge certain manifestations of the respect gap – and correspondingly easier for men, including those who claim to hold progressive views, to overlook or misrepresent the effects of structural sexism.

The gendered economy of attention: speech, silence, and male intrusion

During the 1970s and 1980s, one phenomenon to which many feminist researchers paid close attention was the unequal sexual distribution of speaking rights. Research conducted in English-speaking communities, using data from both public and private settings, showed a clear tendency for men to take more than their fair share of the floor, speaking for longer than women and interrupting women more frequently than they were interrupted by women (e.g. Zimmerman and West, 1975; West and Zimmerman, 1983; Woods, 1988). More recent studies show that this pattern of male conversational dominance has persisted: it has been observed both in experiments (e.g. Rubin and Hancock, 2014) and in a range of real-world settings including academic conferences (Davenport et al., 2014), School Board deliberations (Karpowitz and Mendelberg, 2014), and, according to a more informal study by a linguistically trained insider (Snyder, 2014), tech industry workplace meetings. Though the factors which produce the overall pattern are multiple and complex (see Cameron, 2015 for discussion), the pattern itself is clearly connected to the tendency of both sexes to accord, consciously or otherwise, more respect to men's opinions, expertise, and leadership, and therefore to privilege their verbal contributions – whether actively, by soliciting and supporting them, or passively, by tolerating (or simply not registering) men's infringements on the speaking rights of others. An analogous pattern has been observed in online settings (which for obvious reasons did not figure in earlier feminist research): in these settings interruption as such is not an issue, but women are nevertheless marginalised relative to men by receiving fewer and/or more negative responses. On newspaper comment sites articles by women attract more negative comments than those written by men (Gardiner et al., 2016); on Twitter, political commentators of both sexes are more likely to follow men than women (Marketing Communication News, 2017); in the blogosphere, "men recommend posts by men to other men" (Rigg, 2009). Men's contributions to public discourse typically receive more positive attention and achieve more influence (as measured by shares, retweets, etc.) than comparable women's.

In cases like those just discussed, the lesser degree of respect accorded to women is manifested in a tendency to give women's speech or writing less attention than it would theoretically, in an equal world, receive (a point dramatised by, for instance, the finding of Karpowitz and Mendelberg (2014) that in mixed conversational groups of five people, women were only able to claim speaking time in proportion to their numbers, where they were not merely a majority but a supermajority, outnumbering men four to one). In other cases, however, disrespect may be manifested through an *excess* of attention. When strangers encounter one another in urban public space, they typically observe a norm of what sociologist Erving Goffman (1971) called "civil inattention", comporting themselves in a manner which displays respect for others' right to go about their business without intrusion. Even when forced into close physical proximity with strangers (as on a crowded bus or train), socially competent adults understand that they should avoid staring at others, making unsolicited comments on their appearance and behaviour, or attempting to engage them in interaction beyond polite formulas ("excuse me") and brief episodes of phatic communion ("hot in here, isn't it?") There are some exceptions to this rule: a person in need of assistance may approach a stranger to request it, and it is also permissible to comment on others' behaviour if it is, itself, in breach of normal public etiquette. But as Carol Brooks Gardner, a student of Goffman, pointed out in a series of articles published in the 1980s (see Gardner, 1980, 1989), the most striking apparent exception is the treatment of women by men.

Gardner investigated this phenomenon in the urban public space of Santa Fe, New Mexico, using a combination of participant observation and in-depth interviews. In the case of women and girls, she found that the theoretical right of every person to go about their business without intrusion ("business" here meaning such mundane activities as walking from A to B) was in practice routinely disregarded. While some male intrusions on women took physical and non-verbal forms (e.g. standing too close, touching, staring), Gardner (1989: 48) was particularly struck by the prevalence of "*street remarks*, that is, free and evaluative commentary that one individual offers to an unacquainted other". Such remarks, she goes on, "are one of the ways in which women are socially controlled by talk in public places" (1989: 49).

Some street remarks are clearly instances of sexual harassment (defined in general terms as "unwanted sexual attention"), but others do not rise – or sink – to that level: rather they purport to be compliments, expressions of friendly interest or, genuine requests for assistance (one of the legitimate exceptions to the norm of civil inattention). Their female recipients are thus faced with a dilemma: if they ignore or rebuff a man's apparently innocent overture they make themselves liable to accusations of impoliteness, but if they respond the exchange may turn into sexual harassment (Gardner gives the example of a woman politely thanking a man who complimented her on her dress, only for him to propose "taking it off for you"). Because she responded in the first place, a woman in this situation is liable to be held responsible for whatever happens next. In addition, women know they must approach exchanges of this type as potential precursors to something more dangerous. One effect of being the object of regular street remarks, regardless of the speaker's actual intentions on any given occasion, is to remind women of their vulnerability to male physical and sexual violence. That vulnerability makes it imprudent for women to confront men who intrude on them. Instead they develop a range of avoidance strategies – including, at the extreme, avoidance of public space itself.

Different urban spaces present women with different dilemmas (which may be different again for different groups of women). In her essay "Power walking" the writer Aminatta Forna (2018) reflects on her experiences as a Black African woman walking around the cities of London, New York, and Freetown, Sierra Leone. In London, the sexism of the men who verbally accost her is inflected by racism, and the intrusions may come from men of any race or class. In New York, she is rarely accosted by white men – a pattern she understands as reflecting the way the complicated history of race relations in the USA interacts with "the codes of heterosexual masculinity", producing a tacit agreement that "black men have ownership of and therefore power over black women". In Freetown, and elsewhere in West Africa, she finds that traditional norms prescribing respectful address from younger to older people – including women – are weakening under the influence of globalisation, but it is still possible to challenge disrespect. If a man behaves insultingly to a woman in public, Forna writes, "and she makes it her business to reply, she can expect the crowd to have her back". This has not been her experience in London, however: though men who harass women in public are breaching the norm of civil inattention, bystanders who witness this behaviour are rarely moved to breach it themselves by intervening. What they are witnessing is "only words" – it is rare for a woman to be directly threatened with physical harm – but as Forna comments, the intention and effect of the words is to shame and humiliate; to strip women "not of their clothing, but of their dignity".

Much of what we know about public verbal intrusions on women in the twenty-first century comes from narratives of personal experience like Forna's essay or the testimonies contributed by women to awareness-raising campaigns like the Everyday Sexism project (Bates, 2014). However, a more systematic investigation was recently undertaken by the UK-based researcher Fiona Vera-Gray (2016, 2018), who recruited 50 women spanning a range of ages, occupations, ethnicities, nationalities, and sexual identities and asked them to keep a detailed record both of the intrusions they experienced over a period of up to two months, and of the measures they took to pre-empt, avoid, or de-escalate problematic encounters in public space. These subjects also participated in a series of interviews in which they reflected on their experiences of intrusion. Many reported not just street remarks made in passing, but more prolonged interactions initiated by male strangers. One woman said about this kind of encounter that "it's definitely talking at you" (Vera-Gray, 2018: 37): men are not seeking genuine interaction, but simply demanding women's attention because "they feel like they want to say something" (2018: 37). Another reflected that "you are more interrupted being a woman.... What women do isn't as important and can be interrupted" (2018: 38).

There are reasons to think that men sometimes "feel like they want to say something" to a woman who is otherwise occupied, not because they are interested in her, but because they are affronted by her apparent disregard for them. Interrupting her is a way to remind her of the patriarchal norm that men are entitled to take from women, while women are obligated to give to men (Manne, 2018): attention is one of the commodities to which this principle applies, and any sign that a woman is withholding it may therefore be construed as a provocation. Resentment of women who do not make themselves freely available to men in public, expressed in complaints about their behaviour and advice on how to respond to it, is a recurring theme in the discourse of the online "manosphere", home to misogynist subcultures such as "incels" and "pick-up artists" (PUAs). In 2016, for example, Dan Bacon, a self-styled "dating and relationships expert" described by others as a PUA, became briefly notorious for a post he had published on his website *The Modern Man* entitled "How to talk to a woman wearing headphones".[1] Its premise was that men need not, and indeed should not, accept that a woman wearing headphones (a common strategy for deterring male intrusion, according to Vera-Gray's research subjects) was unavailable for conversation and had the right to be left alone. "Headphones", Bacon acknowledged, "are a great barrier between a person and the rest of the world". But,

> if a guy wants to get a woman's attention he needs to show confidence by being *determined to get her to stop listening to the music* and chat to him. If a guy has a weak vibe or presence about him, a woman usually won't *give in* to his request for her to remove the headphones. *Women love to test guys* to see how confident they really are and a favorite test of women is to ignore a guy's attempts to converse with her and see what he will do next. Will he walk away in *shame*, or will he remain calm and continue talking to her in a confident, easy-going manner?
>
> Bacon (2013, emphases added)

This advice is reminiscent of an old argument justifying rape – that women say "no" when they mean "maybe", or "try harder". A woman who rejects a man's advances (or wears headphones to discourage them) is just testing his mettle: if he takes her at her word and walks away, she will be disappointed and he will be shamed. Often grounded in popular Darwinist theories of natural sex difference (Bacon also notes that "women don't usually go around approaching men" because they are looking for an "alpha male" who is both able and willing to take the lead), this discourse emphasises to men that what women say or do is not a reliable guide to what they think or what they want. That refusal to grant women authority over the meaning of their own words may be the ultimate manifestation of the gender respect gap.

Conclusion: innovations and challenges

Early feminist researchers of language and gender called attention to the prevalence of what West and Zimmerman (1983) dubbed "small insults" (today they might be labelled "micro-aggressions"), revealing experiences like being interrupted in conversation or intruded on in public space as part of the seen-but-unnoticed backdrop to women's everyday lives. These forms of "everyday" or "banal" sexism are still discussed and written about by women, but today they do not feature so prominently in research on language and gender – especially research done by socio- and applied linguists. Why is that, and what might be done about it?

One issue may be the way we define "sexism in language". That phrase has come to be used preferentially if not exclusively in relation to the linguistic *representation* of women and men, with a particular focus on cases where asymmetry is encoded in the system through, for instance, the non-optional lexical and morphological marking of gender. This is the definition most commonly used in reference works and encyclopaedia entries (see, for example, Menegatti and Rubini, 2017), but arguably it is overly narrow: while for analytic purposes it may be necessary to distinguish between system and use, or interaction and representation, there is no reason why those distinctions should limit the scope of an inquiry into sexism in language. From a feminist perspective it would be more logical to begin with the real-world problem, sexism, and on that basis to place within the scope of our inquiry all those language ideologies and linguistic practices (whether interactional, representational, or both at once) which enact, naturalise, and reproduce it. I have followed this principle myself: the practices I have highlighted (ranging from the use of titles in professional contexts to verbal intrusions on strangers in public space) are not, in linguistic terms, a coherent set, but I have suggested they are connected by a shared social function, namely enacting, naturalising, and reproducing the (explicit or implicit, and in either case sexist) understanding that women are not entitled to the same respect as men.

Another challenge is obtaining the kind of data researchers need to pursue the kind of inquiry I am proposing. Many investigations of the influence of gender on face-to-face interaction rely on data elicited under controlled conditions in a psychology lab, often from participants who have been recruited on a university campus. If we are interested in the everyday manifestations of sexism in real-world contexts we need to gather evidence about a wider range of people interacting in a wider range of settings; we also need data from a greater diversity of languages and societies, given that (as Aminatta Forna's discussion of her experiences in London and West Africa illustrates) both respect norms and the associated communicative practices are cross-culturally and cross-linguistically variable. One way forward might be to use the approach that has been labelled "citizen sociolinguistics". Conceived on the model of "citizen science", this can involve using lay language-users' metacommentaries as data, as I have done in this chapter (see Rymes and Leone, 2014); crowdsourcing data by soliciting information from speakers directly (e.g. Leemann et al., 2016 report on a smartphone app developed to investigate variation and change in British English); or designing protocols and guidelines to enable lay volunteers to act as field researchers themselves (e.g. Svendsen, 2018 discusses a project in which Norwegian school students took this role). These approaches might be particularly useful for investigating phenomena like street remarks, which are not easy for an outsider to collect large quantities of data about (though in this case careful consideration would need to be given to issues of ethics and risk-assessment).

There is growing concern about the abuse and harassment of women, both in physical public space and online, and mainstream institutions are increasingly accepting that this is a serious social problem. In Britain, for instance, where feminist organisations are calling for misogynist verbal abuse to be treated in the same way as the racist or homophobic equivalent, i.e. as potentially a hate crime, some police forces have begun to record cases reported to them as "hate incidents". But we should also recognise the negative effects on women of the lower-level forms of disrespect discussed in this chapter. Being interrupted, or addressed by your first name when the man beside you is addressed as "Dr X", is not and never will be grounds for a complaint to the police, but as the writer Marie Shear (most famous for her definition of feminism as "the radical notion that women are people") once observed, such banal instances take a daily toll, not only because they are so relentless, but also because they are so easily dismissed as trivial. "The beauty of sexist language", Shear wrote (2010) "is its Catch-22":

> Protest a given instance of it and we may be scorned for fussing over trifles or cursed out by a speaker, his animus bursting through his cozy veneer. But if we do not protest, the cumulative effect on our spirits is toxic.

Women are, once again, protesting, and feminist researchers of language should be thinking about how our work can support and amplify the message they are sending – that the respect gap exists, and that it matters.

Note

1 The post was originally published in 2013, but after the negative publicity it received in 2016 extensive cuts and other changes were made to the text. In this chapter I quote the earlier version, which is no longer available on Bacon's site but can still be consulted by using the Wayback Machine, an archival resource that captures data from the same websites at different points in time. I used the version that was captured on 30 August 2016, and this is also the version linked to in the reference list.

References

Bacon, D. (2013) "How to talk to a woman wearing headphones", *The Modern Man*. At: https://web.archive.org/web/20160830015428/http://www.themodernman.com/dating/how-to-talk-to-a-woman-who-is-wearing-headphones.html (accessed 2 May 2019).

Bates, L. (2014) *Everyday sexism*. London: Simon and Schuster.

Beinart, P. (2019) "The new authoritarians are waging war on women", *Atlantic*, January/February. At: www.theatlantic.com/magazine/archive/2019/01/authoritarian-sexism-trump-duterte/576382/ (accessed 24 March 2019).

Billig, M. (1995) *Banal nationalism*. London: SAGE.

Bovy, P.M. (2017) *The perils of privilege: why injustice can't be solved by accusing others of advantage*. New York: St Martin's Press.

Cameron, D. (2015) "Why women talk less", *Language: a feminist guide*, 23 May. At: https://debuk.wordpress.com/2015/05/23/why-women-talk-less/ (accessed 1 May 2019).

Campbell, B. (2014) *The end of equality*. London: Seagull Books.

Davenport, J.R.A., Fouesneau, M., Grand, E., Hagen, A., Poppenhaeger, K. and Watkins, L.L. (2014) "Studying gender in conference talks", data from the 223rd meeting of the American Astronomical Society, 14 March. At: https://arxiv.org/pdf/1403.3091.pdf (accessed 1 May 2019).

Eckert, P. and McConnell-Ginet, S. (1992) "Think practically and look locally: language and gender as community-based practice", *Annual Review of Anthropology*, 21, pp. 461–490.

Evans, P. (2018) "'It's Dr, not Ms', insists historian", *BBC News Website*, 15 June. At: www.bbc.co.uk/news/uk-44496876 (accessed 1 May 2019).

Fairclough, N. (1996) "Border crossings: discourse and social change in contemporary societies", in Coleman, H. and Cameron, L. (eds) *Change in language*. Bristol: Multilingual Matters.

Faludi, S. (1992) *Backlash: the undeclared war against women*. London: Chatto & Windus.

Files, J.A., Mayer, A.P., Ko, M.G., Friedrich, P., Jenkins, M., Bryan, M.J., Vegunta, S., Wittich, C.M., Lyle, M.A., Melikian, R., Duston, T., Chang, Y.H. and Hayes, S.N. (2017) "Speaker introductions at Internal Medicine Grand Rounds: forms of address reveal gender bias", *Journal of Women's Health*, 26(5), pp. 413–419.

Fleig, J. (2015) "Doctor locked out of women's changing room because gym automatically registered everyone with Dr title as male", *Daily Mirror*, 18 March. At: www.mirror.co.uk/news/uk-news/doctor-locked-out-womens-changing-5358594 (accessed 5 May 2019).

Forna, A. (2018) "Power walking", *Lithub*, 19 September. At: https://lithub.com/power-walking/ (accessed 3 May 2019).

Gardiner, B., Mansfield, M., Anderson, I., Holder, J., Louter, D. and Ulmanu, M. (2016) "The dark side of Guardian comments", *Guardian*, 12 April. At: www.theguardian.com/technology/2016/apr/12/the-dark-side-of-guardian-comments (accessed 1 May 2019).

Gardner, C.B. (1980) "Passing by: street remarks, address rights and the urban female", *Sociological Inquiry*, 50(3), pp. 328–356.

Gardner, C.B. (1989) "Analyzing gender in public places", *American Sociologist*, 20(1), pp. 42–56.

Goffman, E. (1971) *Relations in public*. New York: Basic Books.

Goodman, S. (1996) "Market forces speak English", in Graddol, D. and Goodman, S. (eds) *Redesigning English: new texts, new identities*. London: Routledge, pp. 145–183.

Gulliver, K. (2014) "Too much informality", *Inside Higher Education*, 6 March. At: www.insidehighered.com/views/2014/03/06/essay-problems-created-students-who-are-too-informal-professors (accessed 1 May 2019).

Hancock, A.B. and Rubin, B.A. (2014) "Influence of communication partner's gender on language", *Journal of Language and Social Psychology*, 34(1), pp. 46–64.

Hardaker, C. and McGlashan, M. (2016) "'Real men don't hate women': Twitter rape threats and group identity", *Journal of Pragmatics*, 91, pp. 80–93.

Jane, E. (2017) *Misogyny online: a short (and brutal) history*. London: SAGE.

Karpowitz, C. and Mendelberg, T. (2014) *The silent sex: gender, deliberation and institutions*. Princeton, NJ: Princeton University Press.

Leech, G., Hundt, M., Mair, C. and Smith, N. (2010) *Change in contemporary English*. Cambridge: Cambridge University Press.

Leemann, A., Kolly, M.-J., Purves, R., Britain, D. and Glaser, E. (2016) "Crowdsourcing language change with Smartphone applications", *PLoS ONE*, 11(1): e0143060. At: https://doi.org/10.1371/journal.pone.0143060 (accessed 5 May 2019).

McRobbie, A. (2009) *The aftermath of feminism: gender, culture and social change*. London: SAGE.

Manne, K. (2018) *Down girl: the logic of misogyny*. New York: Oxford University Press.

Marketing Communication News (2017) "Female UK politics journalists impacted by Twitter gender glass ceiling, Lissted research confirms", 23 October. At: https://marcommnews.com/female-uk-politics-journalists-impacted-by-twitter-gender-glass-ceiling-lissted-research-confirms/ (accessed 1 May 2019).

Menegatti, M. and Rubini, M. (2017) "Gender bias and sexism in language", in Nussbaum, J.L. (ed.) *Oxford research encyclopedia of communication*. Oxford: Oxford University Press.

Nagle, A. (2017) *Kill all normies: online culture wars from 4Chan and tumblr to Trump and the alt-right*. Alresford: Zero Books.

Phillips, S.U. (2003) "The power of gender ideologies in discourse", in Holmes, J. and Meyerhoff, M. (eds) *The handbook of language and gender*. Malden, MA: Wiley-Blackwell, pp. 252–276.

Rigg, J. (2009) "Where are all the female bloggers?", 19 October. At: https://miss-s-b.dreamwidth.org/981399.html (accessed 1 May 2019).

Rymes, B. and Leone, A. (2014) "Citizen sociolinguistics: a new media methodology for understanding language and social life", *University of Pennsylvania Working Papers in Educational Linguistics*, 29(2). At: https://repository.upenn.edu/cgi/viewcontent.cgi?article=1262&context=wpel (accessed 5 May 2019).

Schuman, R. (2014) "That's 'Doctor instructor' to you", *Slate*, 13 March. At: https://slate.com/human-interest/2014/03/what-should-students-call-their-college-professors.html (accessed 1 May 2019).

Shear, M. (2010) "Little Marie and the daily toll of sexist language", *On the Issues*, Summer/Fall. At: www.ontheissuesmagazine.com/2010summer/2010summer_Shear.php (accessed 5 May 2019).

Snyder, K. (2014) "How to get ahead as a woman in tech: learn to interrupt men", *Slate*, 23 July. At: https://slate.com/human-interest/2014/07/study-men-interrupt-women-more-in-tech-workplaces-but-high-ranking-women-learn-to-interrupt.html (accessed 1 May 2019).

Svendsen, B.A. (2018) "The dynamics of citizen sociolinguistics", *Journal of Sociolinguistics*, 22(2), pp. 137–160.

Vera-Gray, F. (2016) *Men's intrusion, women's embodiment: a critical analysis of street harassment*. Abingdon: Routledge.

Vera-Gray, F. (2018) *The right amount of panic: how women trade freedom for safety*. Bristol: Policy Press.

West, C. and Zimmerman, D. (1983) "Small insults: a study of interruptions in cross-sex conversations between unacquainted persons", in Thorne, B., Kramarae, C. and Henley, N. (eds) *Language, gender and society*. Cambridge, MA: Newbury House, pp. 102–107.

Wodak, R. (2015) *The politics of fear: what right-wing populist discourses mean*. London: SAGE.
Woods, N. (1988) "Talking shop: sex and status as determinants of floor apportionment in a work setting", in Coates, J. and Cameron, D. (eds) *Women in their speech communities: new perspectives on language and sex*. London: Longman, pp. 141–157.
Wouters, C. (2007) *Informalization: manners and emotions since 1890*. London: SAGE.
Zimmerman, D. and West, C. (1975) "Sex roles, interruptions and silences in conversation", in Thorne, B., Kramarae, C. and Henley, N. (eds) *Language, gender and society*. Cambridge, MA: Newbury House, pp. 109–129.

3

THE TRANSGRESSIVE, THE TRADITIONAL

Sexist discourses of grandmothering and ageing

Carmen Rosa Caldas-Coulthard
FEDERAL UNIVERSITY OF SANTA CATARINA, BRAZIL

Rosamund Moon
UNIVERSITY OF BIRMINGHAM, UK

> "When old women are not invisible, they may be regarded as figures of fun or objects of contempt."
> *Florence Keyworth (1982: 133)*

Introduction

A letter to the UK newspaper the *Guardian*, protesting at an opinion piece (Harris, 2016) and its reference to the behaviour of Labour Party members at a local constituency meeting, ended as follows: "As a grandmother who has read the Guardian for 50 years, I strongly object to being portrayed in your paper as some sort of spitting extremist."[1] What interests us is not the original article and whether what it said is true, but that this writer asserts her grandmotherhood in order to validate her objection (and denial). She is indexing more than reproductive status: for the implicature to work, readers must believe that there are norms for grandmotherly behaviour, for example that grandmothers are expected to hold moderate views and do not spit. Stereotyping of grandmothers is built on assumptions like these: how grandmothers behave, what they generally do, and what they look like.

In this chapter we will explore how the category "grandmother" and the performance of grandmothering are represented through images and language. This is a topic scarcely addressed within the areas of gender and language studies or critical discourse analysis:[2] a surprising omission since grandparenting and the situation of older women and men in general have been much discussed in other areas, including the sociology and psychology of ageing (e.g. Coupland et al., 1991;

Coupland and Coupland, 1993; Garner and Mercer, 2001), cultural studies (e.g. Greer, 1991; Featherstone and Wernick, 1995; Woodward, 1995; Gullette, 1997; Twigg, 2013), as well as in gerontology and ageing studies more widely (e.g. in the *Journal of Aging Studies* and the journal *Women and Aging*).

Twenty-four years ago, Hamilton (1992: 240) pointed out the important issue that "language, gender and aging are not being addressed simultaneously within the same scholarly studies". The situation has changed little since then – of all the articles published in the journal *Gender and Language* over recent years, only one (Moon, 2014) specifically addresses the lexical representation of age. As older women ourselves, one a semiotician and gender scholar, the other a lexicographer and corpus linguist, we feel that it is more than time to consider how older gender identities and gender roles (that of grandmother in this study) intersect and are recontextualised in public discourses, and what the social effects of these are.

In writing about the category of grandmother, we acknowledge that we cannot fully address its extreme heterogeneity; also, that our focus is clearly anglocentric. Different cultures have different traditions and practices of grandmothering, and therefore there will be different ways of representing these practices, but these are beyond the scope of the present chapter. Further, it is important to add that, though we are only considering grandmothers here, the category of grandfather is similarly neglected: parallel studies, we anticipate, would make many similar but also perhaps different (less sexist) observations.

To explore the question of how "grandmother" is constructed semiotically, we will be drawing on image banks, corpus data, and other texts in order to discuss images, and lexical/textual labelling and their intermodal relations. We are concerned exclusively with semiotic representation since for us, it is through representation, the process of giving meaning to things through language (Hall, 1997) and other semiotic modes of signification (van Leeuwen, 2005) that ideologies are transmitted. With Eckert and McConnell-Ginet (1995: 470) we also believe that:

> social categories and characterization are human creations; the concepts associated with them are not preformed, waiting for labels to be attached, but are created, sustained and transformed by social processes that importantly include labelling itself. And labelling is only part of a more complex sociolinguistic activity that contributes to constituting social categories and power relations among members of a community.

Van Leeuwen (2008: 32) adds that representation "plays a significant part in the work of many critical linguists" since it helps in exposing who is represented as "agent" or "patient" in a given action, in an active or passive role.

In terms of theory, the notion of discourse adopted here relates to the set of attitudes or values of a speaker/writer. Inevitably our linguistic choices in speech or text reflect these attitudes and values and also constitute them. Our concept of discourse follows the body of work from systemic linguistics (Halliday, 1978,

1985), the multimodal social semiotics of Kress and van Leeuwen (1996, 2001), Machin (2007), Machin and van Leeuwen (2007), van Leeuwen (2008), and the "appraisal" theory of Martin and White (2005). We will examine how semiotic resources about grandmothers produce evaluative effects, which influence behaviour, attitudes, and social practices in relation to this specific social category. For us, semiotic resources create meaning and reflect, as part of social action, views and ideologies of interactants.

Grandmothers, in our visual data, are contextualised and resemiotised (Iedema, 2003) in two ways: sharing semiotic resources of childhood or domestic contexts, or presented as transgressive actors, located in incongruous situations or performing behaviours inappropriate for their "age". Our discussion of corpus data complements the multimodal analyses, providing further examples of stereotyping. While references to individual grandmothers are often evaluated positively, there is also strong evidence of generic, figurative, and other usages that trivialise and derogate them. Our conclusions point to processes of social devaluation and gender bias. In many representations, they are "desexed" because they are shown as physically beyond the age of sexual interest and rarely addressed or recontextualised as sexual beings. They are only gendered in the context of family, home, and traditional "female" pursuits. These ageist and sexist representations are naturalised, and deeply embedded, we argue, in practices of exclusion and discrimination. As Fairclough (2013: 71) points out, "if one becomes aware that a particular aspect of common sense is sustaining power inequalities at one's own expense, it ceases to be common sense, and may cease to have the capacity to sustain power inequalities". In exploring the complex category of grandmother, this is our aim.

The broader implications are particularly relevant for the present time, as new forms of grandmothering appear: "new grandmothers", active women doing grandmothering while being partners and professionals themselves. These forms are still largely excluded from public discourses, except those specifically dealing with family issues or directed at older women.

Getting old: invisibility

"Grandmotherhood" is a social, cultural, and uncontested biological category associated with ageing. Greer (1991: 24) links it in with the climacteric, and the fifth of a woman's seven ages: "the end of mothering and the beginning of grandmothering". "Getting old", especially for women, is a conventionalised and a problematic period, since women undergo a profound biological transition (from being reproductive to not being reproductive). Just before or after the climacteric period, therefore, there are too many pressures imposed by a society that does not value women for their intellectual or moral qualities, but simply by their external appearance and sexual performance. Grandmothering, however, is one of the few roles that older women perform, at least in western societies, which may afford them some status and respect, although they are still expected to conform to gendered domesticity. Tahmaseb-McConatha (2013) suggests that research findings show that:

> a satisfying relationship with grandparents has many positive consequences for grandchildren. Research also indicates that there are no clear role expectations for grandparents. Like other social roles, the role of grandmother is culturally contoured and based on social context in which it is played.

A good example of the thin line between negative and positive connotations of this role is provided by Hillary Clinton, with respect to the ways she was talked about in the press and the ways she talked about herself, as in this example from the *Guardian*:

> Can Hillary Clinton run for president AND be a grandmother? Oh, women – always wanting to have it all, aren't they? Well-known US TV journalists have expressed disbelief that the two roles could possibly be combined: "President or grandmother?"
>
> Freeman (2014)

The sexist affirmation that Hillary Clinton could not be a president *because* she is a grandmother brings to the surface all the discriminatory accusations that women suffer because of their domestic status/roles. The binary division public/domestic seems to continue to be enacted in post-feminist times at least as far as old age is concerned. In 2015, Clinton herself took advantage of the positive connotations associated with grandmotherhood and supported her campaign by the creation of a new hashtag: #GrandmotherKnowsBest. And the *Guardian* commentator Suzanne Goldenberg (2015) reported: "'[Hillary Clinton] is going to own the wise, smart grandmother,' [Debbie] Walsh said. 'Embracing the title grandmother – rather than running away – makes her real, makes her human, makes her a more fully rounded candidate.'" These quotes show how the role can be semiotised in different ways connoting profound ideological difference – having political power and being a grandmother do not go together. Knowledge on the other hand is an advantage that the role embodies. And Clinton confirmed: "I'm not a scientist, I'm *just* a grandmother with two eyes and a brain" (Clinton, 2015, emphasis added).

Clinton here used what Thompson (2016) calls "the language of authenticity", a language that privileges emotion and personal experience instead of rationality and political argumentation. By evoking her status as a "grandmother", which is apolitical, she was hoping to draw on the positive qualities that all voters associate with grandmothers. Similarly, the former Brazilian President, Dilma Rousseff, in a speech defending herself against her impeachment (in August 2016), declared "it's not going to be now, after becoming a mother and grandmother, that I will abandon the principles that have always guided me" (Watts and Bowater, 2016). Again here, the same discursive strategies are being used.

The representation of this performed identity is, however, very problematic because it points to stereotypes that are inseparable from those associated with older women in general. Is the role more important than the profession? We cannot imagine that Donald Trump, the competing candidate for the USA presidency in 2016, would have been represented in the press or would have recontextualised himself as a "grandfather": this reference does not occur in political discourses that refer to men.

Caldas-Coulthard (2010: 23) quotes Hepworth (2003: 89), who, in his essay "Ageing bodies: aged by culture", suggests that "the master narrative of human ageing in western culture is biomedical and the biomedical modes of ageing are essentially a reductionist model of decline". Some radical critiques of the decline model, she suggests, especially the work of Margaret Gullette (1997) presented by Hepworth, argue for the "cyclical evolutionary principle within each species – a biologically determined process of continual regeneration and renewal" (Caldas-Coulthard, 2010: 23). Both Hareven (1995) and Gullette (1997) claim that age and ageing as decline are culturally constructed, and that since all stages of life are represented in discourses, they can therefore be contested in other discourses.

The vast majority of public references to old women in general and to "grandmothers" in particular tend to support the decline narrative and its negative associations. Being old for most brings withdrawal from social life: "transition in gender roles and change in the social spheres in which people hold authority as they relate to aging" (Hamilton, 1992: 242). Greer (1991: 20), in her brilliant work on menopausal women, comments that: "Sooner or later the middle-aged woman becomes aware of a change in the attitude of other people towards her. She can no longer trade on her appearance [...] There is no defined role for her in modern society." With age, comes social invisibility. Greer reminds us that even in fiction, most heroines are young. On the topic of ageing and invisibility, Greer (1991: 30) quotes the classic writings of Doris Lessing, who perfectly describes the feelings of the invisible woman:[3]

> It seemed a long time before the food came. Kate sat on, invisible, apparently, to the waitress and to the other customers: the place was filling now. She was shaking with impatient hunger, the need to cry. The feeling that no one could see her made her want to shout: "Look, I am here, can't you see me?" She was not far off that state that in a small child is called a tantrum.
>
> *Lessing ([1973] 2009: 187)*

The decline theory is a manifestation of the ideology of "ageism", which is, according to Copper (1986: 47),

> the negative social response to different stages in the process of aging and it is a political issue. The ageism that old women experience is firmly embedded in sexism – an extension of the male power to define, control values, erase, disempower and divide.

Fairclough (2010: 26) states that "ideologies are a significant element of processes through which relations of power are established, maintained, enacted and transformed". He also highlights that ideology is most effective when its workings are least visible.

One of the consequences of the ideology of ageism is invisibility, silence, and stereotyping. Grandmothers and older people in general rarely have their voices heard in public spaces, but are represented in various derogative ways, as we will demonstrate below. These stereotypes are ingrained in western societies and materialised in many types of discourse. Old women/grandmothers are referred to as "crones" or as "old bats" or "hags", or are othered for being old, weak, or dependent; post-menopausal women are positioned as mentally or physically deranged. Old women are also ridiculed as unattractive, and they are also commonly assumed to be sexually repulsive. As Greer (1991: 302) reminds us "the mythology of temptation is full of beautiful maidens who turn into hell hags with no more gruesome attributes than the normal attributes of age". An association with witches is pervasive in most types of children's literature that allude to grandmothers. These stereotypes are represented in semiotic resources which are not natural or homogeneous but culture-specific, and age and gender bias surface to varying extents in the choices participants of interactions make. We will discuss these choices in our analysis.

Googling grandma

A phrase like "as a grandmother" may assume norms of grandmotherly behaviour; it may also set up expectations of grandmotherly appearance. This corpus example[4] describing a "real grandmother" is strikingly visual:

> as a young child she loved her Nanny but didn't like her Grandma at all because she didn't seem like a "real grandmother." Nanny, wearing wire-rimmed glasses and flowered housedresses, baked cookies and riveted her full attention on Anne's entertainment. [non-fiction]

We will discuss stereotypical grandmothers like the one depicted here in both our visual and textual data. As a preliminary, a quick way of gauging what visual stereotypes we might find is via Google Images: if successive searches consistently produce screenfuls of very similar images, we get some useful information. What we learned from searching for *grandmother* or *grandmothers* is that grandmothers have white hair, frequently permed or set in waves, and wrinkled skin; they are usually smiling; they often wear glasses and diluted pale or dull dark clothes; if engaged in activities, they are interacting with grandchildren, or cooking, or knitting. *Grandma(s)* produces similar results. These are traditional grandmothers, elderly, nurturing, non-dominant, desexualised. Searches for *traditional grandmother(s)/grandma(s)* elicit further such images, though interestingly more non-Caucasian women, and also images purely of foodstuffs, especially baked goods and preserves (traditional grandmotherly products).

Less consistent are the kinds of images elicited by *granny* and *grannies* as search terms: colours are brighter; women pull faces, gesticulate, and are altogether more active. They present alternative grandmotherhoods, perhaps more empowering, often more humorous (but does the viewer laugh with or at these grannies?). More striking still are the sets of pornographic images elicited when the word *granny/grannies* is preceded by an adjective denoting ethnicity, size (*fat/thin/big*), or other characteristic (*sweet, pretty, nasty*): "grannies" are older women, not necessarily elderly though mainly grey- or white-haired, are mostly naked or near-naked, and are engaging in sexual acts or sexual display. Is this liberating, since older women are being afforded sexuality? Or is it sexist and exploitative, often racist as well? Like the acronym GILF (= "grandmother I'd like to fuck"), these images both celebrate and debase.

Clearly there are major limitations in using Google Images as a research tool in this way, particularly since search results are not replicable. However, it draws attention to features that also emerge through methodical analyses of specific images, words, and texts, and also serves as a reminder that shifts in naming and lexical form, though apparently trivial, may well be associated with very significant shifts of meaning.

Grandmas in image banks

The structured and stable nature of commercial image banks offers opportunities for more systematic study. As Machin (2004) and Hansen and Machin (2008) have demonstrated, image banks like Getty and Corbis "stock many millions of images, which can raise revenue of up to $100,000 each a year as they are licensed to designers around the planet" (Machin, 2004: 317). These images, as Machin suggests, do not record reality but evoke an idea or a feeling and "convey particular kinds of scripts, values and identities" (Hansen and Machin, 2008: 781) as well as social relations. Photographs or illustrations in image banks "emphasise photography as a symbolic system and the photograph as an element of layout design, rather than as an image which can stand on its own" (Hansen and Machin, 2008: 783).

Our search for grandmothers in iStock Images (istockphoto.com – a branch of Getty Images), where our photos come from, exemplifies these points. By typing the word *grandmother* we are offered over 12,000 symbolic photos and drawings which represent scripts and identities associated with grandmotherhood – they can be either traditional or not. As with the Google search, grandmothers in our examples confirm social types and values. All images are accompanied by linguistic labels, which classify them into types: *third age, 70 years old, beauty, life style, odd, entertainment, gestures, happiness*.

As Kress and van Leeuwen (1996) have shown so well, there are some parallels that can be drawn between visual and linguistic interpellation. If the participants' eye line makes contact with the viewer, an imaginary contact is established between the represented participants and the viewer. The image is then categorised as a "demand" and the power of "demand" is that the participants are directly addressing

FIGURE 3.1 Beautiful grandma (courtesy of iStock/Getty Images, reproduced with their permission).

the viewer. The small distance between the represented participant and the viewer is also relevant. Proximity between the participants is established because the pictures are taken as *close shots*. Figure 3.1 is an example of a demand picture.

This picture is also generic and decontextualised (Machin, 2004: 320) – the background is out of focus and the only activity performed is the drinking of tea, conveyed by the white cup. According to Kress and van Leeuwen (1996: 165), "by being 'decontextualised', shown in a void, represented participants become generic, a 'typical example', rather than particular, and connected with a particular location and a specific moment in time".

Further examples (Figures 3.2–3.3) show visual variations of the traditional grandmother: if engaged in activities, they interact with grandchildren (not with the viewer) – these are examples of "offer" pictures, offering "the represented participants to the viewer as items of information, objects of contemplation,

FIGURE 3.2 Grandma with child in kitchen (courtesy of iStock/Getty Images, reproduced with their permission).

impersonally, as though they were specimens in a display case" (Kress and van Leeuwen, 1996: 124). They are located again in generic and unfocused settings, generally in domestic spaces: cooking or knitting, playing with children.

Kress and van Leeuwen (2001) also point out that in some domains certain visuals are in fact "truer" than others. Images can represent a person, a thing, or a space according to a scale of "it might look like this" to "it looks like this". The authors call this *coding orientation*, which is a realisation of modality: "naturalistic" (the more the image resembles what we see in reality), "abstract" (how the image

The transgressive, the traditional   43

FIGURE 3.3 Grandma knitting (courtesy of iStock/Getty Images, reproduced with their permission).

shows the essence of what it depicts), and "sensory" (the effect of pleasure or non-pleasure created by the visuals). Other modality markers are degrees of articulation of detail, of background, of depth, of colour modulation and saturation.

Our examples show that the visual choices used by photographers of women symbolising grandmothers index meanings of love and kindness associated with the traditional normative grandmother because they are represented in naturalistic

FIGURE 3.4 Transgressive grandmother (courtesy of iStock/Getty Images, reproduced with their permission).

ways (we believe these are grandmothers because of their convincing friendly smiling faces, white hair, and wrinkles) and sensory ways (e.g. note the vegetables in Figure 3.2). Other choices are the pastel non-saturated colours (whites, beiges, or diluted bluish, pinks, or greens) that could potentially be associated with low or non-sexuality since, as van Leeuwen (2011: 85) points out, "colour plays a particular role in signifying identity". In our case, the pastel colours define asexual women.

The transgressive grandmother's identity (Figure 3.4), by contrast, is materialised through the presentation of demand pictures which interpellate the viewer by aggressive gestures, strong and saturated colours (reds and strong blues), exaggerated attributes (the big glasses). These point to values of non-normativity.

These transgressive representations, of course, have to do with the rejection of the traditional role, but at the same time, they signal the inseparability of humour and denigration. From a multimodal perspective, therefore, grandmothers in image banks are represented clearly from ideological positions, confirming as in other representations, bias against older women.

Texts about grandmothers

While grandmotherhood as a topic is treated in only a limited range of public discourses, this range includes a variety of multimodal genres. There are many procedural texts of how to be a better grandmother (Gransnet, 2013b; Fearnly-Whittingstall, 2011), websites addressed to grandmothers (giving advice and suggestions, hosting discussion fora, etc., e.g. www.gransnet.com), and of course, many children's books with grandmothers as important characters.

A very interesting modal aspect of these genres, including the procedural ones addressed to "older women", is that their meaning potential is always related to childhood and femininity: most book covers present scenarios through drawings (not photos), and the predominant colours are pink, purple, green, and yellow. These choices in colour connote not only childhood but also gender. Caldas-Coulthard and van Leeuwen (2002) have demonstrated that colours can be an important signifier of gender in the world of children and toys. Think of the classic contemporary division of pink for girls, blue for boys. Nor is it only pink and blue that are associated with gender:

> There are all kinds of mauves, pinkish purples, bluish purples ranging from pale to hot and brooding and from light to dark menacing – hardly surprising given that there are different kinds of "femininities". Other colours, like blue for boys or dark colours for men, attach values to the idea of masculinity.
> *Caldas-Coulthard and van Leeuwen (2002: 101)*

As with toys, the pale and non-saturated colours in book covers relating to grandmothers convey not only femininity but also affective positive feelings related to childhood: "Through different shades, the principle of pleasure is enacted. We react positively to colours that attract us" (Caldas-Coulthard and van Leeuwen, 2002: 107).

Further important semiotic modes associated with childhood in these publications are typography (see Kress and van Leeuwen, 1996; Machin, 2007 for the description of the meaning of typography) and illustrations. The types convey playful moods – fonts are cursive, light, irregular, gently curved, and rounded, like children's writing. The illustrations are often in a naïve style, like young children's drawings. There is therefore, through the choices of the modes of colour, typography, and illustration, an association with childhood which is simultaneously reductionist and belittling. These points can be demonstrated simply, for example, by searching the Amazon site for books with "grandmother" or "granny" in their titles, and looking at the design choices of their covers.

Apart from childhood references and allusions, there are other recurrent thematic similarities in texts about grandmothers:

1. of empowerment, positive ageing, purposefulness; but also
2. of frailty and decline, rejection, vulnerability, disempowerment, invisibility; and
3. of specific gendered practices associated with femininity and domesticity; and
4. of desexing (old women are considered physically beyond the age of sexual interest).

These themes are realised through the semiotic system of evaluation, which is the attaching of values to people, things, and actions. Martin and White (2005) label the ways we access the world around us as "evaluative disposition or stance". One of the main functions of evaluative language according to the authors is attitudinal; in other words, "we use language (and semiotic resources) to assign values of 'praising' and 'blaming', by which writers/speakers indicate either a positive or negative assessment of people, places, things, happenings and states of affairs" (White, 2001). For Martin and White (2005), there are three types of attitude: *affect*, which is evaluation that indicates emotional states of affairs (likes and dislikes, such as *I adore my grandmother*); *judgement*, which is the assessment of human behaviour with reference to rules, social acceptability, systems of ethics, legality, etiquette, and social norms (*my grandmother was rather strict on those things*); and finally *appreciation*, which is the evaluation of human artefacts as well as human individuals (*my grandmother was a formidable old lady with a small, round, remarkably unlined face*). And it is through these systems of evaluation, especially through social sanctions, judgments, and aesthetic appreciations, that "grandmothers" are represented – most of the time negatively, we would argue, as our data exemplify.

In the very popular book *Gangsta Granny*, written by David Walliams and illustrated by Tony Ross, the grandmother, as the title suggests, is a gangster (Walliams, 2011). To be transgressive as an old woman can have positive connotations, since transgression, as we mentioned earlier, subverts the social order. However, in *Gangsta Granny*, grandmother as a social actor is constantly being evaluated negatively, especially through references to the body that connote meanings of negative appreciation.

Figure 3.5 shows a 12-year-old boy's visualisation of this Gangsta Granny after he had read the book. Note how the image becomes much more negative if one adds labels to it (as in Tony Ross's original image for the book): "thick glasses, white hair, false teeth, hearing aid, hairy chin, mauve cardigan, smell of cabbage, used tissue tucked up sleeve, a packet of Murray Mints close by, tan tights, floral-print dress, burgundy slippers" (Walliams, 2011: 18).

Gangsta Granny's brain also constantly fails throughout the text: "I am going to put another cardigan on, she said, even though she was already wearing two"; "She probably doesn't understand what you're saying half the time". Also, she smells of cabbage – smell as a semiotic resource is invoked here as negative appreciation/evaluation. Norris (2013) points out that "smell" is a semiotic mode and words that refer to the biological capacity of human beings to smell afford different meaning potentials. In our case, Gangsta Granny would be interpreted differently if she smelt of roses. Nevertheless, "She stinks of cabbage"; "A very slight odour of boiled vegetables"; "She reeked of cabbage"; "rotten cabbage". Another interesting visual clue is that Gangsta Granny never interacts with the viewer/reader. The "offer" pictures of the character are objects of contemplation with whom we do not associate. The transgression therefore, although funny, should not be imitated – it is only for display.

A visual image from iStock typifies a "naughty" granny, similar to the one created by Walliams and Ross (Figure 3.6). Her semiotic features once again point to humorous but derogative meanings – she is very ugly (her profile picture is asymmetrical, her

The transgressive, the traditional 47

FIGURE 3.5 Gangsta Granny illustration by Josh Roberts.

nose and chin are big, her body is curved and unattractive), her colours are saturated (especially her red boots, therefore shocking for her age), she wears comical glasses, a Zimmer frame, and she is outrageous. At the same time, because of these semiotic props, we could derive positive evaluations: she is an old, free, independent woman, not defined by traditional expectations for ageing women.

Another example is the book *My Granny*, written by Nanette Newman and illustrated by Beryl Cook, published in 1983. The cover depicts an old, large woman with white hair, dressed in a bright yellow dress, sitting in a tree and eating a

48 Caldas-Coulthard and Moon

FIGURE 3.6 "Naughty" granny (courtesy of iStock/Getty Images, reproduced with their permission).

sandwich. Other illustrations in the book present "Granny" in a series of further incongruous contexts. For example, she is shown in a dancing class, wearing a leotard and bright red tap shoes. The associated linguistic description categorises her as "odd-type":

> Granny learnt to dance at 82,
> A really odd-type thing to do;
> And when she'd learnt both tap and ballet,
> She changed her name from Maude to Sally.
> *Newman (1983)*

The implicit negative evaluation (old women are not expected to dance and display their bodies at 82!) points to meanings of social judgement and prescriptive behaviour. From a multimodal perspective, the illustrations, like the photos discussed earlier, are very revealing. The images are not used merely to illustrate the text, but also convey subliminal meanings (Barthes, 1977) of fun – and at the same time derogation.

In both books, these are "aberrant" grandmothers, distorted in text and images, intend to entertain the readers. But the conceit of the aberration only works through contrast with a presumed "normal", whether this is the Walliams/Ross caricature of the frumpy smelly old woman, or Newman/Cook's "frightful bore": negative stereotypes of elderly females, albeit disavowed within the narratives. The entertainment value of aberrant and subversive grandmothers therefore has to be considered against a backdrop of widespread concern about ageist as well as sexist stereotyping in children's literature and its prejudicial effect on the young: a concern expressed in a substantial body of work by educationalists, psychologists, sociologists, gerontologists, and others over the last 40 or so years (see, for example, studies by Ansello, 1977; Storey, 1977; Hurst, 1981; Beland and Mills, 2001; Henneberg, 2010; Hollis-Sawyer and Cuevas, 2013; and Iversen, 2015 with respect to digital games).

Grandmothers in corpus data

In this final section of analysis, we explore the category of grandmother as expressed through language, drawing on data from the 450-million-word Bank of English corpus (BoE),[5] and examining its evidence for the word *grandmother*, its pet forms, and cognates. Of the different English words for a parent's mother, *grandmother/s* is by far the most frequent in BoE (16.9 instances per million words), followed by *granny/grannies* (5.8), *grandma/s* (3.5) and *gran/s* (2.8):[6] pet forms such as *gran* and *nan* occur particularly strongly in spoken interaction and tabloid journalism.[7]

Our main use of BoE is as a source of examples in which grandmothers are described or describe themselves, but there are points of interest too in the collocations of these words.[8] For example, the collocational profile for *(great-)grandmother/s* in BoE includes a number of items referring to age, health, lifetime, or lineage (*X-years-old, elderly, aged; frail, sick; died, late, lived; maternal, paternal*); however, more revealing is a subset of its premodifying adjectivals: *beloved, dear, doting, kindly*, also *caring, indulgent*, which point to the affection and significance of the grandmother–grandchild relationship within a family (and evaluate positively). Also foregrounded in the profile for *(great-)grandmother/s* are other female kinship terms and words referring to home and family (*aunt/s, daughter, sister, mother/s; children, parents; family, house*): grandmothers are being sited lexically within a discourse world of domesticity, in the traditional narrative of the family, a female world – as we also found in images.

Corpus data help clarify distinctions in usage between *grandmother* and pet forms *grandma/granny*, etc., though often selection is simply a matter of formality, or realises an individual family's preference or convention.[9]

But the selection may be more heavily freighted. Even though BoE examples concerning individual grandmothers are typically associated with positive evaluations, generic uses, often as plurals, are frequently pejorative. The pet form *granny/grannies*, with its diminutive ending *-y*, is a particular locus of derogation, as examples will later show – diminutives literally belittle, whether for endearment or to show disdain. We have already seen how searching image banks for *granny/grannies* elicited quite different kinds of image from *grandmother/s*. And in the following BoE example from a newspaper advice column, a female correspondent's question about naming shows her particular resistance to *granny* because of the stereotypes it invokes and its implications of ageing:

> The thing is, I don't know what I would like my grandchild to call me. I can't stand the thought of being called granny, which makes me think of a little old greyhaired woman in a rocking chair, or even nan or nana. I am a very youngish 40-year-old. [journalism]

Beyond the corpus, naming practices are regularly discussed in grandparenting texts or on websites: for example, *The new granny's survival guide* has this, with a contributor's quote which echoes the sentiment in the BoE example:

> **What should your grandchildren call you?**
>
> Gran, Granny, Nan, Nanny, Nonna, Nana, Gangy, Grandma, Gumpy, Guk (yes, really), Gorki ... there are no rules for what you should be called when you become a grandmother. For some, the word "granny" is like music to their ears. For others, it's rather more discordant: *It's so ... grey hair and rocking chair. I'm just not ready to see myself like that.*
>
> Gransnet (2013b)

Whether still in her middle years or in deeper old age, a grandmother is de facto an older woman (and *grandmother* collocates with *elderly, frail, sick, died* ...). So grandmotherhood inevitably acquires some of the same connotations as other lexical items that indicate or imply ageing, items generally associated with negative evaluation. See, for example, findings in corpus studies of *elderly* (Baker, 2006, 2010; Mautner, 2007) and *old woman/lady* (Moon, 2014: 21ff).[10] There is no shortage of BoE examples that depict the frailty or vulnerability of grandmothers, including these, where *grandmothers* and *gran* are used for emotive effect:

> But still it seems as if it's a cowardly war. [...] civilians are dying, grandmothers are dying in the streets of Sarajevo? [radio journalism]
>
> A dope-smoking teenager repeatedly beat his 65-year-old gran for two years so he could get her pension money for drugs, a court heard yesterday. [journalism]

What grandmas are like, and what they do

In our discussions of images, we made a number of observations about grandmothers and stereotyping. Examples in BoE help to identify further core features of grandmotherly stereotypes: that is, a set of characteristics traditionally associated with grandmotherliness. Particularly useful in this respect are BoE's examples in which individuals reminisce about their grandmothers – for example, recollecting what their grandmothers looked like:

> I adored my grandmother, who was everything a granny should be – tiny and white-haired, eccentric and fascinating, kind and generous. [journalism]

> I called my grandmother Granno. She was a formidable old lady with a small, round, remarkably unlined face, and was always dressed from neck to toe in black. Her silvery hair was scraped back into a bun. [non-fiction]

> One of my earliest influences was my Granny Fitzsimmons. She wore a starched apron and baked things, and smelled and looked like a granny – with a blue rinse. [journalism]

Recurring elements here and in other corpus examples are references to skin/wrinkles, hair colour, clothing: where colours are mentioned, these are low saturation, pale, or dull (lavenders, blues, white, grey, black; cf. our discussion above of colour in visual images, and see also Twigg's comments about colour in clothing worn by older women: Twigg, 2013: 26–28, 136–139). Recollections also mention smell, but what does it mean to smell like a granny, as in the last of the examples above? To smell of baking? Or something else, as in the following:

> So Anastasia helped her father fold the clothes that still smelled like her grandmother: like soap and powder and lilac cologne. [fiction]

> She dreamed of her grandmother's house. She dreamed the smell of mothballs and turf and fresh-baked cake. [fiction]

> "I shouldn't say it, Daddy, but why does Grandma's house always smell of cooking? [...] It doesn't smell like your cooking, [...] I wouldn't mind if it did. But it's, I dunno, cabbage, stuff like that." [fiction]

Flowery scents, cooking, or grandmothers' homes, usually evaluated positively and through metonymy symbolising the emotional relationship with the grandmother. Though the third is clearly negative: just as with *Gangsta Granny*, *cabbage* in BoE is invariably associated with unpleasant smells and poor, old-fashioned, styles of cooking.

Positive evaluations are also evident in these next examples, describing what grandmothers do and say: nurturing, generosity, moral guidance; homemaking, baking, traditional crafts, and so on. There is a sense of continuity with these women's domestic lives as mothers; also, with a role as guardians of tradition:

> my grandmother on my mother's side was a wonderful wonderful woman. We used to go up there and there was she used to make jam and we sh w I I used to say to her Can I sleep here the night? [unedited transcribed spoken interaction]

> This recipe was handed down to me from my grandmother, who liked to bake this cake on Saturday afternoon and serve it after dinner with vanilla ice cream. [non-fiction]

> a handmade Fair Isle cardigan, the sort grandma stopped knitting for you when you were 10. [journalism]

From examples like these, we can build up an inventory of grandmotherly features, the characteristics frequently associated with grandmothers in BoE:[11] metonymic signifiers of old age such as grey and white hair, wrinkled skin, glasses, etc.; unfashionable or practical clothing in muted colours; scents and cooking smells; family ties and nurturing, domestic skills, traditional knowledge; their homes, their old and old-fashioned belongings; their quiet lives, sitting, knitting, baking. These features situate grandmothers both in the home and in the past: a significant part of the family but merging into the background and into history – becoming invisible.

Such features contribute to, or constitute, stereotypes of grandmotherhood, and many parallel what we have observed in the representations of grandmothers found in image banks. These features are also indexed in allusive references to grandmothers or in generic usage of *grandmother, grandma, granny*, etc. For example:

> a grandmotherly hug of farewell. [fiction]

> It has a homey feeling – slightly stiff on the outside but warm and friendly inside, like a genial grandmother in a starched apron. [journalism]

These seem neutral or even positive in evaluative orientation, but there is no clear cut-off between such uses and those which are more negative, for example where allusions to grandmothers mean "unfashionable":[12]

> The worst time was when I met two university pals at a wedding. They wore sexy dresses while I looked like their granny in my baggy skirt and jacket. [journalism]

> Her pretty, slightly grannyish florals are jazzed up with bands of "lively, fresh colour". [journalism]

Stereotyping features are also indexed in BoE examples where traditional grandmotherhood is resisted, or new models of grandmothering adopted – dressing differently, physically active, having lives beyond the home, and not defined by ageing:

> She hopes to end up like her grandmother, a deliciously eccentric old lady with a penchant for bright red lipstick. "My granny was the type of woman who seized the day. If someone gave her a lovely handbag or perfume she would spray herself all over with it." [journalism]
>
> My Mum is just not a granny-type person. She is only 46, she works and she would sooner go for a night out with the girls. Being a granny is just not her thing. [journalism]

The reference to "bright red" in the first example is significant: cf. the muted colours in visual and textual images of traditional grandmothers, the bright colours observed where grandmothers present themselves or are depicted in non-traditional roles and personae; cf. the "transgressive grandmother" in Figure 3.4, and cf. too Twigg's (2013: 138–139) discussion of the symbolism of older women wearing bright colours, including red and "its brashness, its association with the assertion of sexuality and its repudiation of grey, toned-down, don't-notice-me dress". Grandmothers wearing bright colours stay visible.

Grandmas and sex

We have commented that the category of grandmother is essentially desexualised, and there is some support in BoE, since of its 12,000 or so instances of *grandmother/grandma/granny*, etc., very few include references to sex or sexuality, and fewer than 30 co-occur with any of the words *sex, sexual, sexy*, etc.; further, the majority of these are allusions to grandmothers as asexual, sexually inactive, or prudish (sometimes contrasted with the sexy or sexually active or liberated – and younger; the second example partly desexualises sex):

> Women discovered – or rediscovered – the orgasm and, suddenly, it was okay to have forthright conversations about the clitoris, G-spots and multitudinous positions that would have made our grannies faint. [journalism]
>
> she was aware that being older could have its advantages in our field [sex therapy]. She was unthreatening. For a grandmotherly woman to talk about sex made it no longer illicit or dirty. [journalism]

Only a handful of examples present grandmothers as actually and actively sexualised, *and* do so non-judgementally. Otherwise, they are depicted as ridiculous, pathetic, or transgressive (in the first example, euphemising *older women* is contrasted with dysphemising *grannies*; the second is reminiscent of Googled grannies on pornographic websites):

> Sexuality in older women is not about grannies in hotpants. It is about feeling good about yourself. [journalism]
>
> [Of a magazine for swingers] A granny in her 60s is pictured in stockings and suspenders begging for ANY man for sex. [journalism]

Derogating grandma

We have already said that in allusive and generic uses, *grandmother/grandma/granny*, etc. can acquire negative evaluations: this is particularly common in journalism. Most neutral are those in which the grandmother relationship is referenced to emphasise ruthlessness, certainty, extravagance, and so on:

> Given that most up-and-coming writers would sell their grannies for a commission, that is no mean prize. [journalism]
>
> The former high priest of White House dirty tricks once said he would walk over his grandmother to help Mr Nixon, on whose behalf he plotted revenge against the Washington Post, which investigated the Watergate burglary. [journalism]

These uses are also intended to amuse and entertain: in doing so, they belittle, as do the next group, where references to grandmotherhood mainly serve to signify old, old-fashioned, droll, dull, pathetic. In fact, status as a grandmother often seems irrelevant, since items like *pensioners* and particularly *little old ladies* (Moon, 2014: 24) are used in very similar ways. These are simply allusions to old and elderly women brought under public scrutiny, attributed with antiquated habits and narrow interests and sensibilities, figures of fun. "Grandmother" is merely a trope:

> But instead, I simply drove around at 10 mph, stopping to let grannies across the road and being nice. [journalism]
>
> Panasonic's argument, which their research appears to confirm, is that there is a pent-up demand for an absolutely fool-proof machine [...] that even your granny wouldn't mind using. [journalism]
>
> Is a spa holiday for me? Images of rheumatic grandmeres soothing their pains in sulphurous pools spring to mind. [journalism]

More directly negative are these:

> Then he took me to a bingo hall full of grannies – it was awful. [journalism]
>
> a [fashion] collection based part on clothes that a child has grown out of oddly combined with what eccentric grannies wear to do the gardening. [journalism]

Likewise these, where derogation of the target is effected figuratively through vehicles that reference, and derogate, grandmothers:

> [In a film review] This is as stodgy as Sunday lunch round your granny's. The action's as exciting as her over-boiled brussels sprouts. And the romance is as soggy as a half-cooked Yorkshire pud. [journalism]
>
> We were standing having a drink after the show and they were fighting past me to get to him. It was like being an item in the January sales – he was a half-price designer dress, I was a pair of shop-soiled granny slippers. [journalism]

However humorous the pragmatic intention, it is difficult to read examples like these, drawn from public discourses, as other than evidence of ageism, sexism, and institutionalised contempt. It seems paradoxical that the grandmother figure, which appears iconic and valued in the context of home and family, seems trivialised and demeaned elsewhere – but as Muriel Schulz commented back in 1975, "There just aren't many terms in English for middle-aged or older women, and those which have occurred have inevitably taken on unpleasant connotations" (1975: 68).

Coda

We have demonstrated through our visual and verbal analyses that the major derogation attached to grandmothers is related to a double deviancy – age and gender. We fully acknowledge that to be a grandmother is a biological reality as well as a social role, and that there are different stages or ages of grandmotherhood, just as there are different forms of grandmothering (even within a single culture). But in the images and texts we have examined, we find that grandmothers seem limited through socially constructed values and ideas to domestic milieus and desexualised identities. Furthermore, the serious stereotypes constructed through modes of representation, produce invisibility, disappearance, and marginalisation, trivialisation, and ridicule.

Our main objective was to show that age, like gender is a political issue. And that ageism and sexism are pervasively institutionalised in discourses about grandmothers as with older women in general. Fortunately, signs of women doing grandmothering in new ways are beginning to appear. These grandmothers do not fit the traditional representations that we discussed here: in the public sphere, for example, there are prominent models, actors, artists, politicians, scholars, lawyers, scientists, doctors, businesswomen. These grandmothers are escaping the confines of the role and rejecting the stereotypes. Increasingly, too, grandmothers like other older women are rejecting the physical stereotypes as well.

A voice from Gransnet says:

> I confess that, at 70, I have not yet suffered from appearing invisible. Possibly because I have always been fairly assertive. I spent my working life in predominantly male engineering environments, and holding my own in these

environments where I was often the only woman in a non-clerical position, became second nature and has become part of my personality.

Gransnet (2013a)

Our role as linguists, feminists, and older women is to raise issues that are not addressed in major public discourses. How long will it be before stereotypes associated with grandmothers catch up with contemporary social practices?

Acknowledgements

This chapter is a reprint, with slight modifications, of a paper originally published in *Gender and Language* (Caldas-Coulthard and Moon, 2016): (c) Equinox Publishing Ltd 2016.

Notes

1 The *Guardian*, 18 July 2016, letters page, p. 28 (main section). The original opinion piece was by John Harris (*Guardian*, 15 July 2016, at: www.theguardian.com/commentisfree/2016/jul/15/labour-death-spite-bullying-working-class-base), writing about the current situation of the Labour Party and its leadership crisis; he was referring to a particular faction at this meeting "characterised by what one outsider described as 'a real nastiness', manifested in the caretaker of the building being spat at" and supporters of the current leader being "threatened with violence". There was no direct indication that the letter writer was involved.
2 With the principal exception of work by J. and N. Coupland: see also Caldas-Coulthard (2010).
3 Lessing is one of the writers discussed by King (2013) in her study of older women in fiction.
4 Taken from the Bank of English corpus – see note 5 below.
5 The Bank of English corpus (BoE) was created by COBUILD at the University of Birmingham, UK. BoE consists of a range of texts, drawn mainly from the period 1990–2003 and from public discourses (news media, magazines, print books), but including some transcribed spoken interaction; 71% of texts are British publications, 21% North American, 8% Australian.
6 These figures incorporate *great-grandmother/granny*, etc.
7 See Conboy (2006: 14ff) for discussion of tabloid lexis, including the use of *gran* in relation to their focus on "human interest" stories and "people at the extremes of human experience and behavior" (Conboy, 2006: 15).
8 Collocate analysis is a core method used in corpus analyses of lexis from discourse perspectives. Corpus studies of gendered words include those by Sigley and Holmes (2002), Pearce (2008), Lindquist (2009), Caldas-Coulthard and Moon (2010), and Baker (2014: 133ff), who provides an overview.
9 The names adopted by grandmothers is a topic discussed on grandmothering websites: see, for example, www.gransnet.com/grandparenting/names-for-grandmothers (accessed August 2016).
10 There are also some interesting points of comparison with *spinster* (Stubbs, 1996: 90; Romaine, 2000: 107ff; Baker, 2006: 104ff), which generally implies older age as well as desexualisation and negative loading.

11 Cf. the properties mentioned by Armstrong et al. (1983: 292–299) as markers, or measures, of "exemplariness' in relation to a prototypal (in the Roschian sense) grandmother: they refer to "grey hair, wrinkles, a twinkle in their eye", also elderly, kindly, and dispensing of soup and brownies. These are all features associated with grandmothers in BoE, except for "twinkle": BoE has grandmothers with bright eyes instead.

12 Though just occasionally fashion reclaims the old-fashioned for a while: "granny glasses" were a case in point.

References

Ansello, E.F. (1977) "Age and ageism in children's first literature", *Educational Gerontology*, 2(3), pp. 255–274.

Armstrong, S.L., Gleitman, L.R. and Gleitman, H. (1983) "What some concepts might not be", *Cognition*, 13, pp. 263–308.

Baker, P. (2006) *Using corpora in discourse analysis*. London: Continuum.

Baker, P. (2010) *Sociolinguistics and corpus linguistics*. Edinburgh: Edinburgh University Press.

Baker, P. (2014) *Using corpora to analyze gender*. London: Bloomsbury.

Barthes, R. (1977) *Image, music, text*. London: Fontana.

Beland, R.M. and Mills, T.L. (2001) "Positive portrayal of grandparents in current children's literature", *Journal of Family Issues*, 22(5), pp. 639–651.

Caldas-Coulthard, C.R. (2010) "Women of a certain age: life styles, the female body and ageism", in Holmes, J. and Marra, M. (eds) *Femininity, feminism and gendered discourse*. Newcastle upon Tyne: Cambridge Scholars, pp. 21–40.

Caldas-Coulthard, C.R. and Moon, R. (2010) "Curvy, hunky, kinky: using corpora as tools in critical analysis", *Discourse & Society*, 21(2), pp. 1–35.

Caldas-Coulthard, C.R. and Moon, R. (2016) "Grandmother, gran, gangsta granny: semiotic representations of grandmotherhood", *Gender and Language*, 10(3), pp. 309–339.

Caldas-Coulthard, C.R. and van Leeuwen, T. (2002) "Stunning, shimmering, iridescent: toys as the representation of gendered social actors", in Litosseliti, L. and Sunderland, J. (eds) *Gender identity and discourse analysis*. Amsterdam: John Benjamins, pp. 91–128.

Clinton, H. (2015) "I'm not a scientist, I'm just a grandmother with two eyes and a brain", *Guardian*, 28 July. At: www.theguardian.com/us-news/video/2015/jul/28/hillary-clinton-unveils-climate-change-policy-video (accessed 14 October 2016).

Conboy, M. (2006) *Tabloid Britain*. London: Routledge.

Copper, B. (1986) "Voices: on becoming old women", in Alexander, J., Berrow, D., Domitrovich, L., Donnelly, M. and McLean, C. (eds) *Women and aging: an anthology by women*. Corvallis, OR: Calyx Books, pp. 47–57.

Coupland, N. and Coupland, J. (1993) "Discourses of ageism and anti-ageism", *Journal of Aging Studies*, 7(3), pp. 279–301.

Coupland, N., Coupland, J. and Giles, H. (1991) *Discourse, identity and ageing*. Oxford: Blackwell.

Eckert, P. and McConnell-Ginet, S. (1995) "Constructing meaning, constructing selves: snapshots of language, gender and class from Belten High", in Hall, K. and Bucholtz, M. (eds) *Gender articulated: language and the socially constructed self*. New York: Routledge, pp. 469–508.

Fairclough, N. (2010) *Critical discourse analysis: the critical study of language*. London: Longman.

Fairclough, N. (2013) *Language and power*, 2nd ed. London: Routledge.

Fearnly-Whittingstall, J. (2011) *The good granny guide*. London: Short Books.

Featherstone, M. and Wernick, A. (eds) (1995) *Images of aging: cultural representations of later life*. London: Routledge.

Freeman, H. (2014) "Chelsea Clinton's pregnancy gives birth to new conspiracies", *Guardian*, 22 April. At: www.theguardian.com/commentisfree/2014/apr/22/chelsea-clinton-pregancy-hillary-clinton-grandmother-conspiracies (accessed 14 October 2016).

Garner, J.D. and Mercer, S.O. (eds) (2001) *Women as they age*. London: Routledge.

Goldenberg, S. (2015) "Clinton returns to smash glass ceiling, with gender at forefront of campaign", *Guardian*, 12 April. At: www.theguardian.com/us-news/2015/apr/12/hillary-clinton-2016-presidential-campaign-strategy-politics (accessed 12 October 2016).

Gransnet (2013a) "Ageism". At: www.gransnet.com/forums/other_subjects/a1203153-Ageism (accessed 22 October 2016).

Gransnet (2013b) *The new granny's survival guide*. London: Random House.

Greer, G. (1991) *The change: women, aging and the menopause*. New York: Knopf.

Gullette, M. (1997) *Declining to decline: cultural combat and the politics of the midlife*. Charlottesville, VA: University of Virginia Press.

Hall, S. (ed.) (1997) *Representation: cultural representations and signifying practices*. London: SAGE/Open University.

Halliday, M.A.K. (1978) *Language as social semiotic*. London: Edward Arnold.

Halliday, M.A.K. (1985) *An introduction to functional grammar*. London: Edward Arnold.

Hamilton, H.E. (1992) "Bringing aging into the language/gender equation", in Hall, K., Bucholtz, M. and Moonwomon, B. (eds) *Locating power*. Berkeley, CA: University of California, pp. 240–249.

Hansen, A. and Machin, D. (2008) "Visually branding the environment: climate change as a marketing opportunity", *Discourse Studies*, 10(6), pp. 777–794.

Hareven, T.K. (1995) "Changing images of aging and the social construction of the life course", in Featherstone, M. and Wernick, A. (eds) *Images of aging: cultural representations of later life*. London: Routledge, pp. 119–134.

Henneberg, S. (2010) "Moms do badly, but grandmas do worse: the nexus of sexism and ageism in children's classics", *Journal of Aging Studies*, 24, pp. 125–134.

Hepworth, M. (2003) "Ageing bodies: aged by culture", in Coupland, J. and Gwyn, R. (eds) *Discourse, the body, and identity*. Basingstoke: Palgrave, pp. 89–106.

Hollis-Sawyer, L. and Cuevas, L. (2013) "Mirror, mirror on the wall: ageist and sexist double jeopardy portrayals in children's picture books", *Educational Gerontology*, 39(12), pp. 902–914.

Hurst, J.B. (1981) "Images in children's picture books", *Social Education*, 45(2), pp. 138–143.

Iedema, R. (2003) "Multimodality, resemiotization: extending the analysis of discourse as multi-semiotic practice", *Visual Communication*, 2(1), pp. 29–57.

Iversen, S.M. (2015) "'Not without my kitties': the old woman in casual games", in *Proceedings of the 10th international conference on the foundations of digital games*. At: www.fdg2015.org/papers/fdg2015_paper_44.pdf (accessed 10 September 2016).

Keyworth, F. (1982) "Invisible struggles: the politics of ageing", in Brunt, R. and Rowan, C. (eds) *Feminism, culture and politics*. London: Lawrence & Wishart, pp. 131–142.

King, J. (2013) *Discourses of ageing in fiction and feminism: the invisible woman*. Basingstoke: Palgrave.

Kress, G. and van Leeuwen, T. (1996) *Reading images: the grammar of visual design*. London: Routledge.

Kress, G. and van Leeuwen, T. (2001) *Multimodal discourse: the modes and media of contemporary communication*. London: Arnold.

Lessing, D. ([1973] 2009) *The summer before the dark*. London: Jonathan Cape.

Lindquist, H. (2009) *Corpus linguistics and the description of English*. Edinburgh: Edinburgh University Press.

Machin, D. (2004) "Building the world's visual language: the increasing global importance of image banks in corporate media", *Visual Communication*, 3(3), pp. 316–336.

Machin, D. (2007) *Introduction to multimodal analysis*. London: Hodder Arnold.

Machin, D. and van Leeuwen, T. (2007) *Global media discourse*. London: Routledge.

Martin, J.R. and White, P.R.R. (2005) *The language of evaluation: appraisal in English*. Basingstoke: Palgrave Macmillan.

Mautner, G. (2007) "Mining large corpora for social information: the case of *elderly*", *Language in Society*, 36, pp. 51–72.

Moon, R. (2014) "From gorgeous to grumpy: adjectives, age and gender", *Gender and Language*, 8(1), pp. 5–42.

Newman, N. (1983) *My granny* (illustrations by Cook, B.). London: Collins.

Norris, S. (2013) "What is a mode? Smell, olfactory perception, and the notion of mode in multimodal mediated theory", *Multimodal Communication*, 2(2), pp. 155–169.

Pearce, M. (2008) "Investigating the collocational behaviour of MAN and WOMAN in the BNC using Sketch Engine", *Corpora*, 3(1), pp. 1–29.

Romaine, S. (2000) *Language in society: an introduction to sociolinguistics*, 2nd ed. Oxford: Oxford University Press.

Schulz, M.R. (1975) "The semantic derogation of woman", in Thorne, B. and Henley, N. (eds) *Language and sex: difference and dominance*. Rowley, MA: Newbury House, pp. 64–75.

Sigley, R. and Holmes, J. (2002) "Looking at *girls* in corpora of English", *Journal of English Linguistics*, 30(2), pp. 138–157.

Storey, D.C. (1977) "Gray power: an endangered species? Ageism as portrayed in children's books", *Social Education*, 41(6), pp. 528–533.

Stubbs, M. (1996) *Text and corpus analysis*. Oxford: Blackwell.

Tahmaseb-McConatha, J. (2013) "Learning to be a grandmother". At: www.psychologytoday.com/blog/live-long-and-prosper/201311/learning-be-grandmother (accessed 3 June 2016).

Thompson, M. (2016) *What's gone wrong with the language of politics?* London: St Martin's Press.

Twigg, J. (2013) *Fashion and age: dress, the body and later life*. London: Bloomsbury.

van Leeuwen, T. (2005) *Introducing social semiotics*. London: Routledge.

van Leeuwen, T. (2008) *Discourse and practice: new tools for critical discourse analysis*. Oxford: Oxford University Press.

van Leeuwen, T. (2011) *The language of colour: an introduction*. Abingdon: Routledge.

Walliams, D. (2011) *Gangsta granny* (illustrations by Ross, T.). London: HarperCollins.

Watts, J. and Bowater, D. (2016) "Brazil president Dilma Rousseff comes out fighting in impeachment trial", *Guardian*, 29 August. At: www.theguardian.com/world/2016/aug/29/brazil-president-dilma-rousseff-impeachment-trial (accessed 21 October 2016).

White, P.R.R. (2001) *Appraisal: an overview*. At: www.grammatics.com/appraisal/index.html (accessed 2 June 2016).

Woodward, K. (1995) "Psychoanalysis, feminism, and ageism", in Featherstone, M. and Wernick, A. (eds) *Images of aging: cultural representations of later life*. London: Routledge, pp. 79–96.

4
DISCO DIVAS AND HEROIC KNIGHTS

A critical multimodal analysis of gender roles in "create the world" LEGO cards

Jai Mackenzie
UNIVERSITY OF NOTTINGHAM, UK

Laura Coffey-Glover
NOTTINGHAM TRENT UNIVERSITY, UK

Sophie Payne
UNIVERSITY OF READING, UK

Mark McGlashan
BIRMINGHAM CITY UNIVERSITY, UK

Introduction

In 2017, LEGO teamed up with major UK supermarket chain Sainsbury's for the distribution of a set of 140 "create the world" collectible trading cards. Children were invited to join "Lily" and "Sam" on a round-the-world adventure, with each card featuring a minifigure (small human-like toy figurine) or LEGO creation that they would encounter on their journey. The cards captured a range of the minifigure characters offered by LEGO at the time, and many of these minifigures displayed roles, occupations, hobbies and personality traits associated with "real" life, such as Grandpa, Nurse, Skier and Clumsy Guy. The promotion was extremely popular, and garnered attention from UK regional and national newspapers (*Gazette Live*, 8 May 2017; *Birmingham Mail*, 13 June 2017; *Sun*, 28 June 2017). In this chapter, we investigate the extent to which the minifigures represented in the "create the world" set are gendered, and what particular roles, identities and actions are attributed to these figures. We consider what children may learn about gender roles through playing with the cards, and whether those lessons are likely to help or hinder young people in moving beyond the limiting roles and commonly held stereotypes that perpetuate sexism in the adult world.

We take the position that toys are significant artefacts for social semiotic analysis because they facilitate the imaginative play through which children learn and become socially aware (Caldas-Coulthard and van Leeuwen, 2002; Kahlenberg and Hein, 2010). Toys can also be seen as "texts", with designs that "communicat[e] symbolic and interactive meanings" (Caldas-Coulthard and van Leeuwen, 2003: 19). We therefore suggest that this is an important area of research. Nevertheless, there has been little social semiotic work to date that focuses on children's toys and products, with the exception of Caldas-Coulthard and van Leeuwen's analyses of baby toys (2001), action figures (2002) and teddy bears (2003). Through playing with toys such as the "create the world" cards, children develop their sense of what social roles and relationships are available to them, and what is "normal", expected or desirable behaviour. For example, they may use the representations on the cards as starting points as they engage in role play, building worlds, relationships and qualities for the minifigures alongside their developing sense of their own worlds. Given LEGO's worldwide popularity and success – they reported their highest revenue in 85 years and introduced 355 new products in 2017 alone (*Telegraph*, 9 March 2017) – it is especially important to consider the socialising potential of their products. By examining these cards, we hope to reveal the messages that children absorb when they "create the world" through reading, collecting, and playing with them, and to consider whether these messages may perpetuate discriminatory norms and practices.

Gender and children's toys

In recent years, toys have increasingly been developed and marketed for gender-differentiated audiences, with distinctive sets of gendered semiotic resources coming to signal whether a toy is for boys or girls (Kahlenberg and Hein, 2010; Auster and Mansbach, 2012; Martinez et al., 2013). For example, toys marketed towards boys typically include action figures, vehicles, building toys and weapons, thus promoting strength, outdoor play and physicality, whilst "girls' toys" tend to include dolls, cosmetics and jewellery, promoting the values of beauty, indoor play, domesticity and motherhood (Caldas-Coulthard and van Leeuwen, 2002; Kahlenberg and Hein, 2010; Auster and Mansbach, 2012; Martinez et al., 2013). In terms of colour, boys' toys (and the boys who play with them) tend to be depicted in colours such as red, blue, black, or grey, whilst girls' toys (and the girls who play with them) are usually associated with pastels such as purple and pink (Caldas-Coulthard and van Leeuwen, 2002; Kahlenberg and Hein, 2010; Auster and Mansbach, 2012). The pervasive association of boys with blue and girls with pink has led some to suggest that there is now a ubiquitous visual discourse of gender difference (Baker, 2008: 96), and that the visual (re)production of such difference serves to enforce and perpetuate limiting stereotypes (Cunningham and MacRae, 2011: 608). Pink is shown to be the most gender-marked colour for toys, being strongly associated with girls

(Cunningham and MacRae, 2011; Auster and Mansbach, 2012; Wong and Hines, 2015). This is consistent with Koller's (2008) claim that pink is also used pervasively in marketing that targets women.

LEGO and LEGO bodies

Historically, LEGO has been a toy that boys play with: in 2011, boys made up 90% of LEGO's customer base (*Guardian*, 4 June 2017). However, in recent years, the company has made a number of efforts to target girls. For example, they moved to increase the representation of women in science, technology, engineering and mathematics (STEM) professions, and present women in more intellectually challenging roles, through their introduction of the Research Institute set in 2014, which featured three female scientist figures. In 2017, they went a step further with the Women of NASA set, which included four female scientists who made significant contributions to major NASA missions. Despite their popularity and apparently progressive aims, however, the LEGO group have often been the subject of controversy with regard to the way they represent different groups in society. For example, the "LEGO Friends" range, which was launched in 2012 and includes "mini-doll" figures and sets with themes such as a bakery, riding camp and amusement park (Johnson, 2014; *Guardian*, 4 June 2017), was criticised for the over-use of pastel colours and promotion of stereotypical female roles, with some even condemning the range as a regression to 1970s gender stereotypes (*Telegraph*, 1 June 2017). This range changed the shape of the minifigure for the first time, with its exclusively female characters including slimmer bodies, shaped breasts and small waists. Similar markers are now painted on to the standard body shape for female minifigures in the mainstream range, although there have historically been far fewer of these explicitly marked female minifigures than the standard (presumably male) form (Johnson, 2014).

In this chapter, we are particularly interested in LEGO's representation of human or human-like figures in children's products. Although there has been little social semiotic research that explores children's toy figurines, Caldas-Coulthard and van Leeuwen (2002) have analysed the popular action figure franchises of Action Man and Barbie, focusing on the toys' design and movement, use of colour and the language used in advertising materials. They observe that these semiotic resources are harnessed to demarcate clearly gendered roles for the toys: Action Man appears in professional or action-oriented settings, whilst Barbie occupies settings and roles associated with stereotypical femininity such as shopping, hairdressing, nursing and motherhood. They show that naming strategies for Barbie are linked with idealised notions of womanhood and romance (e.g. Blushing Orchid Barbie, Harpist Angel, Summer Dream), whereas Action Man's personae relate to power, danger and authority (e.g. Dr X, Bungee Jumper, Ninja). The world of Action Man is also characterised by dark colours "evoking mystery or danger", whereas Barbie's world is populated by pinks and purples which create "a sense of romance" (Caldas-Coulthard and van Leeuwen, 2002: 102). LEGO minifigures are quite different from these other action figure toys in size, feel and playability. Most notably, and in keeping with LEGO's primary remit as a building toy, the legs, bodies, heads and hair can be taken apart and reconstructed, enabling different assemblages to be imagined and constructed. The LEGO company themselves seem to encourage play with the bodies of these figures. For example, the "build a minifigure" feature in large LEGO stores invites customers to create their own characters from a range of different body parts. In 2017, the Manchester LEGO Discovery Centre had a "gay pride" display in which traditional gender norms were subverted through the configuration of minifigure parts. One minifigure in this display, for example, had a bearded face, long blonde hair and wore a bikini.

The "create the world" minifigure cards may be a small data-set, but they have been extremely popular with young children in the UK, are part of a large, successful franchise that has made efforts to break gendered stereotypes, and represent many real-world characters and roles. We therefore believe that they are an important site for influencing young people's developing concepts of their own, and others', position in the world. In producing these cards, LEGO and Sainsbury's have the power to offer transformative positions; the creative potential of the malleable minifigures and the inclusion of many fantasy characters means that they have plenty of opportunities to transgress restrictive social norms and boundaries or damaging stereotypes. This chapter will critically examine whether that is achieved.

Methodology

Data collection

The data for this study comprise the names, visual depictions and textual descriptions from a set of 140 "create the world" LEGO collectible cards. These cards were the product of a joint promotion with the UK supermarket Sainsbury's, and were distributed to customers who spent over £10 between 3 May and 13 June 2017. They could also be bought from Sainsbury's for 50p, along with a £2 collector's album to display the cards. We only included cards that featured minifigures for our analysis, resulting in a data-set of 104 cards. We documented these data by first photographing the collection, and then transcribing the textual data, which included the card number, title and full description, into a spreadsheet. This textual data-set amounted to 2265 words.

Each of the minifigure cards is composed in the same way (see Figure 4.1).[1] The visual depiction of a minifigure occupies the centre position, where it is framed by a range of marginal elements, including strongly demarcated frame lines and textual information such as the name of the minifigure character, a description of that character and the number of the card in the series. For example, the Boxer is the central figure of card number 11, framed by a red background with a faded plant motif. Below the image is the typed description (see Figure 4.2). Because it is at the centre of the composition, it may be argued that the image of the minifigure is

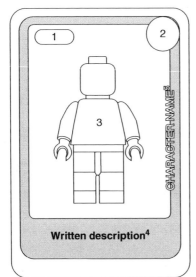

Legend
1. Number of card in series
2. Rock/paper/scissors icon
3. Visual representation of minifigure
4. A written description of the minifigure and their character attributes/characteristics
5. The name of the minifigure

FIGURE 4.1 Composition of a LEGO "create the world" card.

attributed a greater degree of salience than the other semiotic elements, and thus has high "information value" (Kress and van Leeuwen, 2006: 177). The prominence of the visual is not surprising given the young audience for the cards, many of whom will be emergent readers, and pay little attention to the linguistic elements.[2] However, the construction of information value in the cards can also be analysed from top to bottom, with what is nearer the top taking the "ideal" position – the "generalized essence of the information" (Kress and van Leeuwen, 2006: 187), and the information at the bottom being positioned as more "real", detailed, specific information. In this respect, the linguistic resources mobilised in the lower portion of the cards also take a prominent position, and are likely to be read by older children, or adult carers, in prolonged engagement with the cards. Because prominence is given to both visual and linguistic modes in the depiction of the minifigures, our analysis takes account of the range of semiotic resources that are deployed in relation to both of these modes.

Before analysing the content of the cards, we first attempted to categorise each of the minifigures represented therein as either male, female, or gender-neutral. These identifications were checked by all four authors of this chapter and it was agreed that all representations could be identified as either female minifigures (henceforth FMs) or male minifigures (henceforth MMs). We then created two sub-corpora for the text of the FM and MM cards.

Our coding of the minifigures by gender was checked by a group who represent the target audience for these cards: ten children between the ages of 6 and 9.[3] Each of these children was separately shown each minifigure card in turn and asked to state whether the figure on the card was male, female, or they could not say, which

FIGURE 4.2 Card 011: BOXER.

would allow for interpretations of gender-neutrality or non-binary gender. Overall, there was 99% agreement between the authors and the children. The generally agreed lack of gender-neutral or non-binary minifigures is indicative of the binary world depicted on the cards.

The social actor framework

Our analysis of the "create the world" minifigure cards focuses on the following research questions:

1. Are the "create the world" minifigures differentiated by gender? If so, what gendered identities and roles are constructed for them?
2. What actions and functions do the minifigures perform?
3. What wider social norms are indexed and (re)produced through these depictions?

We seek to answer these questions through a multimodal social actor network analysis (van Leeuwen, 2008). In doing so, we treat the minifigures as "social actors", on to which an identity and a place in society is projected, and the cards as recontextualisations of social practices (van Leeuwen, 2008). The social actor framework supports our exploration of the kinds of socio-cultural norms and expectations at work in the construction of the minifigures and, importantly, what they are teaching the children who play with them about their place in the world.

In order to theorise the connections between particular visual and linguistic resources, we draw on the concept of indexicality. An *index* is a type of sign that stands for something else. It is distinguished from other signs because it stands for an object "by virtue of a real connection with it" (Peirce, 1998 [1895]: 14), or as Atkin (2005: 163) puts it, "through some existential or physical fact". Peirce (1998 [1895]) offers as an example "a low barometer with a moist air" as an index of rain; Atkin (2005) suggests that smoke is an index of fire. Both of these indices have a causal connection with the phenomenon to which they point.

In this chapter, we do not employ the concept of indexicality in relation to physical objects or environmental phenomena such as fire and rain, but in relation to social constructs, especially gender. Ochs (1992) has developed the concept of indexicality in this respect, distinguishing two types of index. "Direct" indices, such as the pronouns "he" and "she", or the explicitly gendered categories "man" or "waitress" (all of which are used in the minifigure cards), directly point to the gender of the referent. With "indirect" indices, which are of particular interest here, the connection between the sign and the individual, group, or meaning for which it stands is made through shared cultural knowledge and assumptions. As an example, the word "glamorous" is associated with women in a western cultural context, whereas "stocky" tends to be reserved for men. Visual signs can also carry indexical meanings. For example, as shown above, the colour pink has come to be strongly associated with women and girls. The connection between indirect indices and the social meanings to which they point are not physical. Nor are they static or universal in their reference points – as Johnstone and Kiesling (2008) and Bucholtz (2009) have shown, the indexical meanings of particular signs are variable and context-dependent. The words *dude* and *güey*, for example, have both been associated with male referents, but in certain contexts these words can index a "stance of cool solidarity" (Kiesling, 2004: 282) and a "hip urban Latino identity" (Bucholtz, 2009: 158) that points not only to the gender of the referent, but also their age, ethnicity and the stance of the speaker in relation to them. Our analysis is therefore sensitive to the context-specific social meanings that are indicated through a range of semiotic resources in the "create the world" cards, and to the potential relevance of other factors such as age and body shape.

The analysis that follows will focus on the *categorisation* of the minifigures, which relates to how identities, roles and actions are represented (van Leeuwen, 2008). We explore these categorisations through close examination of the names given to the minifigures in the titles, the visual images and colours (including the minifigure itself and the background), and the language of the descriptions at the bottom of each card. Within van Leeuwen's (2008) framework, categorisation is divided into several sub-types. We focus here on those types that are most prominent in the collection: functionalisation and identification. When social actors are functionalised, they are categorised according to their functions – what they do – such as a paying job, or some other societal role (van Leeuwen, 2008: 42). Identification categories, on the other hand, categorise actors according to what they "unavoidably are" (van Leeuwen, 2008: 42). In relation to identification, we explore the sub-categories of classification, whereby actors are divided according to the contingent socio-historical categories that a given society or institution uses to group and separate individuals, and physical identification, which categorises actors according to their physical appearance or part of their physical body (van Leeuwen, 2008: 44).

Although van Leeuwen's (2008) initial description of the social actor framework focuses on linguistic realisations, he also shows that it can be adapted to analyse visual representations. Our visual social actor analysis focuses on how the minifigures are marked out as male or female through semiotic resources such as the colours used on the card backgrounds and minifigure bodies, and the markings on the faces and bodies of each figure. We consider whether meaningfully placed lines (implying, for example, make-up, facial hair, wrinkles, body fat, or a slim waist), are indexical of gender, and other macro-social categories that may intersect with gender, such as age. We also consider how the items that the minifigures are depicted as wearing or holding contribute to an impression of the characters' roles, activities they engage in, or who they essentially *are*.

Our analysis of the textual descriptions considers how the minifigures are linguistically classified and identified through an exploration of adjectival descriptions. Using Wmatrix (Rayson, 2009), we compare adjectival descriptions that are distinctive to each gendered group of cards, teasing out both qualitative and quantitative differences. We employ a modified version of Moon's (2014) model for classifying adjectival descriptions, grouping them together according to the categories of "classification", "physical characteristics", "personal characteristics" and "appraisement". These also map onto the categorisation types in van Leeuwen's (2008) framework. Where adjectives serve multiple functions (e.g. describing a personal characteristic in addition to appraisement), they are coded in every relevant category.

Assigning the titles, visuals and descriptions of the minifigure cards to analytical categories was not always a straightforward process. In order to achieve some consistency and reliability, two authors of this chapter conducted each analysis separately, before coming together to discuss any divergent categorisations or problematic cases. This process of inter-rater coding helped us to specify and refine the boundaries of each analytical category.

Analysis

The minifigure cards can be grouped into two gender types, male and female, and are recognisable as such by adults and children alike, as explained in the previous section. An important point to note from the outset is that gender representation in the "create the world" cards is not equal, with 67% (N70) of the 104 minifigures being identified as male, but only 33% (N34) as female; male minifigures (MMs) appear twice as often as female minifigures (FMs). This gender imbalance suggests that male is the default gender for a minifigure in this set, whilst the female form is marked (see Mills, 2008 on the prevalence of this pattern in a wider social context). In the analysis that follows, we consider how the gender of the "create the world" minifigure characters is indexed through the full range of semiotic resources available in the cards, through their titles, the visual resources employed in the images, and the linguistic choices made in the textual descriptions. As the section progresses, we draw out key themes, showing what kinds of gendered identities and roles are constructed overall in the "create the world" set.

Identification: classification and physical identification

Identification is the second most frequent type of linguistic categorisation in the naming of the "create the world" minifigures, appearing in 53% (N55) of the card titles.[4] Classification by social category is by far the most common sub-type of identification, with 51% (N53) of the card titles featuring some form of classification. In this section, we begin by exploring the ways in which the minifigures are classified in the card titles, identifying three main sub-types of classification: gender, fantasy figure and personality. As shown in Table 4.1, we found that gender classifications (e.g. Tiger *Woman*, Spooky *Girl* and Pizza Delivery *Man*) were the most common type in the card titles, and that the FM titles were classified by gender more than twice as often (proportionally) as the MM titles.

Table 4.2 shows the linguistic forms used to classify the minifigures by gender. These can take the form of "highly generalised gendered classifications" (van Leeuwen, 2008: 42), such as "man" or "woman", which can appear as pre- or post-modifiers (*Lady* Robot, Spider *Lady*) or as compounds (Cave*woman*). They can also take the form of derivations, created through suffixes such as "ess", "let" and "maid", which in these cases have a diminutive effect, implying youthfulness, innocence, or powerlessness. Others are more specific gendered categories that are part of a gendered pair, such as King, Queen and Witch (the male counterpart of the latter would be Wizard). "Girl" (N7), a category that indicates youth, and "lady" (N3),

TABLE 4.1 Minifigure card titles by classification

Classification type	Proportion of classifications (total N53)	Proportion of MMs (total N70)	Proportion of FMs (total N34)
Gender	62% (N33)	20% (N14)	56% (N19)
Fantasy figure	42% (N22)	21% (N15)	21% (N7)
Personality	17% (N9)	10% (N7)	6% (N2)
Miscellaneous (historical & narrative figures, size, socio-political group)	8% (N4)	3% (N2)	6% (N2)

TABLE 4.2 Gender classification types in minifigure card titles

Form of gender classification	Proportion of MM gender classifications (total N14)	Proportion of FM gender classifications (total N19)
Generalised category: guy	50% (N7)	–
Generalised category: girl	–	37% (N7)
Generalised category: man	43% (N6)	–
Generalised category: lady	–	16% (N3)
Generalised category: woman	–	11% (N2)
Other gendered category (king, queen, princess, witch)	7% (N1)	16% (N3)
Suffixes (-ess, -maid, -let)	–	21% (N4)

which can either indicate status, or be used as a euphemistic alternative to "woman" (avoiding perceived connotations of sexual maturity), are the two most common gendered classifications used for FMs. By contrast, the equivalent denotative gendered counterparts for these categories – "boy" and "gentleman" are not used at all for the male minifigures. Instead, "guy" (N7), a category that is increasingly used in a gender-neutral way in its plural form, yet at the time of writing still retains its gendered meaning in the singular, is the most common gendered classification for the MMs, followed by "man" (N6). These findings reveal that the gender of the FMs is more often linguistically marked, and that gendered labels for the FMs often imply youthfulness or innocence in a way that the MM titles do not (see Mills, 2008 for further discussion of inequalities in gendered categories).

When it comes to the visual resources and textual descriptions that are used to represent the minifigures, appearance takes primacy, and is closely related to the characters' gender classification. Our analysis now turns to the ways in which the minifigures are identified by their appearance through a range of visual and linguistic resources.

Women as youthful with striking features, men as older with hairy faces

Visually, the physical attributes given to the minifigures sharply differentiate the FMs and MMs. For example, facial hair (i.e. moustaches, beards and sideburns) is only found on those minifigures linguistically identified as male. In addition to visual signs of facial hair, linguistic references to hair in the textual descriptions are also restricted to the MMs. The adjectival descriptions of MMs' facial hair often carry positive evaluations, with the adjectives "sensational", "magnificent" and "sweet" premodifying "moustache", "facial hair" and "beard" in descriptions of the Ringmaster, Evil Dwarf and Garden Gnome, respectively. The one reference to "hair" in the FM descriptions relates to head hair from the Medusa card, referring to its functional attributes for this dangerous fictional character: "And don't offer to cut her hair either – it's got some 'sssserious' bite!"

Just as the FMs are more often linguistically classified as female, they are also more often visually identified as female through their physical appearance; all of the FMs have facial markers that index femininity (i.e. implied make-up such as coloured lips and prominent eyelashes), whereas only half of the MMs have facial markers that index masculinity (moustaches, beard stubble, sideburns, or bushy eyebrows).[5] However, since all the FMs' gender is marked through implied make-up, the very absence of feminine indices can be said to distinguish a minifigure as male. This lends further weight to the argument that male is the default gender for a minifigure in this set, whilst the female form is marked.

Another more subtle distinction between representations of the minifigures' faces is that the MMs are more likely to be marked with signs of being older. This is indicated by lines around the face in positions where we would typically expect to see wrinkles, namely across the forehead and next to the eyes. Several of the MMs include such marks, whilst only one of the FMs (Grandma) does. Indices of age therefore seem to intersect with gender here. The implication that the MMs are older than the FMs is supported by the fact that many of the MMs have white or grey hair whereas only two of the FMs do.[6] Those playing with the cards may therefore infer that, whilst it is normal and acceptable for men to age, women are obliged to retain their youth.

Women as slim, curvaceous and well-dressed, men as larger and muscular

In terms of the minifigures' bodies, only a small number of the MMs have visual indices of gender, including chest hair and visible muscles. By contrast, the majority of the FMs have visual indices of gender on their body, namely narrowed waists and/or breasts, making their figures more curvaceous – less square – than the MMs. Of the six who do not have (visibly) narrowed waists, in two cases the bodies are obscured so the waists cannot be seen, two are wearing costumes and one is a robot. Additionally, several of the MMs have lines on their bodies that imply they have fat around their waists, and/or their clothes are baggy, whilst none of the FMs' bodies include such marks.[7] For example, the lines around the bottom of Baseball Player's body suggest he has a tucked-in baggy t-shirt, the lines above the waists of Grandpa, Piggy Guy and Prospector imply a rounded stomach, and the lines around the belts of Elf and Gnome imply body fat around a tightened area. The way the minifigures' upper bodies are presented therefore suggests that it is normal and acceptable for men to have muscles and body fat, whereas women are expected to have small waists and visible breasts. Furthermore, the textual descriptions of the minifigures suggest that appearance in general is more salient and important for women. Adjectives describing clothing, such as "*royal* robes" (Queen) and "her robe is *perfect*" (Kimono Girl) are more frequent in the FM descriptions compared with the MM descriptions.[8] Other adjectival descriptors distinctive to the FM set, such as "glitter-filled" (Unicorn Girl) and "dressed-up" (Bride), as well as references to jewellery such as "sparkly stuff" (Jewel Thief) also imply attentiveness to looking special and striking through clothing and accessories. The inclusion of "glitter" as a premodifier is particularly notable in this regard, given its cultural associations as an indirect index of femininity. Adjectives relating to physical appearance in the MM set are more likely to focus on facial hair (see above).

Pink and blue as visual discourses of gender differentiation

Another feature of visual categorisation that is largely restricted to the FMs is the inclusion of shades and hues of pink. Over half of the FM cards feature pinks and purples somewhere in the visual composition of the cards (mostly in their clothing, but sometimes in the background or number colour), compared with only a handful of the MMs, one of which is Piggy Guy, whose outfit is the colour in which pigs are typically represented. Interestingly, two of the children who acted as second raters for this study identified Piggy Guy as female, presumably because of the strong association of pink with girls and women. The importance of pink as a resource for the ideational representation of femininity is particularly notable when considering the representation of non-human characters. As well as being linguistically marked for gender, the Alien Villainess, Lady Robot and Lady Cyclops cards are also visually marked through the use of pink and feminising facial features, including lipstick (which is always pink) and exaggerated make-up, such as Lady Robot's pink cheeks.

Moreover, pink is integrated into the dress of Alien Villainess and Lady Robot. The most frequently used colour on the MM cards, on the other hand, is blue (closely followed by green); less than half of the FM cards feature these colours. Overall, the use of pink (or purple) for the FMs and blue (or green) for the MMs reinforces and reproduces a visual discourse of gender difference (Baker, 2008).[9] In addition, the higher frequency of both linguistic and visual indices of gender for the FMs, together with the fact that there are double the amount of MMs in total, combine to create the very powerful impression that female is the marked form for a LEGO minifigure.

Functionalisation

Functionalisation is the most frequent type of linguistic categorisation in the naming of the "create the world" minifigures, with 62% (N64) of the card titles referring to the characters' functionalised role (such as a paying job or other social activity). Slightly more MMs than FMs are given a title that refers to a functional role, such as Janitor, Fisherman, Fortune Teller and Disco Diva. These findings are echoed in the visual icons the minifigures are shown to be holding, where again slightly more MMs than FMs hold an item that draws attention to what the character *does* in their role, such as the Janitor and his mop, the Rockstar and his guitar, the Cavewoman and her club, and the Nurse and her syringe.[10] These findings suggest a slight disparity between the kinds of roles the minifigures are given, with the MMs more likely to be categorised in terms of what they *do* in the world, and the FMs more

TABLE 4.3 Functionalisation in card titles, organised by theme

Theme	Proportion of MM functionalisations (total N42)	Proportion of FM functionalisations (total N17)
Entertainment	29% (N12)	18% (N3)
Manual labour	21% (N9)	–
Physical activity	19% (N8)	53% (N9)
War/conflict	10% (N4)	6% (N1)
Adventure/travelling	14% (N6)	–
Crime	5% (N2)	12% (N2)
Service	5% (N2)	6% (N1)
Science	2% (N1)	–
Business	2% (N1)	–
Health	–	6% (N1)
Magic	–	6% (N1)

likely to be categorised in terms of who they *are* and what they *wear*. The difference between the representation of the FMs and MMs becomes more marked when we consider the more specific types of functionalised roles and occupations they are given. Table 4.3 presents a summary of these types in the minifigure card titles, organised by theme.

There are a number of functionalisation themes that apply significantly more often to MMs, namely manual labour (e.g. Plumber and Welder), war/conflict (e.g. Knight and Trooper) and adventure/travelling (e.g. Explorer and Sea Captain). The fact that multiple MMs, but almost no FMs, have functionalised roles that relate to these themes implies that physical work, conflict, adventure and travel are generally available to men, but not to women. Additionally, a higher proportion of the MMs have a functionalised role that relates to an occupation.[11] This disparity is particularly apparent in the male-only manual labour category.

Men as daring and dangerous, women as fun, frivolous and decorative

There are a number of visual and linguistic markers that suggest the MMs are more dangerous and aggressive than the FMs. For example, more MMs than FMs hold an item that can be used to attack, such as Evil Dwarf's axe, Heroic Knight's sword and Alien Avenger's gun. Several MMs, but no FMs, hold some kind of tool that is used to cut or fix, such as Mechanic's spanner, Carpenter's saw and Butcher's knife. The visual implication that MMs do dangerous things becomes even more apparent when looking at what they wear, with many MMs wearing some kind of equipment that protects them from serious injury (usually helmets), whereas only one FM wears such equipment (Snowboarder, who wears a helmet).[12]

The association of MMs with danger is also reflected in the textual descriptions of the minifigures. For example, in the MM descriptions there are a small number of adjectives that imply danger: Gangster is described metonymically as "dangerous" ("there's something *dangerous* in that case and it's not an out-of-tune violin!"); the Pirate Captain is characterised as a "*merciless*, rotten old sea dog", and Ocean King is described as a "*hot-headed* monarch", which implies he is easily angered. There are also some FMs whose descriptions imply they are dangerous, but these characters are more likely to be mythical, suggesting that being dangerous is not an everyday trait for human women. For example, Wacky Witch is evaluated as "wicked", and Medusa is described metonymically as dangerous through reference to her hair: "don't offer to cut her hair either – it's got some *ssserious* bite!" Surfer Girl, a human-like FM, is described as "hot-blooded", but (by contrast with "hot-headed") this phrase has a semantic prosody of sexual, rather than dangerous, behaviour. This implication of sexual behaviour is reinforced with the description "She certainly knows how to make waves at the beach!", which points not only to the literal waves that she rides, but also the metaphorical waves of admiration that she inspires.

The functionalisation sub-category of "physical activity" includes the largest number of FM cards, with more than half of the female minifigures' functionalised titles relating to physical activity.[13] A third of the FMs with physical roles are dancers: performers who depend on viewers' evaluation for success. These functionalised roles are represented both linguistically, through the form "dance + -*er*" (Flamenco Dancer, Hula Dancer), and through the minifigures' clothing: a traditional red and black dress and fan for Flamenco Dancer, and flower garland and grass skirt for Hula Dancer. The items held by the FMs engaging in physical activity tend to be symbolic, decorative, or serve to enhance their performance in some way. For example, Flamenco Dancer carries a fan, Hula Dancer holds maracas and Disco Diva a microphone. In addition, Disco Diva is described in the textual descriptions as "the belle of the glitterball", which echoes the idiomatic English phrase "the belle of the ball", serving as an intertextual reference to the fairy-tale genre, where women traditionally occupy more passive, decorative roles. Even though she is visually active, linguistically Disco Diva is therefore represented as a passive object to be looked at. There are no visual or linguistic references to dancing for the MMs who engage in physical activity. These minifigures instead perform sports and leisure activities such as climbing (Mountain Climber), boxing (Boxer) and weightlifting (Weightlifter).

Discussion and conclusion

In the LEGO "create the world" minifigure cards, a range of semiotic resources combine to create a powerful impression of distinct and binary gender roles, with "female" being the marked form. All of the minifigure cards in the 2017 collection are linguistically and visually gendered in some way, there are twice as many MMs as there are FMs, and the gender of the FMs is foregrounded twice as often, through a range of linguistic and visual indices. Linguistic and visual patterns in the cards suggest that different roles, identities and activities are available to men and women: FMs are represented as younger and slimmer, with more emphasised facial features (such as eyelashes and lips), whereas MMs are depicted as physically stronger, larger and more mature. MMs are also more likely to be functionalised in more dangerous or physical occupations, whilst FMs take up less adventurous, and more frivolous, roles.

It is worth pointing out that there are some exceptions to these general patterns. For example, the MM cards Small Clown, Mime and Thespian break out of their typical gendered moulds because they wear make-up or have slightly narrowed waists. There are also several FMs who wield weapons (such as Alien Villainess, Lady Cyclops and Cavewoman), or who engage in adventurous and/or dangerous activities (such as Surfer Girl and Snowboarder).

However, there are limited types of minifigures that are able to transcend the gender boundaries that pervade the "create the world" set. For example, most MMs possessing visual characteristics more typical of FMs are performers. FMs who wield weapons are all either fantasy figures (Alien Villainess, Lady Cyclops and potentially Tiger Woman, who has a whip) or an exaggerated caricature of an historical figure (Cavewoman). This creates the impression that gender norms can only be transgressed within the confines of role play and fantasy. Even when depicted in violent fantasy roles, however, the femininity of the women in the FM cards is emphasised. Indeed, indices of femininity are particularly prevalent in the textual and visual representations of fantasy figures that are not from the human (or even animal) world, such as Lady Robot, Alien Villainess and Lady Cyclops. This excessive indexing of femininity on fantasy figures restricts the potential of children's imaginative and fantasy play to go beyond the limits of their immediate social worlds.

Our analysis has systematically evidenced the (re)production of gender norms and stereotypes in the "create the world" cards, showing that this is one of many sites in which children learn that their place in the world is sharply determined and restricted along gendered lines. Whilst some of the minifigures do overcome dominant gender norms to an extent, the cards overall are overwhelmingly reliant on restrictive, hegemonic gender norms. The limiting and unbalanced nature of these constructions is not always immediately apparent, but as we have shown, it can be revealed through the kind of critical multimodal analysis deployed here. Given the important role toys play in children's development, it is imperative that we use methods like this to challenge discriminatory messages in children's toys and products, if we are to continue the work of transforming sexist ideologies in wider society.

Notes

1 Due to copyright restrictions, examples of the LEGO cards are included as illustrations. Neither LEGO nor Sainsbury's keep an accessible record of the 2017 cards, although a full list and selection of images can be found at: https://thecollector.io/features/2017/05/lego-create-the-world-complete-list/

2 This claim is supported by the way a group of ten young second-raters engaged with the cards to identify their gender: they all looked first at the image, then at the title, and finally, if necessary, at the written description. Only three of the children read the written descriptions at all.
3 This group consisted of five girls (one aged 6; three aged 7; one aged 9) and five boys (one aged 7; four aged 9).
4 Throughout this chapter, percentages are rounded to the nearest whole number.
5 This statistic includes four "fantasy figure' MMs who have hairy faces.
6 14% (N10) of the MMs have marks that imply wrinkles, compared with 3% (N1) of the FMs. Nineteen per cent (N13) of the MMs have white or grey hair, compared with 6% (N2) of the FMs.
7 10% (N7) of the MMs and 82% (N28) of the FMs have visual indices of gender on their body. Eleven per cent (N8) have lines on their body that imply body fat or baggy clothing.
8 21% (N4) of the FM cards, and 1% (N1) of the MM cards, include adjectives describing clothing.
9 59% (N20) of the FM cards and 6% (N4) of the MM cards feature pinks and/or purples; 69% (N48) of the MM cards and 44% (N15) of the FM cards feature blues and/or greens.
10 60% (N42) of the MMs, and 50% (N17) of the FMs, have a title that refers to a functional role; 61% (N43) of the MMs, and 50% (N17) of the FMs, hold functional items.
11 53% (N37) of the MMs and 35% (N12) of the FMs are given occupational roles.
12 14% (N10) of the MMs, and 9% of the FMs, hold an item which can be used to attack. Nine per cent (N6) of the MMs, but no FMs, hold a tool that is used to cut or fix. Seventeen per cent (N12) of the MMs, but only 3% (N1) of the FMs wear equipment that protects them from serious injury.
13 53% (N9) of the female minifigures' functionalised titles relate to physical activity, compared with 19.04% (N8) of the MMs' functionalised titles.

References

Atkin, A. (2005) "Peirce on the index and indexical reference", *Transactions of the Charles S. Peirce Society*, 41(1), pp. 161–188.
Auster, C.J. and Mansbach, C.S. (2012) "The gender marketing of toys: an analysis of color and type of toy on the Disney store website", *Sex Roles*, 67(7–8), pp. 375–388.
Baker, P. (2008) *Sexed texts: language, gender and sexuality*. London: Equinox.
Bucholtz, M. (2009) "From stance to style: gender, interaction, and indexicality in Mexican immigrant youth slang", in Jaffe, A. (ed.) *Stance: sociolinguistic perspectives*. New York: Oxford University Press, pp. 146–170.
Caldas-Coulthard, C.R. and van Leeuwen, T. (2001) "Baby's first toys and the discursive construction of childhood", in Wodak, R. (ed.) *Critical discourse analysis in post modern societies, Folia Linguistica* XXXV/1–2, pp. 91–110. Austria: Vienna.
Caldas-Coulthard, C.R. and van Leeuwen, T. (2002) "Stunning, shimmering, iridescent: toys as the representation of social actors", in Litosseliti, L. and Sunderland, J. (eds) *Gender identity and discourse analysis*. Amsterdam: John Benjamins, pp. 91–108.
Caldas-Coulthard, C.R. and van Leeuwen, T. (2003) "Teddy bear stories", *Social Semiotics*, 13(1), pp. 5–27.
Cunningham, S.J. and MacRae, C.N. (2011) "The colour of gender stereotyping", *British Journal of Psychology*, 102, pp. 598–614.
Johnson, D. (2014) "Figuring identity: media licensing and the racialization of LEGO bodies", *International Journal of Cultural Studies*, 17(4), pp. 307–325.

Johnstone, B. and Kiesling, S.F. (2008) "Indexicality and experience: exploring the meanings of /aw/-monophthongization", *Journal of Sociolinguistics*, 12(1), pp. 5–33.

Kahlenberg, S.G. and Hein, M.M. (2010) "Progression on Nickelodeon? Gender-role stereotypes in toy commercials", *Sex Roles*, 62, pp. 830–847.

Kiesling, S.F. (2004) "Dude", *American Speech*, 79(3), pp. 281–305.

Koller, V. (2008) "'Not just a colour': Pink as a gender and sexuality marker in visual communication", *Visual Communication*, 7(4), pp. 395–423.

Kress, G. and van Leeuwen, T. (2006) *Reading images: the grammar of visual design*, 2nd ed. London: Routledge.

Martinez, E., Nicolas, M.A. and Salas, A. (2013) "Gender representation in advertising of toys in the Christmas period (2009–12)", *Comunicar*, 41(XXI), pp. 187–194.

Mills, S. (2008) *Language and sexism*. Cambridge: Cambridge University Press.

Moon, R. (2014) "From gorgeous to grumpy: adjectives, age and gender", *Gender and Language*, 8(1), pp. 5–42.

Ochs, E. (1992) "Indexing gender", in Duranti, A. and Goodwin, C. (eds) *Rethinking context: language as an interactive phenomenon*. Cambridge: Cambridge University Press, pp. 335–358.

Peirce, C.S. (1998 [1895]) "Of reasoning in general", in the Peirce Edition Project (ed.) *The essential Peirce: selected philosophical writings*. Indianapolis: Indiana University Press, vol. 2 (1893–1913), pp. 11–26.

Rayson, P. (2009) "Wmatrix: a web-based corpus processing environment", Computing department, Lancaster University. At: http://ucrel.lancs.ac.uk/wmatrix/

van Leeuwen, T. (2008) *Discourse and practice: new tools for critical discourse analysis*. Oxford: Oxford University Press.

Wong, W.I. and Hines, M. (2015) "Effects of gender colour-coding on toddlers' gender-typical toy play", *Archives of Sexual Behavior*, 44, pp. 1233–1242.

5
SEXUAL HARASSMENT AS REPORTED BY THE BRAZILIAN PRESS

Ambivalent and contradictory framings

Branca Telles Ribeiro
LESLEY UNIVERSITY, USA AND FEDERAL UNIVERSITY OF RIO DE JANEIRO, BRAZIL

Liliana Cabral Bastos
PONTIFICAL CATHOLIC UNIVERSITY OF RIO DE JANEIRO, BRAZIL

Introduction

Sexual harassment has been the focus of intense political, social, and gender debate. The charges, hearings, corporate dismissals, embarrassments, and resignations have made sexual harassment a household word, and the implications for changes in schools, hospitals, workplaces, and everyday life (despite the sometimes fierce opposition) appears to be very significant.[1] Yet, at the core of the sexual harassment debate there is explicit and implicit disagreement to what actually constitutes harassment: "when the topic is sexual harassment, people often 'talk past' rather than 'talk to' each other, as if they were discussing different issues" (Bing and Lombardo, 1997: 293). This is what is captured in our discussion.

This chapter examines how some Brazilian public personalities and social commentators interpret the protests on sexual abuse at a much watched American media event in December 2017. Using a frame analysis approach (Bateson, 1972; Goffman, 1974), we investigate how sexual harassment is understood as reported by the Brazilian press. What types of paradoxes and ambiguities are captured in language, communication, and culture when sexism and sexual practices are discussed?

Eight opinion articles, an interview, and 14 letters-to-the-editor published in two leading Brazilian publications constitute our data. The chapter discusses different alignments taken by participants and their implications for sexism and violence. Framing helps us understand different, and often conflicting, perspectives on sexual harassment. Discourse strategies and conversational styles (Gumperz, 1982; Tannen, 1989), such as the use of hyperbole, repetition, and contradiction, point to underlying interactional frames (Tannen, 1993), as well as cultural schemata (Gee, 1992). We examine the effects of these alignments in the media debate and we discuss a range of sexist discursive practices. Social commentators often shift from serious to mocking frames, and we investigate what these shifts accomplish. Is a sexual move to be taken lightly (a joke) or seriously (an attack)? Also of interest are the responses of readers to such framings. The discussion points to a range of different positions regarding sexism, which may vary according to gender, age, and professional status.

Why frames?

"What is not clear to me is the concept of harassment. Is it flirting? ... How could it be defined?" (Leão, 2018b). Sexual harassment is a complex concept to define because it seems to rely entirely on the perspective of those who actually propose a definition and those who participate in a related event. A frame is the interpretation that is crucial to understand any such activity or discourse (Goffman, 1974; Tannen, 1993). Conversationalists, readers, or viewers of a film, must decide whether a message – a statement, question, or laugh – is friendly, aggressive, or flirtatious; intended to amuse, inform, persuade, threaten, or offend; intended as a main point or a side remark. Framing is a matter of conveyed meaning. It is the lenses by which we categorise, remember, and revise what we know, as well as what we say or write, how we mean it, how others hear or read it, and how we do things together linguistically, textually, and interactionally (Ribeiro and Hoyle, 2009). In analysing text, readers (and analysts) define the context(s) of a situation, how its parts fit into the whole, how the whole relates to larger structures of experience, and how what is unfolding at a given moment affects what will come next. Readers dynamically reshape context (reframing it), shifting footing (or alignment) vis-à-vis the content of a text, its author, and his/her own position as a writer or reader. Many elements of a frame are encoded and understood linguistically or textually. In our discussion, we will analyse how different writers/social commentators align themselves in relation to certain events (the #Metoo movement vs. the French response) or take different perspectives on sexual harassment. The discussion indicates that different frames propose different understandings, thus leading to different conclusions.

Particularly relevant to our analysis is the frame discussion that Bing and Lombardo (1997) used in the print media to define sexual harassment: *the judicial frame* (compares behaviours to legal policies and suggests response strategies); *the victim frame* (emphasises harm or injury to the victim(s), suggesting social change); *the initiator frame* (defines the (mis) behaviour as acceptable and implies that no change in behaviour is needed); and *the social science frame* (the objective observer) argues that harassment is contextually and culturally specific and needs to be addressed through integrated approaches. Each frame posits a different understanding and perspective. The following discussion will focus on specific aspects of the *victim frame*, the *initiator frame*, and the *social science frame* in our data.

Contextualising the discussion

To the surprise of Brazilian feminists and social researchers, the women's movement in Brazil returned to street demonstrations in 2015. Often called the "fourth feminist wave", the demonstrators relied on social media and street protests, on new forms of organisation with no specific political leadership, and a focus on making the "personal political" or "the collectivization of personal experiences" (Buarque de Holanda, 2018).[2] Young activists marched in support of legislation against sexual violence, against healthcare restrictions for victims of rape, and for abortion rights. One social media movement called #*meu primeiro assédio* ("my first harassment") was formed after a 12-year-old girl, who had participated in a Master Chef TV programme, was targeted by paedophile and sexist remarks in social media. In May 2016, after a teenage girl was gang raped, protestors marched in many Brazilian cities in a movement called "*mexeu com uma mexeu com todas*" ("messing with one, messes with all"). In Rio de Janeiro, participants staged "a human-microphone performance" collectively sharing experiences. In 2017, TV celebrities endorsed the "*#mexeu com uma mexeu com todas*" slogan after a prominent actor was accused of harassment. These demonstrations were widely reported by the Brazilian TV, newspapers, and online media.

In early January 2018, the Brazilian media devoted extensive coverage to the #Metoo movement. The coverage focused on the Golden Globe Awards ceremony in Los Angeles in December 2017, where most American actresses wore black to protest against sexual harassment in the film and television industries. Opinions about the women's movement and demonstrations by celebrities intensified after a group of 100 well-known French women – actresses, intellectuals, and journalists – led by Catherine Millet (writer) and endorsed by Catherine Deneuve (internationally known actress) published a letter in *Le Monde* that criticised the #Metoo movement. The letter condemned the American movement as a "defamatory campaign" and a "witch hunt" (against men). The letter questioned the elusive nature of "sexual harassment", defended sexual freedom, and criticised some positions of the American protesters as "puritan".

A few days later one of the leading Brazilian newspaper, *O Globo*, reported on the French celebrities' letter, followed by four short opinion pieces (written by a journalist, two anthropologists, and a sociologist) under the headline "What women here think about this topic." *O Globo* continued coverage the next day with four opinion pieces by men: two actors, a philosopher, and a writer, under the title "What these men think about the split between American and French actresses."

The text by the journalist Danuza Leão generated the most controversy. Before we examine this text, we will contextualise it within the group of opinion pieces where it appeared. We believe that a brief description will illustrate how some segments of Brazilian society (artists, researchers, journalists) view sexual harassment and how they perceive the feminist demonstrations. Our observations focused on the ways that the authors frame sexual harassment, and with whom they identify.

The three female writers bring their understanding of the cultures of the USA and France. The anthropologist Miriam Goldenberg, criticises the position of the French authors and asks "whose sexual freedom are we talking about?" She aligns herself with the #Metoo and the Time's up movements. She defines sexual harassment from the victim's perspective (Bing and Lombardo, 1997) and endorses the "end of silence" which, she says, is being confronted "as it stands for abuse of power and sexual violence against women".

Sonia Corrêa (also an anthropologist) writes in a "social science frame" (Bing and Lombardo, 1997). She expands the discussion to include new, progressive definitions. Corrêa supports the #Metoo movement ("very relevant in challenging different types of power"); she also proposes new ways to reduce harassment, which, she says, "affects us all". She does not mention the French letter, but argues against "moral and repressive assumptions", that she attributes to some of the American feminist movement. Similar to the French letter, Corrêa warns about the rise of new conservative social norms that could restrict and censor sexuality, rather than empower women.

Marlise Matos, a sociologist, asks "how should one assess (harassment)?" Her response: "By analysing women's feelings." Matos frames her answer from the women's (victim) perspective. She writes that power is unbalanced in Brazil's patriarchal society, where "men have power over women … even among highly educated people". The issue of power imbalance is not widely discussed, she says. "Speaking out is the only way to redress this situation. … So one needs to say (out loud) 'me too'."

The four men (two actors, a philosopher, and a writer) assume various alignments and framings. Joao Vicente de Castro (a young actor) and Francisco Bosco (a young poet and philosopher) appear to propose nuanced social science frames. Castro sympathises with the #Metoo movement, saying that "most men do not understand the difference between flirting and harassing (or they pretend not to understand it)". Hence, "there is a need for radicalism in the feminist movement … since common sense has not prevailed". However, he argues that the French argument also contains merit, though not at this moment. As a man, he does not want to be excluded from the feminist conversation, given that "the struggle for gender equality is ours too".

Bosco (2018) writes that sexual harassment should be made a crime and that sexual bullying is unacceptable. However, he notes that there is "confusion" in understanding "harassment and even sex". There seems to be a "puritan perception of sex as a traumatic event" which may lead to a misunderstanding about sexual practices. Also, radical American feminists perceive "patriarchal societies as oppressive … and against women's independence rights". He indicates that such societies vary significantly in substance and form, where individuals may have different types of freedom, and may often misunderstand what sex is about.

While Castro and Bosco advocate against sexual harassment (classified as a serious crime), they also emphasise conflicting orientations in a young man's sexual development (Castro notes that informal and street education "requires a man to grow up having as many relationships with women as possible"); they also note the lack of clarity in a young woman's sexual education (Bosco wonders how "sex may be a traumatic event" and "how is sex to be understood"). Their arguments generally fit the social science frame (Bing and Lombardo, 1997). They align as observers of sexual and cultural mores, and note the need for more context specific interpretations.

Paulo Cesar Pereio (2018), at 78, the oldest of the four, and Leandro Narloch (middle aged writer) side with the French position ("I agree with Deneuve's and the other French women's statement", says Pereio; "I thought their statement was great", writes Narloch). While the two generally agree, each frames harassment slightly differently. Pereio takes a defensive position "I am especially respectful, civilised." Then he points out that we live in a world "where people exaggerate about harassment" and tend to generalise that "all men are animals". He uses striking contrastive distinctions ("respectful and civilised" vs. "animals") and bold qualifiers ("the demonstration was a shit"). Pereio says that the #Metoo and similar movements have shifted the focus from "criminality to exaggeration" (on this issue of harassment), and the field needs to be levelled so that men and women have equal power: "both men and women play seduction games". Pereio's statements fit Bing and Lombardo's (1997: 301–302) initiator frame: there is a redefinition of the situation, whereby roles are reversed and the initiator is the victim; women and men are equally powerful; the everyday man is really a nice guy; there is an "alleged harassment" rather than harassment, and thus no truth to the accusation.

Narloch constructs a double framing, writing first from a social science perspective, and placing himself as an objective observer. He briefly alludes to the "Spencer paradox" (British nineteenth-century philosopher) where the incidence of a social problem varies inversely to its actual existence (he paraphrases Spencer on human poverty "which always existed but became a problem only in the industrial revolution" where it gained visibility). Similarly, Narloch points out that it became fashionable, and even "lucrative", to advocate a given position – in this case a feminist position: "A bunch of people (women) are posing as virtuous on stage." Implicitly he accuses women of "capitalising" on sexual abuse and intimidation (for money or publicity). Here he seems to embed an initiator's frame: women (in the awards ceremony) are seen as manipulative, ambitious, and politically motivated. He implicitly points to "alleged harassment" rather than harassment (Bing and Lombardo, 1997: 301–302), questioning the truth of the accusations.

These seven opinion pieces capture very different perspectives and alignments. The first group (Goldberg, Matos, Castro) frame harassment from the victim's perspective (i.e. from the women's feelings, standing for breaking silence); it aligns with the #Metoo and American movement, and opposes the French position. The second group (Correa and Bosco) also view harassment as highly problematic. However, both express concern over what they represent as "sexual moralism" from the American feminists. That is, issues of women's sexuality seem to generate confusion and trauma, which could lead to moralist and repressive attitudes. Both Correa and Bosco alert their readers to the fact that American feminism has a strand of puritan feminism. Finally, the third group (Pereio and Narloch) take a critical stance to frame the discussion in an anti-American and pro-French alignment. They may shift frames from initiator to a social science perspective or vice versa. They strongly align with the French manifesto (distinguishing insistent flirtation from sexual harassment). The tone seems ironic in its grandiloquence (citing a British nineteenth-century philosopher; presenting contrastive hyperboles; or using euphemisms to mitigate a potential crime). In sum, these well-known opinion writers offer radically different positions. Their texts evoke two larger frames: a serious text (Goldenberg, Correa, Matos, Castro, and Bosco) and a mocking and critical text (Perreio and Narloch). This discussion also serves as background to Danuza Leão's position, which generated much press attention as well as letters, opinion statements, and interviews.

Danuza Leão's opinion statement and interview

Danuza Leão's opinion article generated the most controversy. The text supports conservative and sexist ideas, even while it advocates an independent feminine sexual life. The strong reaction to her opinion article is connected to her public image: Leão is an 84-year-old Brazilian journalist and outspoken celebrity, who has been a public personality since her youth. She has written bestselling books on social etiquette, and has, for decades, regularly contributed opinion pieces to top Brazilian newspapers. She opens the text with a central question:

> What is not clear to me is the concept of harassment. Is it flirting? Sexual invitations between men and women always start from one side. Sometimes the other side is not interested, and this is standard. How could it be defined?

Leão begins by stating that the concept of harassment is unclear and subject to interpretation. However, this brief neutral alignment is rather tenuous. In her next question ("is it flirting?"), she mitigates blame from the initiator (typically a male subject), while shifting responsibility to the target (typically a female). She describes shared roles (men and women) pointing to symmetrical power relations, while the action (flirting) and the reference (an invitation) describe and point to benign activities. She implicitly says that a woman can refuse an invitation yet still be flirtatious. She assumes a position of a cultural observer who sees no harm in an activity where participants (men and women) share power more or less equally.

Next, she expresses concerns, and implicitly criticises the demonstrations at the Awards:

> I hope this trend of denouncing sexual harassment does not become commonplace in Brazil. What happened at the Golden Globe Awards seemed like a large funeral. In spite of their gorgeous dresses, I think most of the women [that is, those who wore black] went home alone.

Leão challenges women's contemporary attitudes "of denouncing sexual harassment", framing such attitudes as a "trend" which she hopes will not be imitated in Brazil. She criticises the Golden Globe Awards by using contrastive hyperboles ("large funeral" vs. "gorgeous dresses"). Women in black – a powerful group identity often symbolising loss, sorrow, or pain – is twice reframed as a "large funeral" to which no one is attracted. Instead of an exciting show, the Golden Globe Awards is portrayed as sad and somber, where women failed to attract admirers and "went home alone".

While aligning with traditional positions, Leão expresses a tone of mockery throughout this segment. She trivialises the women who spoke out. She reaffirms this criticism and continues to align with cultural stereotypes in her next closing statements:

> I don't think denouncing harassment would generate a "witch hunt" because it is sort of ridiculous to start with. It's painful to see that a woman can make an accusation and a man can lose his job. This is something sinful. But this is an American thing. There they don't understand sex. It's great to pass by a construction site and be noticed. I lived in this era. I think women should be harassed at least three times a week to be happy. Long live the men!

Disagreeing with the French celebrities, Leão does not believe there could be a "witch hunt", which she ridicules. Next, she takes a critical position against the Americans, which she articulates in a crescendo: "ridiculous", "painful", "sinful", "an American thing". The final "American thing" culminates with the statement "they don't understand sex" whereby Leão aligns with the French celebrities and disqualifies the American women in black (who could only trigger ridicule, pain, and shame). She pins both alignments (the sexy French versus the puritan American) to an entire generation "I lived in this era." And she expands its meaning by affirming how women of her generation ventured into prototypical working-class male environments (such as a construction site) and were rewarded by "a compliment". This challenging move (Goffman, 1981) on the part of middle-class women ("passing by a construction site to be noticed") is met with a thrill that Leão strongly affirms when she states "women should be harassed at least three times a week to be happy" and concludes by claiming the value of men publicly, exclaiming, just as people would acclaim kings, "Long live the men!"

What broader frame would capture Danuza Leão's tone and intended meaning? Is it play (mock insult) or hostility (real insult)? How should a reader interpret her positions? First one could infer that Leão displays a consistent alignment with women of her generation, who resolutely supported their men and were, in exchange, protected. Men risk losing their jobs (traditionally they are the breadwinners), they control specific territories (the workplace with its social and cultural demarcations), and they are expected to uphold social norms (one could only voice "compliments" and "invitations" to a lady, and certainly not threats or intimidations). Second, Leão aligns herself as an accomplice to men in performing a traditional gender role (Giddens, 1992). She denies women's claim for victimhood by mitigating a male's intended action (as "a compliment" and "an invitation") and consequently modifying its resulting effect (an "invitation" is not an "imposition", and much less a forceful coercive action). In performing this role, Leão emphasises extreme positions by using hyperboles, a direct style and expressive language. She also belittles the cultural positions of a younger generation. If one considers gender-related ways of speaking (Kendall and Tannen, 2003), it seems that Leão seeks to position herself in status to men (her choice of stylistic discourse strategies is often associated with male speech patterns),[3] while also aligning with women of her own generation. Firm in these two conservative footings, Leão challenges modernity and contemporary women's stances on sexuality.

Two weeks later, the national weekly magazine *Veja* interviewed Leão (2018a) about her earlier remarks and the controversy they generated. The interview was prominently displayed in the magazine, of which we include a few sections.

Q. *Did you find out what harassment means?*
A. I realised I was wrong after I wrote [my opinion piece]. Harassment is a crime. In the sexual field or any other.

Q. *Why did you write about harassment if you did not know what it was?*
A. They asked me to talk about the Golden Globe Awards. I noticed that it looked like a funeral. I thought that all those women in black would return home alone …

Q. *But it's not always good enough to say "no", right? [after Leão declared that "it is simple: I say no".]*
A. I'm not generalising. There is rape. When a woman is in a dark street and three guys stop her, there is no way out. Now if a young woman goes to a young man's home, that's different. People say that she can go to his bedroom, take off her clothes in bed, but if she says no, it's no. It's really not like that. What people are doing makes one feel that women are stupid, idiots, as if they don't know anything. But a woman knows a lot. She needs to behave in a way so that bad things don't happen.

Q. *You said that this "trend to speak out against harassment" had not yet happened in Brazil. Did you forget about the recent episodes in public transportation, and specifically the case of actor José Mayer?*
A. If a man masturbates against a woman's back on the bus or subway, he needs to go to a psychiatric hospital. This is not harassment. This is mental illness. Now I read about José Mayer's story in the newspapers. They had an affair for eight months. After eight months the woman couldn't put a stop to this?

Q. *Do you really believe that women enjoy going by construction sites to get some praise from workers?*
A. This thing … was a joke that we all heard when we were young. A woman would say: "oh, I'm feeling terrible, fat, ugly. My hair is bad." Someone would then turn

around and respond: "Walk by a construction site at lunch time, and you will lift your ego with all the whistling!"

Q. *Do you think that sexual relationships used to be easier?*
A. There was a time when men were expected to always be flirting with women … It was as if that was part of their masculinity. I used to work in nightclubs, people would drink; you can imagine how much flirting took place. And there is nothing more simple than just saying "no". One just says "no". It's great to flirt, one feels pretty, wonderful, powerful. … Seduction cannot end in the world because it is a wonderful thing.

In this interview, Leão seems to take three major alignments. In her first alignment, she reviews some key prior positions: she asserts that sexual harassment is a crime not to be taken lightly; she also says that violence and rape happen in society; and finally, she claims that no woman of her generation would walk by a construction site (a prototypical male territory) to be complimented. She recants her prior declarations, reframing them as a joke (hence, not to be taken seriously) or a misunderstanding, for which she apologises. In doing so, Leão asserts that harassment is a crime and violence against women is a serious problem.

In a second alignment, Danuza Leão reaffirms traditional prior positions from her first written statement in *O Globo*. She restates that women who challenge traditional sexual mores will not attract men (they would return alone); implicit is the assumption that outspokenness would break tacit sexual understandings between women and men (such as flirting), which would leave women that speak out isolated. Related to her initial statements, Leão implies that women who stand up for themselves have traditionally been left alone.

In a third alignment, Leão seems to *endorse* the social system in place letting "boys be boys", which would also mean understanding rape in a traditional and sexist way, believing that "real rapes" only happen in dark corners ("When a woman is in a dark street and three guys stop her, there is no way out") as discussed by Ehrlich (2002). Here women need to defend themselves and "(a woman) is no dummy", she knows what she is getting into (or she should know). Also, a woman needs to be careful: "She needs to behave in a way so that bad things don't happen."Within this alignment, Leão also takes a critical stance to the women's movement. In the section on José Mayer (a TV celebrity whose case had been denounced in street demonstrations), Leão blames the woman for taking so long to denounce. She implicitly raises doubts about the woman's credibility. In this social system, men are (or may be) expected to act aggressively, while women are expected to act defensively. To this respect, Leão affirms that sexual masculinity is violent, while sexuality for women is different. These alignments convey metamessages which reinforce traditional social positions and stereotypes.

The above discussion points to Danuza Leão's initial denial of her prior claims: it is not true that harassment is a sexual game that women enjoy playing; neither is it true that there was much fun flirting across social classes in construction sites. However, she tells her interviewer that all these prior positions need to be taken with a grain of salt (a joke, a misunderstanding). While she reframes her positions, she also maintains traditional alignments: women need to be self-protective; they know – or should know – what they are likely to get into. In doing so, Leão naturalises unequal power relations.

Leão concludes by aligning herself with the French women on seduction ("without flirting there is nothing", "it is such a wonderful thing"). Aligning with the French is also present in her first opinion piece, where she says that the #Metoo movement could lead to a "witch hunt", and agrees that the American feminists are puritan (and know nothing about sex). But Leão often assumes a mocking/play frame, differing from the French statement which takes a more serious criticism of the #Metoo movement.[4]

Responses to Danuza Leão: letters from readers

O Globo's initial report (10 January 2018) presented the eight opinion pieces discussed above. On 11 and 12 January, *O Globo* published six letters supporting and one letter criticising Ms Leão's opinions. The national news magazine, *Veja*, published the Q&A interview of Leão in the 24 January edition. On 31 January, *Veja* published five letters supporting Leão and two criticising.

In the following discussion, we analyse these 14 reader-response letters published by *O Globo* and *Veja*. Three major frames stand out: first, many readers align with Danuza Leão's communicative style, praising her bluntness and clarity; second, the readers align with Leão's positions in distinguishing women from men, in valuing flirting and seduction, and in agreeing with the French women; finally, some readers criticised Leão's assessments and extended that criticism to her generation.

Readers respond positively to Leão's communication style, which they described as "direct, straight to the point, clear". Often descriptors for her style follow a crescendo "without hypocrisy, without half words, without the hellish 'politically correct' (mantras)!" (Saade, São Paulo) or "simple, truthful, objective" (Azevedo, Rio de Janeiro). Objectivity and clarity were frequently paired with truthfulness, and political correctness with hypocrisy. A number of these assessments were restated as "the world is so tiresome, so it's a relief when someone writes exactly what you'd like to say" (Saade, São Paulo, 2018), where the reader identifies herself clearly with the writer. Leão is seen through her speaking/writing style, and interpreted as someone "practical, objective and classy", to be celebrated "bravo to bright women" (Oliveira, São Paulo, 2018) and congratulated as a top star "this is a lady who knows the World better than Catherine or Oprah" (Scarpa, São Paulo, 2018). Identity and speaking/writing style are evoked as one and the same thing, triggering various compliments from the readers (Bravo Danuza! Bright woman! Congratulations!).

Second, readers support Danuza Leão's alignment with the French women, pointing to specific cultural expressions of flirting: "Let those who don't understand an elegant and respectful 'fiu-fiu' (whistling), throw stones. Abuse is another thing altogether" (Saade, São Paulo); "insistent or awkward flirting is not wrong, and a male paying a compliment is not being aggressive" (Peralva, Niteroi). These writers also point to American women as extreme ("way too much") and puritanical ("make sex into something that must be censored"). Differences of behaviour between men and women should be celebrated ("long live the difference!"). Writers also claim that women are not victims ("except of ourselves") and should make conscious decisions ("every woman must know what she wants and choose her own path, aware of her decisions" (Azevedo, Rio de Janeiro).

Finally, some writers confront Leão. A few describe her style as "rude" (Barros, Rio de Janeiro) and her opinions as "silly" and revealing a "lack of knowledge and a lack of understanding" (Oliveira, São Paulo). Most of these critical letters describe Leão's positions as traditional or "old", as Goris (Minas Gerais) says "this lady is living in a distant past where women needed to be 'complimented' to feel 'good'. Today, women have learned to feel happy without needing to involve men, flirting, or their sexuality." Some letters emphasise a difference in generational outlook ("it would be better for the planet – and mostly for women – that she be quiet and learned to knit", says Oliveira, São Paulo). A few writers point to the French vs. the American vs. Danuza Leão controversy, as a woman reader from Rio de Janeiro writes:

> Catherine Deneuve's opinion is suspicious ... she defended movie director [Roman] Polanski from a prior rape accusation of a minor ... So are Danuza Leão statements wrong, because she claims that for a woman to be happy she should be harassed three times a week. What she is referring to is a "compliment" within basic rules of respect. The women's movement is not against that, but it is against sexual harassment imposed to women on the workplace and any harassment which is offensive and in bad taste.
>
> *Barros, Rio de Janeiro*

What can we learn from the framing of these letters? First, O Globo and Veja present readers' responses to Danuza Leão's opinion piece and to her interview. Conspicuously missing are readers' reactions to the other seven writers. This editorial decision makes Leão appear as a prominent Brazilian public voice (or counter voice) to the #Metoo movement and the French celebrities' statement.

Readers (both men and women equally) praise Leão's style as objective, clear, rational, and honest. These traits have often been associated with the speech/writing style of men, described as "report talk" rather than "rapport talk" (Kendall and Tannen, 2003). Leão's style is assessed as competitive and strong, a woman who does not mince words ("without detours"). This assessment is also conveyed through Leão's criticism of political correctness. Readers value Leão's anti-intellectual and blunt positions, which are described as "honest" because she avoids "half words" and "hypocrisy".

Finally, it is relevant to note that readers who criticised Leão were in the minority. They often presented a social science frame (Bing and Lombardo, 1997) searching to balance different views (to compliment "within basic rules of respect" is quite different from harassing "which is offensive and in bad taste"; "we need to take history into consideration … we are condemning a large group of people without having a just assessment"; "let's eliminate rude ways of behaviour but not give up light flirting"). A small group of readers directly confronted her position and her generation.

Conclusion

"I conclude with a sermon" – this is how Ervin Goffman (1976) opens his final remarks in the essay "Gender Display", in which he discusses the importance of denaturalising the ways we deal with gender in society, and of how profoundly unfair these ways are, especially for women. In this "sermon", he observes that analysis must go beyond stating the presence of sexism. Goffman (1976: 69) notes how "male domination is of a very special kind", how "gender stereotypes run in every direction", and how these stereotypes emerge in the "most loving moment apparently without causing strain".

> Whereas other disadvantaged groups can turn from the world to a domestic scene where self-determination and relief from inequality are possible, the disadvantage that persons who are female suffer precludes this; the places identified in our society as ones that can be arranged to suit oneself are nonetheless for women thoroughly organized along disadvantageous lines.
>
> *1976: 69*

Though not intending to engage in a sermon, Goffman underlines the importance of denaturalising sexist and patriarchal structures that organise our daily social life. He considers specifically the question of violence against women, and how difficult and confusing public debates on this topic can be. Our study followed Brazilian researchers who have analysed asymmetrical gender relations in printed media, and indicated that gender relations not only reflect, but reinforce and make these social asymmetries seem like the natural order of things.

Gender studies recognise today a "very complex and intertwined view of relationships within sex, gender, sexuality and language" (Ostermann and Moita Lopes, 2014: 424), and have expanded to other media and settings. In this chapter, which clearly does not support a dualist perspective on gender, we discussed male and female stereotypes in the written media, addressing a recent event that had significant public attention. We believe that looking at local examples of the written press can help us understand the public debate on the unfair "arrangement between the sexes", to quote Goffman (1977) again.

Using frame analysis, we discussed inconsistencies, conflicts, and paradoxes that emerged in the printed press debate on sexual harassment. The analysis articulated frame as a larger structural and cultural perspective, a type of schema, with a particular interactional view of framing, related to how writers and interviewees aligned themselves when speaking about harassment, sexuality, feminism, and power. We observed, for example, that: (1) alignments can be critical of the #Metoo movement, but not of feminism in general; (2) alignments can be against violence, but also against denouncing violence; (3) some alignments support women's independence, but oppose denouncing violence; and (4) some alignments are against violence, but question the existence of violence against women. Not only harassment, but also the understanding of sex and sexuality was problematised in serious and in ironic framings. Paradoxically conservative ways of reacting to feminist movements align with French liberal views of sexuality. Ms Leão was praised for her objective (masculine) style in defence of a traditional view of women and of feminism itself. She projects a powerful gender performance. She does not shy away from "compliments" from men in construction sites (a hyper-masculine location). She evokes certain language games (such as teasing and mock insults) in sites that can be problematic for most women. In the interview she reframes as "play" – "we were never (at the construction site) … it was a joke". Even if this statement is reframed as play, readers still support and applaud ("Let those who don't understand an elegant 'fiu-fiu' [whistle] throw stones"). Leão reasserts her position of strength as a woman who held and defended her own territory (in men's traditional space as bars/nightclubs), and as an older woman who is proud of having lived in a given "period of time, that era". If Leão's statements are considered transgressive by some readers ("rude", "silly", "terrible statement"), her alignments permit her to straddle the line between playful and serious talk. At one moment she challenges and is defiant; at the next moment she teases and poses rhetorical questions. Most readers responded enthusiastically in support to such alignments ("Bravo Danuza!", "I love you Danuza!"). What seems to be at stake here is the power that non-serious frames have to create involvement (Tannen, 1993) and captivate readers in a given direction.

A brief observation should be made about the "post-truth" contemporary scenario, where information is often manipulated by the press and social media. In the letters, for example, we observed how Ms Leão's style is praised for not being politically correct, and described as clear, direct, simple, and truthful. She is congratulated as a hero. As Blommaert (2018) observes, in this new post-truth era, truth is what ordinary and decent people feel to be true. Truth is conceptualised as a matter of moral identity, since it includes a moral judgement of social actors. For her supportive readers, Ms Leão "writes exactly what you'd like to say", with no intellectual or academic hypocrisy (or linguistic barriers). In doing so, she seems to create the right text and context to avoid a serious discussion on the devastating rates of violence against women in the Brazilian society.

This discussion illustrates that written media matters, and that it is still relevant to examine how a specific sector of society (celebrities and intellectuals) expresses itself in the press. As mentioned before, these celebrities' statements, particularly Danuza Leão's, were also subject to extended responses in the digital media. In a typical event of our globalised world, local events are modelled by discussions in other geographical and distant regions (Giddens, 1991), boundaries are blurred between written and digital medias, and what is published in one media or platform can be accessible immediately in others.

Finally, we must add that in the various texts analysed in this chapter, two important trends seem to emerge. First, younger men clearly align with contemporary feminist positions and struggles. Second, although always subject to change, there seems to be a generational shift towards a more progressive vision, with a traditional outlook among older professionals. In the 1960s and 1970s, most Brazilian social activists and intellectuals were not focused on a feminist agenda. Many considered feminism a minor social question in a country of so many inequalities (Ostermann and Moita Lopes, 2014; Buarque de Hollanda, 2018). Now gender issues are not only gaining more space in the media (printed and digital), but seem to be placed at the forefront of many cultural and social debates, increasingly gaining attention and support of more sectors of society.

Notes

1 Tarana Burke started the #Metoo movement to support survivors of sexual harassment and violence in 2006. The hastag went viral in 2018 when women used it to tell their stories. Yet, few accused men have taken responsibility or offered private apologies. Since the Weinstein report, some 200 prominent men lost their jobs after public allegations of sexual harassment. A few face criminal charges. As reported by the *New York Times*, "Americans disagree on how people accused of sexual misconduct should be held accountable and what the standard of evidence should be" (23 October 2018).
2 Brazilian feminist movements have faced struggles and victories. In the 1970s and 1980s, Women's Police Stations (*Delegacias da Mulher*) were instituted nationally. In 2006, the federal law *Maria da Penha* (named after a woman was crippled by her husband) for the criminalization of violence against women was approved. Another judicial landmark was the *Lei do Femicídio* (the Femicide Law, 2015) on the killing of women motivated by misogyny. Since then, news articles on violence against women and femicide crimes have been reported in the printed press almost daily.
3 Linguistic and discourse strategies are resources available to all speakers (Gumperz, 1982), although distributed unequally (Mills, 2003). And certain styles of speaking have been associated with men's talk, who seem to draw on more directness, dominance, hierarchical, and competitive speech (Kendall and Tannen, 2003).
4 After the publication of the French statement, much of the international press (*Le Monde*, the *New York Times*, the *Washington Post*, among others) showed a large divide in discussing harassment and violence against women. Even in France, what constitutes harassment seemed to be greatly subject to interpretation, as several writers, intellectuals, and politicians criticised misunderstandings and lack of empathy for victims of violence in the original letter.

References

Bateson, G. (1972) *Steps to an ecology of mind*. New York: Balantine Books.
Bing, J.M. and Lombardo, L.X. (1997) "Talking past each other about sexual harassment: an exploration of frames for understanding", *Discourse & Society*, 8(3), pp. 293–311.
Blommaert, J. (2018) "Ergo: exploring the world of alternative facts". At: https://alternative-democracy-research.org/2018/09/19/ergo/ (accessed 8 April 2019).

Bosco, F. (2018) "Ha uma percepção do sexo como trauma", 11 January, p. 24. At: https://oglobo.globo.com/sociedade/homens-comentam-polemica-entre-francesas-americanas-sobre-assedio-22275871 (accessed 19 July 2018).
Buarque de Hollanda, H. (2018) *Explosão feminista: arte, cultura, política e universidade*. São Paulo: Companhia das Letras.
Gee, J.P. (1992) *The social mind*. New York: Bergin & Garvey.
Giddens, A. (1991) *As consequências da modernidade*. São Paulo: Editora Unesp.
Giddens, A. (1992) *Sexuality, love and eroticism in modern societies*. Stanford, CA: Stanford University Press.
Goffman, E. (1974) *Frame analysis*. New York: Harper & Row.
Goffman, E. (1976) "Gender display", *Gender Advertisements: Studies in the Anthropology of Visual Communication*, 3, pp. 69–77.
Goffman, E. (1977) "The arrangement between the sexes", *Theory and Society*, 4(3), pp. 301–331.
Goffman, E. (1981) "Footing", in *Forms of talk*. Philadelphia, PA: University of Pennsylvania Press, pp. 124–159.
Gumperz, J.J. (1982) *Discourse strategies*. Cambridge: Cambridge University Press.
Kendall, S. and Tannen, D. (2003) "Discourse and gender", in Schiffrin, D., Tannen, D. and Hamilton, H. (eds) *The handbook of discourse analysis*. Malden, MA: Blackwell, pp. 548–567.
Leão, D. (2018a) "Dizer 'não' é facil", *Veja*, 24 January, pp. 15–16. At: https://veja.abril.com.br/revista-veja/dizer-nao-e-facil/ (accessed 19 July 2018).
Leão, D. (2018b) "O Globo de Ouro me pareceu um grande funeral", *O Globo*, 10 January, p. 21. At: https://oglobo.globo.com/sociedade/danuza-leao-globo-de-ouro-me-pareceu-um-grande-funeral-22271999 (accessed 19 July 2018).
Mills, S. (2003) *Gender and politeness*. Cambridge: Cambridge University Press.
Oliveira, L.A. (2018) *Veja*, 31 January, p. 25. At: https://veja.abril.com.br/revista-veja/leitor-2567/ (accessed 19 July 2018).
Ostermann, A.C. and Moita Lopes, L.P. (2014) "Language and gender research in Brazil: an overview", in Ehrlicht, S., Meyerhoff, M. and Holmes, J. (eds) *The handbook of language, gender and sexuality*, 2nd ed. Malden, MA: Wiley Blackwell, pp. 412–430.
Pereio, P.C. (2018) "Parece que todos os homens viraram animais", *O Globo*, 11 January, p. 24. At: https://oglobo.globo.com/sociedade/homens-comentam-polemica-entre-francesas-americanas-sobre-assedio-22275871 (accessed 19 July 2018).
Ribeiro, B.T. and Hoyle, S. (2009) "Frame analysis", in Brisard, F., Ostman, J.O. and Verschueren, J. (eds) *Grammar, meaning and pragmatics*. Amsterdam: John Benjamins, pp. 74–90.
Saade, A. (2018) *Veja*, 31 January, p. 25. At: https://veja.abril.com.br/revista-veja/leitor-2567/ (accessed 19 July 2018).
Scarpa, C.C. (2018) *Veja*, 31 January, p. 25. At: https://veja.abril.com.br/revista-veja/leitor-2567/ (accessed 19 July 2018).
Tannen, D. (1989) *Talking voices: repetition, dialogue and imagery in conversational discourse*. Cambridge: Cambridge University Press.
Tannen, D. (1993) *Framing in discourse*. New York: Oxford University Press.

PART II
Sexism and institutional discourses

6

"UNTIL I GOT A MAN IN, HE WOULDN'T LISTEN"

Evidence for the gender order in New Zealand workplaces

Janet Holmes
VICTORIA UNIVERSITY OF WELLINGTON, NEW ZEALAND

Introduction

Nearly 30 years ago, feminist sociologists described New Zealand as a "gendered culture", a culture in which "the structures of masculinity and femininity are central to the formation of society as a whole", a culture in which "the intimate and structural expressions of social life are divided according to gender" (James and Saville-Smith, 1989: 6–7). Gender, they suggested, is the motif and preoccupation of New Zealand society, as class is in Britain. Women and men are still more effectively trapped in gender roles in New Zealand than in Britain, they claimed. More recently a marketing lecturer at Auckland University commented that for various reasons "I think our gender roles in New Zealand are very ingrained" (cited in *Dominion Post*, 13 September 2018). Even if one has reservations about the extent to which such claims can be sustained, they suggest that little has changed in terms of gender relations in New Zealand in the last 30 years. Our sociolinguistic research in New Zealand workplaces over this period provides a rich source of evidence about the ways in which gender may influence workplace interaction. This chapter reviews some of this evidence.

In the last two decades, New Zealand has experienced a marked improvement in the number of women who have succeeded in gaining senior leadership positions in certain work domains. During this period, for example, among several other senior women political leaders, three women have taken on the role of Prime Minister: Jenny Shipley between 1997 and 1999; Helen Clark for nine years (three Parliamentary terms) from 1999 to 2008; and in August 2018 Jacinda Ardern completed her first year in that office. The roles of Governor-General and Chief Justice are currently filled by women and there was also a small increase in the percentage of women in senior management positions in the public service from 39.6% to 44.2% over the five-year period to 2016 (Human Rights Commission,

2016). However, the latest Human Rights Commission Report (2018) notes that "while women comprise 61% of public servants, they comprise only 42% of chief executives of public service departments and 48% of the top three tiers of senior management". And the story in the private sector is worse; there has been a sharp decline in women's representation in senior management roles from 33% in 2011 to 22% in 2018, and 56% of businesses have no women in senior roles. "In one global report, New Zealand ranks 33 out of 35 countries surveyed for the proportion of senior leadership roles held by women" (Human Rights Commission, 2018).

In this rather depressing context, I consider the extent to which the "gender order" (Connell, 1987; Eckert and McConnell-Ginet, 2013) continues to influence attitudes and behaviour in New Zealand workplaces drawing on evidence from workplace interaction (in the Language in the Workplace Project database), including analyses of how women in leadership positions negotiate the complex and often confusing demands imposed by this ideology.

The gender order

The Language in the Workplace Project (LWP) team uses a social realist approach in the analysis of workplace interaction (see Holmes et al., 2011: 19ff). Social realism provides an account of the relationship between wider social structures and ideologies and individual agency, proposing that individual behaviour (including language) is influenced by outside "reality" (Coupland and Jaworksi, 2009: 17). In other words, our behaviour is constrained by the parameters of broad societal norms and "inherited structures" of belief, power, opportunity, and so on (Cameron, 2009: 15). These constraints involve institutional norms and ideologies which members of society are typically aware of, whether they conform to them or contest them (Bucholtz and Hall, 2005). Our recent research has focused more particularly on how these macro-level societal constraints are instantiated at the level of micro-level face-to-face interaction (e.g. Holmes et al., 2011, 2012). Gender is an unavoidable consideration in this approach.

The "gender order" (Connell, 1987) is one example of a strong ideological constraint which influences what is regarded as appropriate behaviour for women and men in different contexts (e.g. Jackson and Parry, 2011). Connell (1987) introduced this concept to describe the patterns of power relations between masculinities and femininities that are widespread throughout many societies and which influence the construction of gender identity. Emphasising the importance of attending to large scale macro-level structures, she points to the hegemony of masculinities in most western societies and the influence of hegemonic power relations which shape notions of masculinity and femininity. Through socialisation processes and increasing familiarity with societal norms and expectations, we learn how to behave appropriately as gendered individuals in our society (Eckert and McConnell-Ginet, 2013). The gender order thus acts as a societal level constraint to which members of society orient in their interactions. Moreover, it seems reasonable to suggest that the workplace constitutes a prime site for investigating awareness of the gender order and its influence on the way leadership is enacted by women and men in different organisational contexts. As Cameron (1997: 30) points out, we cannot deny "the materiality of gender and power relations", just as we cannot ignore the relevance of "the institutional contexts and the power relations within which gender is being enacted".

The concept of the gender order directs the attention of analysts to gendered assumptions which undeniably influence the behaviour of individuals, and encourages analysis of taken-for-granted presuppositions about gender appropriate behaviour which impact interaction, often in quite subtle ways. Eckert and McConnell-Ginet (2013: 20) note that gender is a social arrangement, "not primarily an individual matter but a practice connecting the individual to the social order", and they argue that "[i]nequality is built into gender at a very basic level" (2013: 21). Drawing on a wide range of research, they perceptively identify some of the myriad ways in which gendered assumptions influence everyday interaction. While the feminist research of the last 40 years has had a significant impact on New Zealand society, with a large increase in public awareness of the need to avoid overt gender discrimination, there is also evidence that the gendered ideologies, expectations, and norms identified by Eckert and McConnell-Ginet continue to influence social behaviour (including language). The analysis in this chapter makes a small contribution to the enterprise of demonstrating awareness of the continuing impact of the gender order in workplace interaction.

Gender stereotypes and leadership discourse

Extensive research among gender and language scholars over the last few decades supports the claim that the norms for behaviour, including interaction, in many workplaces, especially in the business sector, are often predominantly masculine norms, and in many workplace contexts in a range of countries men's discourse styles have been institutionalised as ways of speaking with authority (e.g. Holmes, 2006a, 2017; Mullany, 2007; Schnurr, 2009; Baxter, 2010, 2011, 2012; Angouri, 2011; Liu et al., 2015).

In many work areas, stereotypes of effective leaders are typically masculine in conception. The tendency to "think leader, think male" is discussed by a number of feminist analysts (e.g. Kendall and Tannen, 1997; Holmes, 2006a, 2009; Mullany, 2007; Baxter, 2012), and references to "hero" leaders (e.g. Jackson and Parry, 2001) reinforce this tendency. A recent edited collection (Ilie and Schnurr, 2017) directly addresses this issue, with a rich compilation of analyses from scholars complexifying and contesting these constraining stereotypes.

Researchers have also examined ways in which workplaces can be experienced as gendered through the use of workplace discourse which alienates women in particular (e.g. Holmes, 2006a; Mullany, 2007; Baxter and Wallace, 2009; Baxter, 2010). Nielsen (2008: 173), for example, describes Danish bakeries as "masculine workplaces", characterised by "masculine discourse" (2008: 185), which is perceived by the women as "really rough and unpleasant" and as having an "aggressive and nasty" tone (2008: 185). Similarly, Plester and Sayers (2007) explore the use of aggressive humour in male-dominated IT companies, identifying a style of humour which they characterise as banter or "taking the piss". Baxter (2011: 234) has theorised that whole corporations are gendered, and claims that "[in] a 'male-dominated' corporation women leaders still face many prejudices about their competence". In such workplaces "feminine" styles of interaction may be side-lined and regarded as ineffective, and women are positioned as "other" (Baxter, 2011: 234). These analyses illustrate ways in which gender seems to be embedded within the institutional structure of many workplaces.

Despite the predominantly masculine stereotypes of leadership, and evidence of gendered work contexts where feminine interactional styles are marginalised, considerable evidence has accumulated indicating that effective leaders, both female and male, exploit a diversity of styles to achieve their interactional goals (e.g. Holmes, 2006a; Eagly and Carli, 2007; Mullany, 2007; Baxter, 2010). Current theories of leadership and management highlight the importance both of assertiveness and authority, attributes normatively associated with masculine styles of interaction, as well as well-honed relational skills, attributes associated with feminine interactional styles (Eagly and Carli, 2007). Jackson and Parry (2011: 20) discuss, for example, the "feminization" of the leadership prototype, emphasising the gendered nature of the different characteristics that are associated with effective leadership rather than the gender of effective leaders, and arguing that "leaders who conform to the feminized stereotype, that of a balance between relationship-orientation and task-orientation, will be the better leaders, irrespective of whether they are women or men". I return to this point in the conclusion.

Taking account of this research, the analysis below focuses on evidence that women in New Zealand workplaces continue to be aware of the constraints of the gender order, and the pressure of gendered norms and stereotypes, as well as the effects these norms exercise on workplace discourse, and especially on the discursive resources available to women who aspire to leadership positions. My analytical approach has its roots in interactional sociolinguistics (Gumperz, 1999), examining discourse in its wider socio-cultural context and drawing on the analysts' knowledge of the community and its norms to interpret what is going on. I use this approach within a social constructionist framework to analyse evidence of gendered influences on leadership identity work. First however, I briefly describe the methodology and database.

Methodology and database

The material discussed below derives from the Wellington Language in the Workplace Project (www.vuw.ac.nz/lals/lwp). Our data collection takes an ethnographic approach: after a period of participant observation, we ask volunteers to record samples of their everyday workplace interactions over a period of two to three weeks. This is followed by debriefing interviews to collect comments and reflections on this process. Where possible we video-record meetings of groups, using small cameras which are fixed in place and left running for the whole meeting.

As far as possible, our policy is to minimise our intrusion as researchers into the work environment.[1]

The LWP Corpus currently comprises more than two million transcribed words from 2000 interactions, involving 700 participants from 30 different New Zealand workplaces which include commercial organisations, government departments, small businesses, factories, building sites, and eldercare facilities. The data analysed in the next section draw from material recorded in meetings in professional white-collar workplaces, as well as interviews conducted after the recording phase with workplace leaders.

Analysis

The analysis in this section provides evidence that women in New Zealand workplaces continue to be aware of the constraints of the gender order, and the pressure of gendered norms and stereotypes. Detailed qualitative analysis of daily workplace discourse provides an invaluable means of relating such macro-level social ideologies to micro-level interactions in specific contexts.

I recently coined the term "the culture order" as a parallel concept to the gender order to account for the ways in which individuals orient to the construction of their ethnic or cultural identity (Holmes, 2018a). Just as the gender order acts as a societal level constraint to which members of society orient in their interactions, so the culture order identifies the hegemonic ideologies influencing the ways in which individuals orient to ethnicity. The concept of the culture order encourages analysis of taken-for-granted presuppositions about appropriate cultural behaviour which impact interaction, especially in intercultural contexts. Similarly, the concept of the gender order directs attention to gendered assumptions which unavoidably influence the behaviour of individuals. My analysis of intercultural interactions indicated that minority culture group members tend to be most aware of the constraints of the culture order (Holmes, 2018a, 2018b). Majority group members typically take societal norms for granted and simply assume their ways of behaving are normal. Similarly, it is normally, though not exclusively, women who are most aware of the constraints of the gender order.

In some workplaces there are explicit references to the challenges for women of working in "a boys' club" (e.g. IT workplaces, hospitals). Excerpt 1, a chat between a nurse and a patient, provides a short example.

Excerpt 1

Context: In a hospital ward cubicle, Tara, a staff nurse, is discussing a woman surgeon with Mia, a patient.

1. Mia: cos she's such a a definite woman
2.   but I mean that's what I've done
3.   it's a tough old world out there
4.   //(just) knowing\ where you're going

5. Tara: /yeah exactly\\
6.   it's a real boys' club as well
7. Mia: sure is

Mia is a well-informed patient: *that's what I've done* (line 2) refers to the fact that she has consulted widely about her condition. She is thus well aware of the dominance of male surgeons in the area and she comments on the challenges facing even a *definite* ["confident"] *woman* (line 1) in the medical sphere, *it's a tough old world out there* (line 3). Tara, the staff nurse follows up with *it's a real boys' club as well* (line 6), explicitly referring to the challenges and constraints raised by the gender order in this working sphere.

In earlier articles (Holmes, 2005, 2006b) I analysed in some detail a more complex discussion by senior policy analysts in a government department of the influence of the "old boys' network" in the workplace. Excerpt 2 testifies to awareness of the gender order among the women participants in particular. Connie, the executive officer, is updating the team on a recent meeting with the Minister, and she mentions the name of a particular businessman. Jake interrupts her with some information about the businessman's local standing.[2]

Excerpt 2

Context: Regular meeting of mixed gender group of 13 people in a government department.

1. Jake: he's he's got a quite high profile
2.   and he's considered to be + //you know=
3. Connie: //a good chap\
4. Stu: /a good guy\\
5. Jake: =a bloody\ good bloke
6. Stu: a good guy //oh okay\
7. Jake: /and the\\ Minister thinks so as well so you know
8.   //an- and\ he's quite an honourable guy
9. Wendy: /( )\\
10. Connie: [quietly] mm
11. Jake: he's a sort of a handshake and I trust you type guy
12.   so you know + when you've got another good bloke
13.   talking to another good bloke then you've got a
14.   [general laughter]
15. Stu: they didn't go to the same school //did they\
16. Jake: /us good\\ blokes have gotta stick together

         [general laughter, buzz of sceptical noises and comments
         including "oh right" from more than one woman]

17. Wendy: //bloody good bloke\
18.   /[general laughter]\\

19.	Jeff:	bet he doesn't employ many women workers
20.		[general laughter]
21.	XM:	no
22.	Connie:	(oh) I probably wouldn't want the job either

The men and women (who are all of similar professional status) appear at first to be in agreement, as reflected in the development of a collaboratively shared floor between Jake and Stu and Connie (lines 1–6). Connie's contribution *a good chap*, is practically simultaneous with Stu's synonymous *a good guy* (lines 3–4), and Jake's *a bloody good bloke* (line 5). This is maximally cohesive, collaborative, and supportive discourse, with all three clearly on the same wavelength, developing a single shared floor.

However, gender gradually emerges as an alternative and contentious issue as the men develop the notion of the pervasiveness and power of the old boys' network (lines 7–16). The issue of gender is gradually foregrounded as Jake expands the concept of *a good bloke* (lines 5, 11–13), and Stu's comment *they didn't go to the same school did they* (line 15) refers to one common source of the old boys' network. Jake picks up this reference in an overlapping turn *us good blokes have gotta stick together* (line 16), an explicitly gendered development of Stu's humorous comment. The women protest and contest the men's scenario with comments such as *oh right*, and sceptical noises, and Wendy contributes a challenging and sarcastic echo *bloody good bloke* (line 17). By now, gender is very explicitly the focus of the discussion and Jeff joins in (line 19) with a taunt to the women *bet he doesn't employ many women workers*, to which Connie responds challengingly *I probably wouldn't want the job either* (line 22). In the course of this exchange, then, the women and men explicitly articulate rather different views about the characteristics of *a good bloke*, and some of the implications of the constraints imposed by the gender order, such as the exclusion of women from significant workplace interactions and of women employees from some workplaces, are explicitly referenced. The systemic nature of men's more powerful position in the workplace is very apparent in this exchange which focuses on the discursive strategies men use to maintain economic power, and the dependence of women on powerful men to provide them with opportunities for employment. Both female and male participants are clearly aware of these gendered societal norms with the men explicitly endorsing them, albeit semi-humorously, and the women vigorously contesting them.

In a contrasting example (Excerpt 3), Clara, the section manager in another organisation makes a joke about a male team member's inability to manage a complex job.

Excerpt 3

Context: Regular meeting of mixed gender project team within a commercial organisation.

1.	Clara:	[smiling voice]: he can't multi-task:
2.	Females:	[laugh]

3. Peg: it's a bloke thing
4. [general laughter]
5. Clara: [laughs]: yeah yeah:

Clara begins by specifically teasing Harry about his limitations in not being able to take on additional tasks; her comment *he can't multi-task* (line 1) elicits laughter from the other women in the group. The need for multi-tasking skills in the workplace had been a focus of discussion in the New Zealand media, with feminists pointing out that women have always needed to multi-task because of the demands of running a household. It is thus an issue which immediately makes gender differences salient, referring obliquely to the gender order which requires women to take primary responsibility for household tasks. Peg then draws an explicit gender boundary with her generalising comment *it's a bloke thing* (line 3), which elicits laughter from the group. This brief example provides further evidence of the impact of expectations generated by awareness of the gender order in the workplace.

Another set of examples illustrates sexist attitudes among clients who treat women as inadequate or unsatisfactory representatives of their organisations, and who demand to deal with men. Again, these are evident in explicit reports from participants. Excerpt 4 is a particularly egregious example. Anna is contributing to the general discussion of a difficult client.

Excerpt 4

Context: Meeting of the sales and production team in a commercial company. The team members, three men and four women, agree that the client under discussion is troublesome.

1. Imogen: it's gonna be trouble
2. Chrissie: it's trouble
3. Anna: you know the amount of time
4. I've wasted on these people the last week
5. when I can pop into [company] for half an hour
6. (and sort things)
7. yeah I mean my regular clients don't talk to me
8. the way I've been spoken to the last three weeks

[Description of an episode where the angry client swore in a meeting]

9. Molly: [name] was just rude…
10. Anna: he was just seemed to be getting angrier and angrier …
11. and I said look [name] I'm really trying hard to explain this here
12. but you you do need to to listen to what I'm saying
13. Paul: mm

14.	Anna:	and he didn't until I got a man in he wouldn't listen
15.		but I mean that that's you know a one-off sexist issue
16.		that we do have from time to time with [company]
17.		but what I'm saying is are they worth it

This is a short excerpt from a very extended discussion about the competing claims of the need to get new business vs. the need to be "treated with respect". While the discussion about difficult clients is quite general, with all participants engaged and largely in agreement that the company needs to weigh up the cost of such demanding, time-consuming customers, the specific point which is my focus here is Anna's claim that the male client would not listen to her *until I got a man in* (line 14). This is a very explicit instance of an attitude which was evident in other workplaces too.

In an interview with the female CEO of another commercial company, I raised this issue overtly. Her response indicated that the situation was not an unfamiliar one and that she simply sent a man along to clients who did not want to deal with a woman. Excerpt 5 is a section from the relevant discussion.

Excerpt 5

Context: Interview between the CEO of a commercial company and the researcher. The Chief Executive Officer has just described someone who she suspects finds her interactional style "overwhelming".

1.	Yvonne:	so there have been a few individuals like that
2.		but you see it doesn't hold me back I just
3.		but if I if I notice it then I just I I
4.		oh actually another one is [name]
5.		who has problems with women
6.		so I just sent Hone you know
7.	Janet:	just be strategic about it
8.	Yvonne:	yeah you've just got to think you know
9.		he doesn't I mean I get on sort of with [name]
10.		but I can't make headway with him
11.		that's why I send Hone over
12.		Hone will come back with a whole lot of information
13.	Janet:	interesting yeah
14.	Yvonne:	you know it's just boys like to share
15.	Janet:	yeah boys' networks
16.	Yvonne:	but on the other hand there are also women
17.		who relate much better to me
18.		and so Hone will say oh they need a girl you know so
19.	Janet:	so the girls' networks are getting established too yeah yeah
20.	Yvonne:	yeah they work in the same sort of way I mean
21.		I ( ) a lot of women I work with um
22.		they just prefer to work with women

Yvonne's solution to the fact that some clients clearly talk more comfortably to a man than a woman is to send along a man to elicit the information she needs: *I just sent Hone* (line 6). But she also goes on to indicate that some women *just prefer to work with women* (line 22), and so for some business interactions *a girl* is needed (line 18). This very interesting discussion suggests that women are beginning to challenge the dominance of men in the business world, but it also of course provides further testimony to the influence of the gender order.

In a number of workplaces, there are explicit sexist comments about women's appearance and indications of men's preoccupation with women's appearance, as well as patronising comments, such as "good girl" addressed to competent professional women, providing further evidence of the pervasiveness of the gender order. (Note that in Excerpt 5, Yvonne reports Hone as saying *they need a girl* (line 18) rather than a woman.) However, I turn now to more subtle indications of the ways in which the gender order plays out in workplace interaction. There is abundant anecdotal evidence of the pattern where women propose an idea and it is ignored, only to be later suggested by a male participant, when it is welcomed and lauded. Indeed, there are even cartoons making this point.[3]

Another similar strategy which is almost as offensive is when a woman's contribution is treated as unimportant or side-lined. Excerpt 6 illustrates one of the ways in which the concerns of a participant in a workplace discussion can be "managed".

Excerpt 6

Context: Regular meeting of a large group (18 participants) in a government department. Henry is the Chief Executive and is chairing the meeting. Selene is a manager. They are checking through the items on the agenda.

Due to space constraints, I have edited Selene's comment to less than half its actual length.

1. Hen: okay thank you Georgia + er check ins.
    [An agenda item is mentioned]
2. Sel: can I make a comment on it ...
3. I've only been away for ten days +
4. um + I didn't come back till last night ......
5. and I find today an unconsulted paper on approving new capital bids
6. + and a [XX] paper for decision
7. and I have skimmed them not read them
8. and I don't feel very + well prepared to participate
9. particularly in the [XX] one where I have been very strongly involved
10. + so I feel I don't I'm not at the stage
11. that the papers not be handled today

12.		but I don't feel very comfortable about participating in the decision …
13.	Hen:	yeah okay Selene what what as I understand
14.		you're registering your concern about that
15.		but not asking for us not to consider the paper is that right
16.	Sel:	[drawls]: no: but I mean um ++
17.		yeah you you've summed it up correctly that I'm uncomfortable
18.	Hen:	okay + well let let's um er if during the course of that discussion
19.		you you continue to be uncomfortable
20.		let's um discuss it at the time
21.	Sel:	right
22.	Hen:	any other check ins

This interchange could be considered an illustration of stereotypically gendered interactional styles. Selene expresses her concerns at considerable length. In the process, she uses many of the strategies associated with a normatively feminine style of interaction. She is indirect, she is polite, and she is self-deprecating. The information she conveys could be summarised as "I don't think we should discuss these issues because I haven't had time to read the documents". Instead she is apologetic – *I have skimmed* [the papers] *not read them* (lines 7–8), and indirect: *so I feel I don't I'm not at the stage that the papers not be handled today but I don't feel very comfortable about participating in the decision* (lines 10–12). These are stereotypically feminine deferential strategies which could be regarded as making Selene appear subservient. Instead of explicitly insisting on stopping the discussion (which might be considered reasonable if, as she says, she has been *very strongly involved* (line 9)), she says *I don't feel very comfortable about participating in the decision* (line 12).

Henry, by contrast, is direct, forthright, and authoritative, making use of discursive features associated with a normatively masculine style of interaction. He summarises Selene's words concisely: *you're registering your concern about that but not asking for us not to consider the paper* (lines 14–15), and he quickly makes the decision that they will deal with this issue when and if they need to (lines 18–20), and then moves the discussion along *any other check ins* (line 22).

At this point it is important to consider how perceptions and context are very important in analysing and interpreting workplace discourse. This interchange could be interpreted in a different way. Selene could be seen as making a strong case for delay, providing convincing reasons, such as her position as someone who has been *strongly involved*, and as someone who for legitimate reasons has not had time to prepare for the meeting. In response to her lengthy expression of concern, the CEO's response is brief. Selene's reply suggests she is not happy with his rather summary dismissal of her concerns. She appears to reluctantly agree drawling *no*, then adds *but I mean*, and pauses before stating *yeah you you've summed it up correctly that I'm uncomfortable* (lines 16–17). In fact, later in the meeting, though she has been promised she could raise her concerns again, she finds herself at a point where the decisions have been made and her concerns have been effectively ignored. While this interactional pattern could have involved a female chair and a male participant, I draw attention to it as an example of how such behaviour can appear gendered when it is repeatedly the women participants who are shut down in this way and when the strategies used to do so could be perceived as overbearing.

Women in leadership positions are very aware of the influence of such perceptions as well as the society-wide stereotypes which reinforce the gender order. Leaders are expected to be decisive, authoritative, competitive, confident, single-minded, goal-oriented, etc. (e.g. Kendall and Tannen, 1997; Holmes, 2006a; Baxter, 2010). These are attributes strongly associated with "masculinity" rather than "femininity", and consequently women in leadership positions in countries as diverse as New Zealand, England, Europe, and Hong Kong are faced with additional challenges compared to men (as documented in detail by Holmes, 2006a; Mullany, 2007; Schnurr, 2009; Baxter, 2010; Angouri, 2011, among others). Excerpt 7, from an interview with Penelope, a woman who has been CEO of a number of organisations, testifies to this awareness. She here reflects on her experience at organisation X where she was required to manage a major structural change.

Excerpt 7

Context: interview with Penelope, Chief Executive.

1.	Penelope:	several people said to me at organisation X
2.		it's such a relief to have somebody in this role
3.		who will make decisions + and so actually
4.		I found that it did actually work to be decisive
5.		and to ++ um + n- not think oh I can't make this decision
6.		until I've talked to six other people [laughs]: you know:
7.		just sort of like I'm in charge (of you) here
8.		and I am the chief executive and I can make this decision
9.		and I will [sniffs]

There is some hedging, and a number of interactive pragmatic particles in this excerpt – *actually* (lines 3, 4), *you know* (line 6), *just sort of like* (line 7) – perhaps indicating Penelope's reluctance to self-promote as well as her orientation to her addressee. However, she also clearly describes her awareness of the need for assertive leadership behaviour, as well as people's positive reaction to it.

Our recordings of Penelope's interactions with her senior management team provide abundant evidence that she is a consultative and supportive leader in appropriate contexts. She pays compliments and thanks people generously for their work; she encourages discussion and negotiates agreement rather than imposing decisions (see Holmes, 2006a). Moreover, there is a good deal of humour at various points indicating the relaxed atmosphere she encourages. However, she also moves discussion along and makes sure that clear decisions are reached and recorded on key issues. Contentious views are exhaustively discussed until a solution is negotiated, and Penelope then succinctly summarises and indicates the action to be taken (see Holmes, 2017 for detailed analysis.)

In the course of our work in New Zealand workplaces, we have documented in some detail many such examples of the complexities of constructing an effective leadership identity and the challenges facing women in particular in negotiating the widely recognised "double bind" regarding "professionalism and femininity" (Kendall and Tannen, 1997: 92) imposed by the gender order. Stereotypical feminine behaviour is considered inconsistent with a leadership role.

Women leaders respond in varied and sophisticated ways to the constraints of the gender order. To take just one further example, Clara who featured in Excerpt 3 making fun of a male team member and demonstrating collegiality with women participants, adopts the persona of "Queen" to enact an authoritative leader identity when required. At other times she constructs a more motherly or even flirtatious identity (Holmes, 2006a). In instances where she has made an autocratic decision which others are unhappy with, either she or a member of her team typically soften it with a follow-up humorous comment as in Excerpt 8. One of Clara's team's tasks is to develop a new call centre for the organisation and as part of this assignment they need to decide on an appropriate greeting to be used by call centre staff when answering calls from the organisation's clients.

Excerpt 8

Context: Regular weekly meeting of project team in large commercial organisation; Sandy is the chair, Clara is the manager.

1. Sandy: we were going to have a vote on
2. it's um welcome or is it [in Māori]:kia ora:
3. Clara: oh it's welcome
4. Vita: yeah
5. Sandy: you sure?
6. Clara: yes
7. Peggy: you phone up and say whatever (you)
8. /want to outside business hours\ =
9. Vita: /[laughs]\
10. Peggy: = but in business hours it's welcome
11. Vita: [laughs]: where did that come from anyway: [laughs]
12. Sandy: just made that up

Clara has no hesitation in disagreeing with Sandy's suggestion that they vote on the greeting to be adopted. She is not at all conciliatory in her rejection of Sandy's suggestion of *kia ora* as one possibility for a greeting (line 2).[4] Rather she is authoritative and direct *oh it's welcome* (line 3). Her uncompromising declaration of the greeting to be adopted seems to cause tension which other participants use humour to release. Peggy teases Sandy that he can do what he likes at home but Clara's in charge here (lines 7–8, 10), and Sandy backs down claiming that this was not a well-thought-out idea, but instead something that had just occurred to him, he *just made that up* (line 12). Here then, Clara is relatively forceful and uses stereotypically masculine strategies to assert her point of view, while other team members collaborate to ease the tension and thus the process of accepting her ultimatum.

We identified this pattern repeatedly throughout our data-set. Powerful women would "do power" authoritatively, issue orders peremptorily, summarise action points succinctly, and then follow up with a humorous comment or anecdote, sometimes even a self-deprecating remark, thus attenuating the effect of their "masculine" behaviour (see Holmes, 2000; Holmes and Stubbe, 2015 for further examples). In Clara's team it is often another team member who does this relational work, typically her second-in-command Sandy. It seems, then, that while it is superficially acceptable for women to "do power" explicitly in the workplace, there is an underlying pressure to counter or neutralise the effects of the authoritative and "masculine" strategies entailed in doing so with more "feminine", supportive, and collegial or self-deprecating behaviours. This is further evidence that societal assumptions about appropriate behaviour, in this case the gender order, continue to operate and impose restrictions and constraints, even when women have apparently broken through the glass ceiling.

Discussion

The analysis has identified a range of evidence that the gender order continues to influence interaction in New Zealand workplaces. Overt reference is sometimes made to the fact that women are excluded from influential discussions and decisions by the *boys' club* in Excerpt 1 or the "old boys' network" referred to extensively in Excerpt 2 (*us good blokes have gotta stick together*), as well as in Excerpt 5. A second type of explicit evidence comprises the demand by some clients to deal with a man, as reported in Excerpts 4 and 5. Overt discourse patterns, such as ignoring a woman's contribution until repeated by a male, or closing down a discussion point raised by a woman (Excerpt 6) make the point that women's contributions may be treated as unimportant.

Finally, and most interestingly, perhaps because it is so much more subtle, is the evidence from gender identity construction work in interaction. There is extensive evidence that constructing gender identity in interaction is a dynamic process, and both women and men draw creatively on features of both normatively masculine and feminine communication styles in this process. But there is equally extensive evidence that women leaders walk a tightrope between enacting authority by adopting decisive stances in interaction (Excerpts 7 and 8), while maintaining their femininity through the use of epistemic devices such as hedges, interactive pragmatic particles, and supportive feedback (Excerpt 7).

This pattern is also well documented by other feminist analysts in the UK, such as Mullany (2007) and Baxter (2010, 2011), and for Hong Kong (Schnurr, 2009) and Europe (Angouri, 2011). Indeed Baxter (2011: 231) includes it as one category of "double-voiced discourse", a category that describes the way that women appear to "monitor and regulate their use of language more than men", adjusting it to take account of "their colleagues' concerns and agendas". Baxter (2011: 243) proposes that use of double-voiced discourse provides women leaders with "a self-regulatory mechanism to monitor, police, review and repair the way they appear and sound to their colleagues in order to avoid negative judgement". In New Zealand this tendency is reinforced by the Pākehā (European-based) culture order which endorses an egalitarian ethic discouraging overt displays of status and power, especially in less formal contexts (Holmes et al., 2012). So, New Zealand women leaders are subject to pressure from the gender order and this is compellingly reinforced by the dominant culture order in many contexts.

Conclusion

While roles available for women in workplaces internationally have steadily expanded, the influence of gendered norms and socio-cultural expectations undoubtedly constrain those available to female rather than male workers in all those countries and cultures where research has been undertaken. This chapter has provided a range of evidence describing how the gender order continues to influence workplace interaction. It is important to ask in conclusion then are there any signs of change? My analysis suggests there are precious few, but some can be found.

Overt sexism seems to be decreasing and when it does occur it is likely to be called out and challenged as in Excerpt 2 (*good bloke*) and Excerpt 4 (*until I got a man in*). However, while recognising the economic pressures, Yvonne's compliance with her client's gender preferences (Excerpt 5) is not so encouraging. On the other hand, Clara's criticism of a male team member for his inability to *multi-task* (Excerpt 3) could be regarded as evidence that some women are fighting back and asserting the advantages that women bring to workplace interaction. Moreover, in Excerpt 5, Yvonne says *a lot of women I work with um they just prefer to work with women*, suggesting, as noted in the interview, that *the girls' networks are getting established too.*

Another interesting development which suggests a direction of change that could be regarded as indirectly challenging the gender order is the growth of, or perhaps the increasing recognition of, "co-leadership" and "distributed leadership" (e.g. Holmes et al., 2011; Clifton, 2017). Heenan and Bennis (1999) first developed the notion of "co-leadership" which they define as two leaders in vertically contiguous positions who share the responsibilities of leadership. We have many examples in our data of just such relationships (Holmes et al., 2011). In terms of relevance for the gender order we found repeatedly that when a female manager behaved in an authoritative way, making a decision which could be perceived as autocratic or even unwelcome, her second-in-command (female or male) would frequently attend to relational aspects of the interaction and re-establish rapport through a mitigation technique such as humour (as illustrated in Excerpt 8). Thus "double-voiced discourse" may be accomplished through more than one participant to maintain good workplace relations. And since in many of the workplaces where we recorded the second-in-command to a woman was typically a male, this stereotypically "feminine" role of attending to relational aspects of interaction may over time increasingly become disassociated from gender.

In the introduction to this chapter I drew attention Jackson and Parry's (2011: 20) claim that "leaders who conform to the feminized stereotype, that of a balance between relationship-orientation and task-orientation, will be the better leaders, irrespective of whether they are women or men." If they are right, greater recognition of the positive aspects of normatively feminine talk in the workplace may contribute not just to greater acceptance of the effectiveness of women leaders, but also to the erosion of aspects of the gender order which disempower women at work.

Acknowledgements

I here express appreciation to Alexandra Birchfield for assistance with references and statistics, to Shelley Dawson and Emily Greenbank for helpful discussion, and to Meredith Marra and Bernadette Vine for unfailing support in locating data and examples from our database, and for reading a draft of this chapter. I also acknowledge the generosity of those who allowed us to record their workplace interactions.

Notes

1 See Holmes and Stubbe (2015: ch. 2) for more details.
2 See Holmes (2005) for greater detail.
3 Cartoons and Agony Aunt columns in magazines and blogs provide a rich source of information on components of the gender order, the former often contesting and the latter sometimes reinforcing gendered behaviours.
4 *Kia ora* is now widely accepted as an appropriate greeting from call centre staff.

References

Angouri, Jo (2011) "'We are in a masculine profession…': Constructing gender identities in a consortium of two multinational engineering companies", *Gender and Language*, 5(2), pp. 373–403.

Baxter, Judith (2010) *The language of female leadership*. Basingstoke: Palgrave Macmillan.

Baxter, Judith (2011) "Survival or success? A critical exploration of the use of 'double-voiced' discourse' by women business leaders in the UK", *Discourse and Communication*, 5(3), pp. 231–245.

Baxter, Judith (2012) "Women of the corporation: a sociolinguistic perspective of senior women's leadership language in the UK", *Journal of Sociolinguistics*, 16(1), pp. 81–107.

Baxter, Judith and Wallace, Kieran (2009) "Outside in-group and out-group identities? Constructing male solidarity and female exclusion in UK builders' talk", *Discourse & Society*, 20(4), pp. 411–429.

Bucholtz, Mary and Hall, Kira (2005) "Identity and interaction: a sociocultural linguistic approach", *Discourse Studies*, 7(4–5), pp. 585–614.

Cameron, Deborah (1997) "Theoretical debates in feminist linguistics: questions of sex and gender", in Wodak, R. (ed.) *Gender and discourse*. London: SAGE, pp. 21–36.

Cameron, Deborah (2009) "Theoretical issues for the study of gender and spoken interaction", in Pichler, P. and Eppler, E. (eds) *Gender and spoken interaction*. London: Palgrave Macmillan, pp. 1–17.

Clifton, Jonathan (2017) "Taking the (heroic) leader out of leadership: the in-situ practice of distributed leadership in decision-making talk", in Ilie, Cornelia and Schnurr, Stephanie (eds) *Challenging leadership stereotypes: discourse and power management*. New York: Springer, pp. 45–68.

Connell, Raewyn (1987) *Gender and power: society, the person and sexual politics*. Stanford, CA: Stanford University Press.

Coupland, Nikolas and Jaworski, Adam (2009) "Social worlds through language", in Coupland, Nikolas and Jaworski, Adam (eds) *The new sociolinguistics reader*. Basingstoke: Palgrave Macmillan, pp. 1–21.

Eagly, Alice and Carli, Linda L. (2007) *Through the labyrinth: the truth about how women become leaders*. Boston, MA: Harvard Business School Press.

Eckert, Penelope and McConnell-Ginet, Sally (2013) *Language and gender*, 2nd ed. Cambridge: Cambridge University Press.

Gumperz, John J. (1999) "On interactional sociolinguistic method", in: Sarangi, Srikant and Roberts, Celia (eds) *Talk, work and institutional order: discourse in medical, mediation, and management settings*. Berlin: Mouton de Gruyter, pp. 453–471.

Heenan, David A. and Bennis, Warren (1999) *Co-leaders: the power of great partnerships*. New York: John Wiley and Sons.

Holmes, Janet (2000) "Politeness, power and provocation: how humour functions in the workplace", *Discourse Studies*, 2(2), pp. 159–185.

Holmes, Janet (2005) "Power and discourse at work: is gender relevant?", in Lazar, M. (ed.) *Feminist critical discourse analysis*. London: Palgrave, pp. 31–60.

Holmes, Janet (2006a) *Gendered talk at work*. Oxford: Blackwell.

Holmes, Janet (2006b) "Sharing a laugh: pragmatic aspects of humor and gender in the workplace", *Journal of Pragmatics*, 38, pp. 26–50.

Holmes, Janet (2009) "Men, masculinities and leadership: different discourse styles at work", in Pichler, P. and Eppler, E. (eds) *Gender and spoken interaction*. London: Palgrave Macmillan, pp. 186–210.

Holmes, Janet (2017) "Leadership and change management: examining gender, cultural and 'hero leader' stereotypes" in Schnurr, Stephanie and Ilie, Cornelia (eds) *Challenging leadership stereotypes: discourse and power management*. New York: Springer, pp. 15–43.

Holmes, Janet (2018a) "Negotiating the culture order in New Zealand workplaces", *Language in Society*, 47(1), pp. 33–56.

Holmes, Janet (2018b) "Intercultural communication in the workplace", in Vine, B. (ed.) *Routledge handbook of language in the workplace*. London: Routledge, pp. 335–347.

Holmes, Janet and Stubbe, Maria (2015) *Power and politeness in the workplace*, 2nd ed. London: Routledge.

Holmes, Janet, Marra, Meredith and Vine, Bernadette (2011) *Leadership, discourse and ethnicity*. Oxford: Oxford University Press.

Holmes, Janet, Marra, Meredith and Vine, Bernadette (2012) "Politeness and impoliteness in New Zealand English workplace discourse", *Journal of Pragmatics*, 44, pp. 1063–1076.

Human Rights Commission (2016) "Annual report 2016–2017". At: www.humanrights.gov.au/ (accessed 1 January 2020).

Human Rights Commission (2018) "Women's rights in New Zealand. Submission of the New Zealand Human Rights Commission for the Seventh Periodic Review of New

Zealand under the Convention on the Elimination of Discrimination Against Women". At: www.hrc.co.nz/ (accessed 20 October 2018).

Ilie, Cornelia and Schnurr, Stephanie (2017) *Challenging leadership stereotypes through discourse*. Singapore: Springer Verlag.

Jackson, Brad and Parry, Ken (2001) *The hero manager: learning from New Zealand's top chief executives*. Auckland: Penguin NZ.

Jackson, Brad and Parry, Ken (2011) *A very short, fairly interesting and reasonably cheap book about studying leadership*, 2nd ed. London: SAGE.

James, Bev and Saville-Smith, Kay (1989) *Gender, culture and power: challenging New Zealand's gendered culture*. Auckland: Oxford University Press.

Kendall, Shari and Tannen, Deborah (1997) "Gender and language in the workplace", in Wodak, R. (ed.) *Gender and discourse*. London: SAGE, pp. 81–105.

Liu, H., Cutcher L. and Grant, D. (2015) "Doing authenticity: the gendered construction of authentic leadership", *Gender Work and Organisation* 22(3), pp. 237–255.

Mullany, Louise (2007) *Gendered discourse in professional communication*. Basingstoke: Palgrave.

Nielsen, Mie Fema (2008) "Pulling in opposite directions", *Communications Director*, 2008(4), pp. 173–185.

Plester, Barbara A. and Sayers, J. (2007) "'Taking the piss': Functions of banter in the IT industry", *Humor*, 20(2), pp. 157–187.

Schnurr, Stephanie (2009) *Leadership discourse at work: interactions of humour, gender and workplace culture*. Basingstoke: Palgrave.

Transcription conventions

All names are pseudonyms.

[laughs]::	paralinguistic features, colons indicate start and finish
... //.....\ ...	simultaneous speech
... /......\\ ...	
...	section of transcript omitted
()	unclear utterance
(hello)	transcriber's best guess at an unclear utterance
...	section of transcript omitted
+	pause of up to one second
=	turn continuation
XM	unidentified male

7
SEXISM AND MEDIATISED RECONTEXTUALISATIONS

The case of a battered woman who killed[1]

Sibley Slinkard
NORTHEASTERN UNIVERSITY, BOSTON, USA

Susan Ehrlich
YORK UNIVERSITY, TORONTO, CANADA

Introduction

In her introduction to the second edition of *The Feminist Critique of Language*, Deborah Cameron (1998) highlights the limitations of a word-based critique of sexist language, arguing that the focus on single words and expressions that characterised early efforts at gender-based language reform makes difficult the identification of problematic *discursive* features in texts. Cameron drew her examples from reports of rape in the British print media at the time and showed how a constellation of linguistic features (mostly grammatical features) functioned to represent rape of women as a crime against men, thereby reinforcing antiquated conceptions of rape as "damage to the property" of fathers or husbands. As noted, Cameron's (1998: 12) primary point was the absence of any expressions within these media reports that would have been deemed problematic by advocates of non-sexist language reform and, thus, her scepticism about "the centrality of naming in The Feminist Critique of Language". Instead, Cameron (1998: 12) argued for a more nuanced and contextually specific understanding of sexist language in which the sexism of "particular practices of representation", such as the sexism of rape reporting or the sexism of advertising, is interrogated.

It is over 20 years since Cameron published this introduction, but we would contend, in keeping with Cameron's argument, that even if many of the sexist lexical items and expressions targeted by the non-sexist language reformers of the 1970s and 1980s are less problematic today (see Freed, Chapter 1 in this volume), sexist discursive practices are still an important site of feminist critique. Thus, in this chapter, like Cameron, we focus on the discursive features of print media representations, in particular, representations of a trial in which a battered woman was charged with the murder of her abusive husband. We are interested in the media coverage of women who kill their abusive partners as previous research has shown that there is a public fascination with *women* who kill and that their stories are deemed to be especially newsworthy, in fact, much more newsworthy than stories about violent men who kill their abused partners and wives (Meyers, 1997). According to Nicolson (1995: 202), public interest in the "women who kill" narratives comes from society's interpretation of such women as "doubly deviant" – not only have they violated the law, they have also transgressed the norms of appropriate femininity. Indeed, Noh et al. (2010: 111) claim that although the rates of intimate partner homicide committed by men far out-number those committed by women, there is more media attention and "extant sensationalism" afforded to cases where women kill men. And, of course, the "deviance" of battered women who kill their abusive partners is an overarching theme of these sensationalised reports (Noh et al., 2010): they are either portrayed as *mad* women, suffering from mental illness as a result of the violence they have experienced, or as *bad* women, in Noh et al.'s (2010: 120) words, as "rational manipulative cold-blooded killers". Crucially, it is rare for the news media to represent the women's actions as reasonable responses to violent circumstances and, in many cases, actions taken when their own lives are threatened.

Following Cameron's (1998) emphasis on the specificities of sexist representational practices and the need to unpack the *particular* manifestations of sexism in different contexts and registers, we focus in this chapter on the print media's sensationalist portrayal of a battered woman who killed her abusive partner, arguing, in line with previous research, that this portrayal fails to capture the complexities of intimate partner violence and the fact that many battered women kill their abusive partners in self-defence. As Noh et al. (2010: 127) point out, the characterisations of battered women who kill as either *mad* or *bad* "not only make for sensational news, they reinforce belittling … social attitudes towards women and victims of domestic violence".

The remainder of the chapter is structured as follows. We first provide a general description of the legal case that formed the basis of the media reports, followed by a more detailed description of aspects of the case (e.g. the accused's police interview) that are crucial to understanding the excerpts we analyse. We then turn to our analysis, which focuses on multi-layered recontextualisations of the accused woman's police interview in media reports, and end with some concluding remarks about the significance of this kind of critique.

Description of the legal case, *R v Craig* (2011)

On the night of 31 March 2006, Teresa Pohchoo Craig (hereafter Teresa) stabbed her husband, Jack Craig (hereafter Jack), four times with a knife while he slept in the couple's motorhome outside of Ottawa, Canada. Jack had returned home earlier that night from the gas station the couple owned. He was intoxicated and was threatening to break one of his customer's legs. Teresa stated that she was afraid of Jack, especially because he was intoxicated, and believed that he would follow through on his threat. He elbowed her and pushed her as she helped him use the washroom. She testified that after he had gone to sleep, she sat at the kitchen table and worried about her life with Jack and how he would behave in the morning. She then stabbed him. After the stabbing, she ran to a neighbour's house, where she stated that she had killed her husband and asked the neighbour to call 9-1-1 emergency services. Jack was pronounced dead during the ambulance ride to the hospital and Teresa was detained, subjected to an official police interrogation and charged with first-degree murder under the *Criminal Code of Canada 1985*.

The trial began on 14 April 2008. The Crown prosecution in the case argued that Teresa's actions were intentional, deliberate, and planned, all consistent with a first-degree murder conviction. It further argued that Teresa killed Jack because she hated him and was unhappy with her life and their mounting financial problems. Teresa pleaded not guilty to the charges, and her defence initially attempted to advance a plea of self-defence at trial. She testified that, over the course of her marriage, Jack subjected her to psychological, verbal, and chronic low-level physical violence and was physically abusive towards their young son, Martyn. Jack also utilised tactics of coercive control, which include patterns of domination, isolation, and control meant to subordinate women and impede their autonomy (Stark, 2007: 15). The defence argued that Jack's coercive control left Teresa in a constant state of fear for herself and her son, a fear which led her to kill Jack for both their safety. The defence also argued that Teresa suffered from significant psychological issues consistent with Battered Woman Syndrome (Walker, 2009) and that her actions on the night of Jack's death needed to be contextualised within the framework of a battered woman's experiences.

At trial, the judge disallowed the self-defence plea. The defence then changed her plea to manslaughter and took the position that Teresa, suffering from significant psychological issues, was unable to form the intent to kill and ultimately snapped and killed her husband out of impulse. In this way, she lacked the necessary *mens rea* for murder. The defence asked for a conditional sentence in line with sentencing for similar cases where battered women had killed abusive partners.

The jury found Teresa guilty of manslaughter and the trial judge sentenced her to eight years in prison (in line with the Crown's recommendation at trial). With new counsel, Teresa appealed her conviction and sentence to the Ontario Court of Appeal. The appeal to conviction was denied but Teresa's appeal to sentence was affirmed, as the Court argued that the trial judge had not adequately considered Teresa's status as a battered woman in determining her sentence. After serving approximately three years in prison, Teresa was released in 2011.

It should be noted that Teresa was originally from Malaysia and had secured landed immigrant status in Canada. While she was a non-native speaker of English, she did not have an interpreter during her police interview and at trial she was provided with a Cantonese interpreter, although she did not take advantage of this service.

Media recontextualisations

News reports are invariably *recontextualisations* (Caldas-Coulthard, 2003: 273) and, given that much news involves the reporting of *speech* events – what Bell (1991: 60) characterises as "talk about talk" – this "talk" is susceptible to change and transformation as it is decontextualised from its original occasion of production and recontextualised in other contexts (Bauman and Briggs, 1990). As Attenborough (2014: 184) says, like all recontextualisations, media recontextualisations may differ in "rhetorically consequential ways" from their original referents. However, in spite of the intertextual gap (Briggs and Bauman, 1992) that can exist between a source interaction and its recontextualisation, recontextualisations are often displayed in the media (and elsewhere) as faithful to their source interactions. In the analysis that follows, we focus on media recontextualisations of Teresa's case that we view as "rhetorically consequential". More specifically, we show how the majority of the news reports were devoted to the prosecution's theory of the case and this, in turn, allowed the media to advance a narrative of Teresa as a *bad* woman who committed murder rather than as an abused woman who may have acted in self-defence in response to her abuse. The media's adoption of the Crown's (i.e. prosecution's) theory of the case depended to a large extent on its recontextualisation of portions of Teresa's police interview; thus, in the remainder of this section, we provide more details on the police interview.

Recontextualisations of Teresa's police interview

As noted above, Teresa was charged with the first-degree murder of her husband and, consistent with this charge, the Crown argued that Teresa killed Jack with intent and premeditation. In putting forward this argument during the trial, the Crown relied upon, and extensively cited from (i.e. recontextualised), Teresa's police interview, perhaps not a surprising strategy given that it is well known that police interviews tend to be biased in favour of the prosecution. Auburn et al. (1995: 356), for example, contend that the police interview privileges a version of events preferred by the prosecution, one that "constructs the assumption of the suspect's guilt"; in a similar way, Kassin and Gudjonsson (2004: 41) characterise the police interview as a "guilt-presumptive process". In our media analysis, we focus on two different portions of the police interview recontextualised in the media reports, both of which were used by the Crown to argue that Teresa's killing of Jack was intentional and premeditated. We discuss each of these in turn.[2]

"Enough is enough", "get rid of him"

There were two phrases produced by Teresa in her police interview that played a significant role in *R v Craig* (2011) and subsequently in the media representations of the case: "enough is enough" and "get rid of him". Teresa made these comments in response to questions about why she killed her husband and, as can be seen in Excerpt 1, the police interviewer (KP) then "parsed" them as indicative of Teresa's "pure hat[red]" for Jack (lines 10–11).

Excerpt 1 (Police Interview, *R v. Craig*, 2011: 204–205)

1. KP Okay. Well, I'll tell you what. I…we…that is more information
2.   and you know what, to be fair, you have lots of rights here. But
3.   I guess what I'm getting at is I…I don't know…
4. TC Oh, you all want to know I hate him if I kill him.
5. KP Is that why you did it? Because you know what? You know what? I
6.   think it's that simple.
7. TC Yeah…(pause)…Like Michael say, enough is enough.
8. KP Why'd you kill him? Is that why?
9. TC Enough is enough. Get rid of him.
10. KP Is that what you thought? Are we just talking about pure hate
11.   here, is that what it is?

In previous work, Slinkard (2019), the first author of this chapter, has argued that this "parsing" of the two phrases supplied the prosecution with a motive for Teresa's killing of Jack (i.e. pure hate) and the Crown prosecutor, in turn, recontextualised the phrases in his closing address in order to signal intent or *mens rea*. Consider Excerpt 2 where the Crown cites Teresa's producing of the two phrases from her police interview and equates them with her "intent to kill" in line 16.

Excerpt 2 (Crown Closing, *R v. Craig*, 2011: 3504)

12. She says, when asked why, "**Enough is enough, get rid of him.**" So,
13. she knows what she's saying during that video. And the labels
14. don't matter, whether it's shock or whatever you want to call it,
15. it doesn't matter. The point is she knew what she was saying. She
16. had the intent to kill.

The phrases were then subjected to another layer of recontextualisation in the Final Jury Charge when the trial judge summarised the Crown's position. There, the trial judge recontextualised the phrases in such a way that a further layer of meaning was added, i.e. Teresa's premeditation in killing Jack. Whereas the Crown prosecutor had presented the phrases as produced by Teresa during her police interview (as indeed they were), the trial judge represented them as thoughts she had *before* she killed Jack, as can be seen in Excerpt 3, lines 17–18 and line 21.

Excerpt 3 (Final Jury Charge, *R v. Craig*, 2011, Theory of the Crown: 93–94)

17. On March 31, 2006, Teresa Craig came to the conclusion that
18. **enough was enough**. Their business was failing, their financial
19. situation was bleaker than it had ever been before and showed no
20. signs of improvement, their marriage had their share of problems.
21. So, "**enough is enough**" she thought, "**get rid of him**". Those are
22. her words, not the Crown's words. While the vast majority of
23. people would not see these problems as reason to take their
24. spouse's life, these reasons were good enough for Teresa Craig to
25. kill her husband.

Of course, it would be impossible to know what Teresa thought before killing Jack; yet referring to Teresa's thought process prior to her killing of Jack, as the trial judge does, presumably helps to establish intention and premeditation, something necessary for the first-degree murder conviction that the prosecution sought. While this part of the jury charge is supposed to be a mere summation of the prosecution's theory, Heffer (2005) and Johnson (2014) have argued that a judge's presentation of evidence in judicial "summing ups" can subtly direct juries towards a particular perspective: in Excerpt 3, the jury is directed to the Crown's theory of the case, i.e. that Teresa killed Jack with intent and premeditation.

Excerpts 2 and 3 above show that the prosecution and the trial judge invoked the phrases, "enough is enough" and "get rid of him", to support a charge of murder; yet, this was in stark contrast to the meanings ascribed to the phrases by the defence and ultimately the Ontario Court of Appeal. Consider Excerpts 4 and 5 from the opinion of the appellate court.

Excerpt 4 (Appellate Opinion, *R v. Craig*, 2011: 5)

After her arrest, the appellant gave lengthy videotaped statements to the police in which she acknowledged stabbing her husband to death. When asked by the officer to explain why she had done so, the appellant said, "**enough is enough**". The appellant's explanation that "**enough is enough**" can only be understood in the context of her relationship with the deceased.

Excerpt 5 (Appellate Opinion, *R v. Craig*, 2011: 14)

On the evidence, the appellant fit the description of a battered wife. She was trapped in a relationship that belittled and dehumanized her to the point where she suffered a serious and ongoing mental disorder rendering her unable to perceive the obvious consequences of her actions.

We are satisfied that the effect that the long-term abuse had on this appellant should have been treated as a substantial mitigating factor on sentence.

In Excerpt 4, we see that the appellate court, consistent with Teresa's defence, argued that "enough is enough" had to be interpreted within the context of Teresa's relationship with Jack and, in Excerpt 5, we see a more detailed description of the dehumanising and abusive nature of this relationship. Excerpt 5 also shows the appellate court's contention that leniency in sentencing was warranted based on the "long-term abuse" that Teresa suffered. By contrast, what is conspicuously absent in the media coverage of the trial exemplified below is any connection between Teresa's use of the phrase "enough is enough" and the chronic abuse that she suffered at the hands of Jack. Indeed, Teresa's use of this phrase, along with the phrase, "get rid of him", is consistently used in the media reports to bolster a depiction of Teresa as a cold-blooded murderer, rather than as a battered woman who acted in self-defence.

"He's strong so you had to wait til he's asleep to kill him, right?"

Other portions of the police interview that were subject to recontextualisation in the media reports analysed below concern the question of whether Teresa's killing of Jack was premeditated. Teresa stabbed Jack while he was sleeping and the Crown argued, in keeping with a first-degree murder charge, that the killing occurred with forethought and planning, i.e. that it was premeditated. The defence, by contrast, argued self-defence, and once the self-defence plea was disallowed, it maintained that Teresa, suffering from Battered Woman Syndrome and the effects of coercive control (as a result of Jack's abuse), "snapped" on the night in question. In other words, she did not kill Jack with forethought and planning. Teresa herself testified that she did not remember what had happened on the night of the killing, as her "mind went blank".

Excerpt 6 occurs at a point in the police interview when the police officer, KP, is attempting to probe Teresa's claim that she would not have been able to kill Jack when awake because he was "really strong".

Excerpt 6 (Police Interview, *R v. Craig*, 2011: 212–214)

26. TC   When he's awake he really awake and he really strong.
27. KP   What do you mean by strong? What's that matter…what's that
28.   matter about him being awake? What're you trying to say that? I
29.   don't understand that.
30. TC   When he awake I can take…I cannot kill him.
31. KP   **Okay. Okay. And so you're waiting for him to be asleep 'cause**
32.   **he's stronger when he's awake.**
33. TC   Yeah.

(some intervening lines)

34. KP   Okay. Was there a time before this when he was asleep you thought
35.   you could maybe do it? Wasn't...wasn't there another time he was
36.   asleep?
37. TC   Oh, that time I never think of doing it because my mind is not
38.   focus on it.
39. KP   M'hm. But when you do get focus on what did you think?
40. TC   I don't know why I did it. Yesterday sometime...
41. KP   M'hm.
42. TC   But just down in the cell I was regret. I shouldn't kill him.
43. KP   But it's done.
44. TC   We...we...we should talk.
45. KP   Okay. But we have to get past that, Mrs. Craig, right. 'Cause
46   that didn't happen right.
47. TC   Yeah, that's right.
48. KP   It didn't happen so let's not talk about what didn't happen,
49   let's talk about what happened. How's that. Is that at some time,
50.   Mrs. Craig-Mrs. Craig, at some time a knife was...was brought
51.   into the RV and it was used on your husband, right. Okay. And now
52.   you...you've told me that you're...you're angry at him sometimes,
53.   that he didn't sleep and when he's awake, **he's strong so you had**
54.   **to wait til he's asleep to kill him, right?**
55. TC   Yeah.

In lines 31–32, KP reformulates Teresa's responses about Jack's strength so as to suggest planning and forethought on her part – Teresa is characterised as "waiting" for Jack to fall asleep "because" he is less strong then. (Note that Teresa has only said that she could not have killed Jack when he was awake, not that she was *waiting* for him to fall asleep *so that* she could kill him.) Although Teresa, in line 33, confirms TC's reformulation, her own utterances (lines 37–38, 40, 42) do not suggest forethought and planning but rather a kind of confusion and bewilderment about Jack's killing, consistent with the defence's contention that she "snapped" on the night in question. She, for example, says in line 40: "I don't know why I did it." In lines 53–54, KP again depicts Jack's killing as premeditated, producing a reformulation much like that in lines 31–32, and once again, Teresa confirms this formulation in line 55.[3] In the same way that the Crown and the trial judge recontextualised the phrases "enough is enough" and "get rid of him" in their arguments for intent and premeditation on the part of Teresa, so they invoked the notion, supplied by the police interviewer in excerpts such as Excerpt 6, that Teresa "waited" for Jack to fall asleep in order to kill him. And, as we will see below, the media reports also relied on this characterisation of Teresa in constructing her as a *bad* woman who murdered her husband.

Analysis

The data for this chapter come from a corpus of newspaper articles and online news reports obtained from three different electronic sources: the academic research database LexisNexis, the research database Factiva, and the search engine Google. Through LexisNexis and Factiva, keyword searches were conducted on Canadian newspapers for reports of the trial, using the terms *Teresa Craig* and *Teresa Pohchoo Craig*. Google was used to search for newspapers that were not available under LexisNexis or Factiva, as well as for reports of the trial written for online-specific sources. The final corpus consisted of 40 news articles that reported on the case, 36 of which dealt explicitly with the trial. We present representative examples from this corpus of 36 articles in the analysis below.[4]

The first example comes from the *Ottawa Citizen* on the first day of trial testimony.

> **Excerpt 7 (*Ottawa Citizen*, 15 April 2008)**
>
> *Accused waited until husband slept, then stabbed him: Crown*
> 1. The jury in the murder trial of Teresa Craig has heard that she sat in the dark, waiting for her husband to fall asleep, and when Jack Craig began to snore, she got the sharpest knife in the kitchen and stabbed him four times.
> 2. Crown attorney Jason Neubauer told the jury that when police told Ms. Craig her husband had died, she replied: "Good for him. I always suffer verbal abuse, not physical abuse."[5] He said she also told police, "I hate him. Yeah, enough is enough. I kill him."
> [...]
> 3. In his opening address in Ms. Craig's first-degree murder trial at the Elgin Street courthouse Tuesday, Mr. Neubauer told jurors they will hear evidence that Mr. Craig was never violent with the accused.

The headline of the story, "Accused waited until husband slept, then stabbed him: Crown", represents the Crown's theory of the case – that Teresa is a murderous woman who preyed on her husband when he was vulnerable (i.e. when he was asleep). Like the headline, we see in the first paragraph of Excerpt 7 that Teresa's actions are represented as premeditated; for example, "she sat in the dark, waiting for her husband to fall asleep" suggests that Teresa planned to murder Jack and is reminiscent of the police officer's reformulations in Excerpt 6 that characterised Teresa as "waiting" for Jack to fall asleep in order to kill him. However, not surprisingly, the news report provides a particularly sensationalised version of these events: not only is Teresa "waiting" for Jack to fall asleep, she is "[sitting] in the dark" while she waits. This description conjures up an image of an evil woman, hiding in the dark, waiting to pounce on her unsuspecting victim. The reader is also led to believe that Teresa planned an especially vicious killing as she is represented as securing "the sharpest knife in the kitchen" in order to carry it out.[6] Consistent with previous research, we see that Teresa is framed as a *bad* or evil woman here, i.e. not as a battered woman who may have killed Jack in self-defence.

In the second paragraph of Excerpt 7, the authors explicitly reference the Crown's opening address. The newspaper here is engaging in a multi-layered recontextualisation of Teresa's statements: the newspaper is reporting on what the Crown said during his opening address, who himself is quoting from Teresa's police interview.[7] Thus, the versions of Teresa's statements from the police interview are twice removed from their original producer (Teresa). But, interestingly, the phrases are still represented as Teresa's direct speech. Bell (1991: 60) has called these kinds of quotes *pseudo-direct speech* or *pseudo-quotes* – quotes which are written by a press officer but attributed to another source. While Bell found in his work that pseudo-quotes were at least sometimes approved by the original source in question, it is hard to imagine that either the Crown or Teresa had any say in how the statements in Excerpt 7 are reproduced in the newspaper.

Even though represented as an exact reproduction of what Teresa said in her police interrogation, the pseudo-quotes in paragraph 2 are misrepresentations of this speech event in a variety of ways. First, the fact that all of Teresa's statements in the police interview were answers to (persistent) questioning from the police officer is not captured in this news report. Second, Teresa's actual utterances have been altered. For instance, in the original police interview, Teresa's phrases "I hate him" and "enough is enough" do not appear adjacent to each other, but in the article they do. And, interestingly, when "I hate him" and "enough is enough" are immediately juxtaposed, it appears that what Teresa could no longer tolerate was her "hateful" husband, not the chronic abuse that the defence associated with "enough is enough". Third, we see that something that Teresa did not say in her police interview, "I kill him", is included as part of Teresa's utterances in the news report: "I hate him. Yeah, enough is enough. *I kill him*" (emphasis added). Note that such an utterance could be construed as a blatant confession to murder, especially when it follows "I hate him" and "Yeah, enough is enough." Taken together, then, the recontextualisations of Teresa's words in paragraph 2 (of Excerpt 7) function to frame Teresa as a "cold-blooded killer". And, significantly, while this article is representing the Crown's theory of the case and not the one put forward by the defence, this particular vantage point might be something that is missed by the average reader. Given that many of Teresa's utterances in Excerpt 7 are represented as direct speech, there is a sense of "veracity and authenticity" (Stokoe and Edwards, 2007: 339) that comes from this verbatim rendering of Teresa's speech (see Matoesian, 2000 for discussion), even if readers do recognise the story as emanating from the Crown.

Excerpt 8, from the *Times Colonist*, like Excerpt 7, reports on the Crown's opening address, which itself includes recontextualisations of Teresa's statements to the police.

Excerpt 8 (*Times Colonist*, 19 April 2008)

Woman admitted stabbing husband to death, court told

1. A former Protection Island resident on trial for her husband's murder admitted to a neighbour she was the killer, an Ottawa court heard this week.
[…]
2. In his opening address to the jury, Crown attorney Jason Neubauer said she agreed to the marriage even though she never liked Jack Craig.
[…]
3. The jury heard that Teresa Craig had waited in the dark for her husband to fall asleep on the pull-out coach. Their son was asleep in a bedroom at the rear of the 32-foot RV.
4. When Jack Craig began to snore, Neubauer said she got the sharpest knife in the kitchen and stabbed him four times.
   Neubauer said that when police told Craig her husband had died, she replied: "Good for him. I always suffer verbal abuse, not physical abuse."
5. He said she also told police, "I hate him. Yeah, enough is enough. I kill him."

Excerpt 8 also sensationalises the killing with language about Teresa "wait[ing] in the dark for her husband to fall asleep" (paragraph 3) and securing the sharpest knife in the house (paragraph 4). A further similarity between Excerpt 7 and 8 is the inclusion of pseudo-quotes that misrepresent Teresa's answers to questions in the police interview: "I hate him. Yeah, enough is enough. I kill him" (paragraph 5).[8] (See discussion above.) However, in Excerpt 8, not only does this pseudo-quote appear in the body of the article, it also appears as the caption to a photograph of Teresa (Figure 7.1). Captions help to contextualise images, which are themselves "recontextualized by the news process" (Huxford, 2001: 47), and, according to Teo (2000: 16), they "can have a very powerful ideological effect on readers' perception and interpretation of people and events". We see with the caption in Figure 7.1 that Teresa's statements to the police are wholly decontextualised from their source interaction and reproduced under an undated, and not particularly flattering, photograph of Teresa. Indeed, the caption provides readers with an especially negative framing of the image, and therefore of Teresa herself: she appears to be confessing to an intentional, premeditated killing, further reinforcing the Crown's theory that she is guilty of first-degree murder.

While Excerpts 7 and 8 focus on the Crown's opening address, the focus of Excerpt 9 is the replaying of Teresa's police interview in court.

Teresa Craig: "I hate him. Yeah, enough is enough. I kill him."

FIGURE 7.1 Photograph of Teresa Craig, *Times Colonist*, 19 April 2008.

Excerpt 9 (*Ottawa Citizen*, 2 May 2008)

"Maybe there is some evil in me": accused unable to explain reason for stabbing husband

1. In a rambling three-hour statement to police, accused murderer Teresa Pohchoo Craig came across as a hard-working, loving mother who saw herself as submissive to a husband she had grown to hate.
2. But Mrs. Craig was unable to supply a straightforward answer when asked again and again by police why she had repeatedly stabbed Jack Craig as he was asleep in the couple's RV motorhome on Donnelly Drive near Kemptville.
3. "Maybe there is some evil in me," she told Ottawa police Sgt. Michael Hudson, the lead investigator in the case.
"Something keep pushing me. ... Do it. Do it," she said.
4. The video of the statement was played yesterday in the courtroom where Mrs. Craig is on trial, charged with first-degree murder in her husband's death.
5. "I hate him, that's why I kill him. Enough is enough. Get rid of him," she said on the recording.

6. But earlier in the statement she said, "I didn't mean to kill him."
7. Asked if she had any message for her nine-year-old son, Mrs. Craig said, "Just tell him I'm sorry I kill his dad. He's going to miss him for a long time. I wish I didn't do it."
8. She said that she worried her son will hate her "because I kill his dad."
9. Mrs. Craig said she waited until her husband fell asleep before stabbing him in the early hours of March 31, 2006.
10. "When he's awake, I cannot kill him. He's strong."

The headline, "Maybe there is some evil in me", immediately characterises Teresa as a *bad* woman and, as a headline, this characterisation informs the reader's understanding of the news report as a whole. This particular phrase is taken from Teresa's police interview when the police officer asks Teresa why a "good mother, a hardworking person ends up in this situation" to which she responds: "maybe there is something … some evil in me. I don't know why I did it. Now I regret" (Police Interview, *R v. Craig*, 2011: 12). In using this particular quote as the headline, the reporter sensationalises the story, emphasising the individual pathology of a *bad* woman and the "evil" impulse that seems to have motivated a killing that is otherwise inexplicable.

We see that the *bad* (i.e. "evil") woman narrative is further reinforced with the recontextualisation of "enough is enough" and "get rid of him" in paragraph 5. Teresa's utterances are once again misrepresented (see discussion above) in that "I hate him" immediately precedes "enough is enough" and "get rid of him" although this is not the case in its source interaction. What is also interesting about this particular pseudo-quote is the addition of material that does not exist in the source interaction. That is, "I hate him" is followed directly by the clause, "that's why I kill him" (*not* a part of the original police interview), which explicitly establishes a causal link between Teresa's hatred of Jack and her killing of Jack. Thus, while the point of this article, as shown in the sub-headline ("Accused unable to explain reason for stabbing husband"), seems to be that Teresa was unable to explain her reasons for killing Jack, through the recontextualisation of Teresa's words from the police interview in paragraph 5, the article at the same time conveys the idea that Teresa's hatred for Jack motivated the killing. And, as in the previous excerpts, much of this material is represented as verbatim rendering of Teresa's words, adding an air of objectivity and neutrality to the media account. That is, while the explanation for Jack's killing put forward in Excerpt 9 is one that was advanced by the Crown, there is no mention in this report that this is the Crown's theory; indeed, the recontextualisations of Teresa's words are represented and understood as coming directly from the videotape of Teresa's police interview as this was played in court and therefore as a confession to murder.

In paragraph 9 of Excerpt 9, we see a somewhat different manifestation of media recontextualisations: here the dialogic nature of Teresa's police interview is obscured. It is well documented that the narratives emerging from police interviews are co-constructed by a police officer *and* a suspect given the significant role that questions play in shaping and constraining suspects' responses (Haworth, 2017). However, when these interviews are transformed into written documents, information that was "introduced through a question or a suggestion from the police officer" may appear as an utterance that the suspect has spontaneously produced. In other words, the sources of utterances "are systematically *blurred*" (Jönsson and Linell, 1991: 434, emphasis added). In her investigation of the Pinkenba case, for example, Eades (2008) found that one way source distinctions were *blurred* was through the switching of authorship attribution such that propositions uttered by lawyers during the cross-examination of three Aboriginal boys were later attributed to the boys themselves when this information was recontextualised in the media.

In a similar way, we see that the source distinction of a key utterance from the police interview (Excerpt 6, lines 53–54) – "you had to wait til he's asleep to kill him, right?" – is *blurred* when this portion of the police interview is recontextualised in the media. That is, even though Teresa merely provides confirmation of KP's utterance of lines 53–54 with a "Yeah" (line 55), she is nevertheless represented as having uttered a similar statement to that of KP in paragraph 9, Excerpt 9 of the media report: "Mrs. Craig *said* she waited until her husband fell asleep before stabbing him" (emphasis added). In switching authorship and representing this utterance as spontaneously produced by Teresa, the media report is, arguably, giving greater weight to the Crown's theory – that Teresa premeditated her husband's killing – than is warranted by lines 53–55 of Excerpt 2 from the police interview where she merely confirms this idea. As Eades (2008: 322) points out, this kind of blurring of source distinctions fails to recognise the role of coercive questioning in shaping the testimony of witnesses in courtrooms and the statements of suspects in police interviews.

We also find blurring of sources in the next news report (Excerpt 10), a report that focuses on Teresa's cross-examination.

Excerpt 10 (*Ottawa Sun*, 22 May 2008)

Woman changes story on the stand; denies plotting to kill husband during sleep

1. A 51-year-old woman, charged with the first-degree murder of her husband, denied under cross-examination Thursday she plotted to kill him as he slept on March 31, 2006.
2. But Teresa Craig's only explanation for her damning statements to police later that day was that her mind was "messed up."
3. "My mind was blank at the time … not thinking anything," she insisted of the moment she picked up a kitchen knife and repeatedly stabbed Jack Craig, 54, in the trailer parked outside their gas bar about 60 kilometres south of Ottawa.
4. She also denied thinking what she later told police, that she wouldn't be able to kill her husband if he were awake.

The headline summarises the report: Teresa originally confessed in the police interview to "plott[ing] to kill" Jack, but later denied or recanted her confession under cross-examination; that is, she "chang[ed] her story on the stand". Teresa's original story, as represented in this report, is that she "plotted to kill" her husband, Jack. Like Excerpt 9, this excerpt involves a blurring of sources, specifically, the switching of authorship attribution. That is, while KP originally produced the "story" about Teresa's plan to kill Jack, in Excerpt 10 (headline and paragraph 1) the story is ascribed to Teresa and is sensationalised as a "plot". Teresa is then said to have "chang[ed] her story" under cross-examination. This report presents Teresa in a negative light by suggesting, first, that she confessed to murdering her husband and doing it in a particularly secretive and conniving way (i.e. she "plotted to kill" her husband) and, second, that she then denied it under cross-examination. The problem, of course, with this characterisation of Teresa is that she never said in her police interview that she "plotted" to kill her husband nor even that she "planned" to kill him. Following Eades (2008: 323), the most that could be said of Teresa is that she *conceded to* or *acquiesced to* KP's proposition that she waited for Jack to fall asleep in order to kill him and this was done in the context of persistent and coercive questioning. Nonetheless, the media report transforms Teresa's (possibly coerced) concession or admission ("Yeah") into a full-fledged utterance that she *alone* has produced about her "plot" to kill her husband.[9]

Conclusion

Consistent with other research on media representations of battered women who kill their abusive partners (e.g. Sheehy, 2014), this examination of media reports of *R v. Craig* (2011) has demonstrated that the vast majority of the coverage focused on the Crown's theory of the case – that Teresa acted with intent and forethought and committed first-degree murder.[10] What was generally absent in the media reports was mention of the defence's position that Jack's tactics of coercive control left Teresa in a constant state of fear for herself and her son, a fear that led her to kill Jack in the name of their safety. That the media overwhelmingly reported on the Crown's version of events is perhaps not surprising given the sensationalist and "newsworthy" nature of this particular narrative: "Teresa was a 'bad' woman, who sat in the dark, plotting to kill her husband and choosing the sharpest knife in the kitchen in order to do so."

Our analysis supports Noh et al.'s (2010) findings regarding the "mad/bad" depictions of battered women who kill, but, as a linguistically oriented discourse analysis, it also offers a new perspective on such findings. That is, our ability (given our access to the transcripts of the police interview) to assess the *veracity* of the media's recontextualisations of Teresa's police interview means that we have been able to demonstrate clearly how such recontextualisations can differ from their source interactions in "rhetorically consequential ways" (Attenborough, 2014: 184). We have also been able to show how the two intertextual devices that form the core of our analysis – pseudo-quotes and the blurring of source distinctions – can obscure the transformative work that these kinds of recontextualisations do. In our excerpts (and corpus, more generally), for example, even when it is clear that it is the Crown's theory of the case that is being presented (and this was *not* always the case in our excerpts), the pseudo-quotes and the blurring of source distinctions give readers the impression that they have direct access to Teresa's words, even when these words have been misrepresented or have not in fact been uttered by Teresa at all but rather by a police officer. And, as noted above, this kind of verbatim misrendering of a speaker's words, especially in the case of the pseudo-quotes, can lend an air of neutrality to an account as "'direct access' to an event" may lead recipients to believe they are "assess[ing] it for themselves" (Stokoe and Edwards, 2007: 339).

Attenborough (2014) has argued that one of the ways in which public perceptions of social problems are formed is through mediatised recontextualisations. Like Attenborough, we suggest that the recontextualisations of *R v. Craig* (2011) exemplified above would not only have influenced public perceptions of Teresa, but also the public perception of battered women who kill more generally. Moreover, we submit that the kind of analysis we have conducted has particular significance in light of the potentially far-reaching effects of media recontextualisations in reproducing sexist understandings of intimate partner violence and battered women. Specifically, by attending to the subtleties of media recontextualisation practices, this type of analysis can help to denaturalise a (sexist) perspective whose empirical underpinnings might otherwise go unnoticed.

Notes

1 This chapter is based on a chapter from the first author's Ph.D. dissertation (Slinkard, 2019).
2 The police interview data were provided to the first author by Teresa Craig's appellate counsel, Susan Chapman (now the Honourable Justice Susan M. Chapman).
3 While twice seeming to confirm TC's propositions in lines 31–32 and 53–54, Slinkard (2019) has made the argument that Teresa's confirmations may be instances of gratuitous concurrence, a phenomenon whereby speakers, often non-native speakers of a language, "freely say … *yes* to a question, regardless of belief of the truth or falsity of the proposition questioned" (Eades, 2008: 31, emphasis in original). Gratuitous concurrence has been widely observed in legal contexts where witnesses in court (especially in crossexamination) and suspects in police interrogations are subject to "repeated and pressured questioning" over an extended period of time (Eades, 2008: 97). Thus, Teresa, as a nonnative speaker of English in the context of a police interview, may not in fact be signalling agreement when she produces "yeah" in response to KP's formulations of her "plan" to kill her husband.
4 The corpus is comprised of a range of newspaper formats, including both broadsheet (*Ottawa Times*, *Times Colonist*) and tabloid/popular press (*Ottawa Sun*).
5 Teresa denied any physical violence in her police interview, but later testified to what the defence expert witness, Dr Evan Stark, classified as "low-level" violence (such as pushing and shoving). Stark also concluded that Teresa was likely "underreporting the nature and extent of the abuse" (*R v Craig*, 2011: para. 29).

6 When asked about the murder weapon, Teresa stated she used a chef knife from their kitchen knife block "cause it's sharp" (Police Interview, *R v Craig*, 2011: 227).
7 These multi-layered recontextualisations thus misrepresent both Teresa's utterances *and* the Crown's utterances in the sense that the Crown generally, in his opening and closing addresses, rendered Teresa's words (from her police interview) verbatim.
8 As both the *Ottawa Citizen* and the *Times Colonist* were part of the Canadian media company, Canwest, at the time, it is possible that these identical pseudo-quotes come from the same news agency or that one was copied from the other.
9 Note that if Teresa's confirmations of KP's proposition in the police interview were in fact instances of gratuitous concurrence (see note 3), then it is possible that Teresa's confirmations did not signal her agreement with the proposition.
10 In contrast to the articles written before the appeal decision was handed down, those written after portrayed Jack as abusive and situated Teresa's killing of Jack within the context of this abuse, in line with the appellate decision.

References

Attenborough, F. (2014) "Rape is rape (except when it's not): the media, recontextualisation and violence against women", *Journal of Language, Aggression and Conflict*, 2(2), pp. 183–203.
Auburn, T., Drake, S. and Willig, C. (1995) "'You punched him, didn't you?': versions of violence in accusatory interviews", *Discourse & Society*, 6(3), pp. 353–386.
Bauman, R. and Briggs, C.L. (1990) "Poetics and performance as critical perspectives on language and social life", *Annual Review of Anthropology*, 19, pp. 59–88.
Bell, A. (1991) *The language of news media*. Oxford: Blackwell.
Briggs, C.L. and Bauman, R. (1992) "Genre, intertextuality, and social power", *Journal of Linguistic Anthropology*, 2, pp. 131–172.
Caldas-Coulthard, C. (2003) "Cross-cultural representation of 'otherness' in media, discourse", in Weiss, G. and Wodak, R. (eds) *Critical discourse analysis: theory and interdisciplinarity*. New York: Palgrave Macmillan, pp. 272–296.
Cameron, D. (1998) "Introduction to part one", in Cameron, D. (ed.) *The Feminist Critique of Language a reader*, 2nd ed. London: Routledge, pp. 1–30.
Eades, D. (2008) *Courtroom talk and neocolonial control*. Berlin: Mouton de Gruyter.
Haworth, K. (2017) "The discursive construction of evidence in police interviews: case study of a rape suspect", *Applied Linguistics*, 38(2), pp. 194–214.
Heffer, C. (2005) *The language of jury trial: a corpus-aided analysis of legal-lay discourse*. New York: Palgrave Macmillan.
Huxford, J. (2001) "Beyond the referential: uses of visual symbolism in the press", *Journalism*, 2(1), pp. 45–71.
Johnson, A. (2014) "'Dr Shipman told you that…': the organising and synthesising power of quotation in judicial summing-up", *Language and Communication*, 36, pp. 53–67.
Jönsson, L. and Linell, P. (1991) "Story generations: from dialogical interviews to written reports in police interrogations", *Text*, 11(3), pp. 419–440.
Kassin, S. and Gudjonsson, G. (2004) "The psychology of confessions: a review of the literature and issues", *Psychological Sciences in the Public Interest*, 5(2), pp. 33–67.
Matoesian, G. (2000) "Intertextual authority in reported speech: production media in the Kennedy Smith rape trial", *Journal of Pragmatics*, 32(7), pp. 879–914.
Meyers, M. (1997) *News coverage of violence against women: engendering blame*. Thousand Oaks, CA: SAGE.

Nicolson, D. (1995) "Telling tales: gender discrimination, gender construction and battered women who kill", *Feminist Legal Studies*, 3(2), pp. 185–206.

Noh, M., Lee, M. and Feltey, K. (2010) "Mad, bad or reasonable? Newspaper portrayals of the battered woman who kills", *Gender Issues*, 27, pp. 110–130.

R v Craig (2011) ONCA 142.

Sheehy, E. (2014) *Defending battered women on trial: lessons from the transcripts*. Vancouver: UBC Press.

Slinkard, S. (2019) *"She chose to get rid of him by murder, not by leaving him": discursive constructions of a battered woman who killed in R v Craig*. Unpublished Ph.D. dissertation, York University, Toronto.

Stark, E. (2007) *Coercive control: how men entrap women in personal life*. New York: Oxford University Press.

Stokoe, E. and Edwards, D. (2007) "Black this, black that: racial insults and reported speech in neighbour complaints and police interrogations", *Discourse & Society*, 18(3), pp. 337–372.

Teo, P. (2000) "Racism in the news: a critical discourse analysis of news reporting in two Australian newspapers", *Discourse & Society*, 11(1), pp. 7–49.

Walker, L. (2009) *The battered woman syndrome*, 3rd ed. New York: Springer Publishing.

Newspapers cited

"Accused waited until husband slept, then stabbed him: Crown" (2008) *Ottawa Citizen*, 15 April.

Ward, B. (2008) "Maybe there is some evil in me: accused unable to explain reason for stabbing husband", *Ottawa Citizen*, 2 May.

"Woman admitted stabbing husband to death, court told" (2008) *Times Colonist*, 19 April.

"Woman changes story on the stand; denies plotting to kill husband during sleep" (2008) *Ottawa Sun*, 22 May.

8

THE DISCOURSE OF (RE)EXPLOITATION

Female victims in the legal system

Nicci MacLeod
NORTHUMBRIA UNIVERSITY, UK

Introduction

This chapter is concerned with police–victim interviews in cases of rape. It aims to uncover some of the ways in which gender normative ideologies are manifested through discursive practices, and how skewed representations of gendered violence as consensual encounters are constructed and resisted through talk. Low conviction rates for rape have long been at the centre of political and scholarly attempts to address the issues of victim-blaming and rape-supportive culture. Within the current adversarial criminal court system in England and Wales, there are only two possible verdicts: "guilty" or "not guilty", and this has been cast by many as lying at the root of the problem. An accused attacker not proven "beyond a reasonable doubt" to have committed the offence receives a "not guilty" verdict, thus casting suspicion on the victim herself as being a liar[1] – there is no option, as there is in Scotland for example, for a "not proven" verdict. It is easy to see why the legal system has often been accused of working against the interests of women.

The fact that some 90% of rapes are committed by someone known to the victim means that often the only issue over which there is disagreement is that of consent. In their interviews with suspects and victims, investigators must establish their "points to prove" for the offence in question – namely, for the suspect to be prosecuted for "rape" according to the Sexual Offences Act (SOA) (2003), that:

(a) he intentionally penetrates the vagina, anus or mouth of another person (B) with his penis,
(b) B does not consent to the penetration, and
(c) A does not reasonably believe that B consents. (Sexual Offences Act, 2003: s. 1(1))

This throws up the issue of what consent is – the SOA (2003: s. 74) defines it thus: "a person consents if he (*sic*) agrees by choice, and has the freedom and capacity to make that choice", and as set out in Grant and Spaul (2015), it is most appropriately conceived of as a communicative act, albeit sometimes a non-verbal one.

Police interviews are traditionally characterised as displaying an asymmetrical power relationship (see Fairclough, 1989), with differential rights and obligations imposed upon the participants and particular constraints imposed upon their contributions (see Drew and Heritage, 1992; Thornborrow, 2002). Furthermore, they are goal oriented, which is to say that one participant – in this case the interviewing officer – is focused on achieving some institutionally prescribed goal, of which the less powerful participant, the interviewee, is not necessarily aware. For police interviewers, this is the "points to prove" as described above – establishing specific and particular details "on the record" that collectively point to a particular offence as having taken place (see Haworth, 2015). Relatedly, police interviewers, who know they are not just interacting with the victim but also collecting evidence for a potential future trial, are also cognisant of the potential subsequent "overhearing audiences" (Heritage, 1985; Heydon, 2005), such as their colleagues, the Crown Prosecution Service, and, ultimately, a jury. While the naïve interviewee positions herself as one of two participants in a dialogue, and orients to the interviewer as the sole audience for her utterances, many of the latter's contributions can be heard to orient to the future listeners (see Haworth, 2013). Interviewers often invoke a participation framework (Goffman, 1981) in which they are merely the animator of a message for which the police institution is the principal, while their audience role is institutionally ambiguous, torn between being a primary recipient for the talk and a neutral elicitor on behalf of future audiences (see Haworth, 2013; MacLeod, 2019).

Sexual violence in the justice system

Since at least as far back as Estrich's (1987) book *Real Rape*, there has been substantial interest in the ways in which sexual violence is discursively conceptualised within the legal system. Estrich's pioneering work demonstrated that, in order to be considered rape and treated as such by the justice system, incidents needed to fulfil certain criteria. Occasions of acquaintance rape, in which a known man attacks a woman, which account for by far the majority of rapes, do not usually attract the same level of vigorous prosecution as stranger rapes. In contrast to attacks by strangers, those carried out by acquaintances are likely to be viewed as the outcome of a misunderstanding, or of poor communication on the victim's part – at any rate, the question more often than not comes down to consent, as discussed earlier. As Ehrlich (2007) points out, the discourses surrounding these types of case shape societal and legal understandings of what makes for a "good" complaint, i.e. one which is likely to be taken seriously. Tiersma (2007) echoes this sentiment, arguing for a legal (re)definition of rape that accounts just as well for acquaintance rape situations as it does for attacks by strangers. As Tiersma (2007: 101) depressingly concludes, however, the most important improvements will not come simply from legal reform, but only if we "learn to reform ourselves".

The discursive complexities of the police interview noted in the introduction are further compounded when the content concerns sexual violence. Our collective attitudes have been described as "rape supportive", which is to say that in discussions of rape – whether in the media, online, even in legal contexts – rapists are often exonerated and their behaviour normalised, while victims attract blame and are often cast as at least in part responsible for the attack, and as regulators of their attackers' behaviour (see Anderson and Doherty, 2008). Rebuttals of accusations of sexual assault are underpinned by cultural assumptions about gender and sex (Burt and Estep, 1981), with heterosexual norms supporting, or providing a "cultural scaffold" for rape (Gavey, 2005). Many past studies have suggested that the police hold even more negative views of rape victims than do other professionals (e.g. Lee and Cheung, 1991, in Anderson and Doherty, 2008) with victims often facing judgement and/or disbelief at the hands of the police. As Gregory and Lees (1999: 4) point out, "the police stand accused of employing harsh methods of interrogation on women reporting such attacks, on the assumption that they might be making false allegations". As Lea (2007: 497) points out,

> perceptions of the act of rape, the perpetrators of this crime and the victims thereof are not best understood by seeing those perceptions as individual, private interpretations or attitudes … The attributions people make … are constructed by, and constructive of, the ideological context they inhabit.

Put another way, people's attitudes towards sexual violence are shaped by ideologies pervasive throughout society, rather than being independently constructed viewpoints. As we shall see throughout this chapter, however, the onus is largely placed on individual women to avoid situations in which they might find themselves victims of rape, rather than on addressing the ills of a society that produces rapists, or on rapists themselves not to rape.

Negative societal responses to victims of sexual violence have been shown to seriously undermine victims' post-rape recovery, and this "secondary victimisation" (Williams, 1984 in Anderson and Doherty, 2008), realised either through self-blame (see MacLeod, 2016) or through interactions in institutional settings such as the police interview, show the pervasive nature of socio-cultural support for rape, "structurally integrated at all levels of society" (Anderson and Doherty, 2008: 10). As evidenced by, among others, Gregory and Lees (1999), such patterns manifest themselves as low reporting rates, high attrition rates, and low conviction rates, as discussed earlier (CPS, 2018; ONS, 2018).

Ehrlich's (2007) analysis of a civil trial demonstrates how the sense-making resources available to complainants of sexual violence are restricted by their cultural context, allowing only for representation of incidents of sexual aggression in the language of consensual sexual encounters. This finding echoes that of Coates et al. (1994), who reported judges in acquaintance rape cases using ill-chosen terms to describe the violence, such as the defendant "offering" his penis to the complainant's mouth.

Coates and Wade (2004) examined a corpus of sexual assault trial judgments, and identified several categories of excuse that are routinely given for offenders' behaviour, including drug and alcohol abuse, psychopathology, and loss of control, among others. Explaining the actions of perpetrators of sexual violence in this way, they note, conceals violence and mitigates perpetrators' responsibility, as well as blaming or pathologising victims. In light of the respective expectations of the genders in terms of how their sexuality "should" be realised, an alleged perpetrator's behaviour is often treated as unproblematic, in that his actions are construed as part of "normal" heterosexual behaviour (Anderson and Doherty, 2008).

The data

The data drawn on here are a set of police interviews with rape complainants conducted in England. As a matter of routine these interviews are video-recorded, and these video recordings were transcribed by the author as part of a wider project examining discursive patterns of police interview interaction (MacLeod, 2010).

Constraints on victims' narrations

The excusing and justification of sexual violence has been explored at length in the accounts of convicted sex offenders. Auburn and Lea (2003), for example, demonstrate that offenders construct a moral identity for themselves through talk, mitigating their culpability and managing blame and responsibility for their offences.

The production of these "defence components" by witnesses in court when they anticipate some form of blame allocation may result from their answer to an examining lawyer's question has also been discussed (Atkinson and Drew, 1979). The concept of victim responsibility is a well-established one in terms of research into perceptions of rape (Lea, 2007). Thus, it follows that even in the accounts of those reporting rape, we might expect there to be evidence of the speaker's attempts to "excuse" or "justify" their own behaviour, in relation to culturally defined norms. Indeed, in the specific context of the police interview, MacLeod (2016) shows how interviewees (IEs) reporting rape rely on prevalent discourses around sexual violence to account for their behaviour in relation to the attack, often entirely unprompted by the interviewer (IR) – for example, providing reasons for why they waited in a particular area, such as "I thought I'd be safe there", without this information being explicitly pursued by the IR. This chapter shifts the focus from interviewees accounting for their own behaviour to looking in more general terms at how the events in question are represented in their talk. I aim to elucidate the relationship between these representations and culturally pervasive sexist discourses around sexual violence.

As we might expect of the asymmetrical context of the police interview, it is often the IR's contributions that constrain the response of the IE. In the following extract

(Extract 1), for example, the IR's question in line 8 is arguably blame-implicative. The parties have been discussing the IE's health problems. The "he" referred to in line 10 is a family member of the IE, who she reports as having gone on to rape her.

Extract 1

1.		IR:	e:rm what kind of (.) effect does that h- have on you healthwise?
			(1)
		IE:	I get drunk very easily (.5) takes me about two or three days to (.5) pick myself up I've been out and had a good drink ·shih
5.			(4)
		IE:	I tend to drink coke after about eleven. ·shih (.)
	→	IR:	so why didn't you go on the coke this time?
	→	IE:	cos he was persistent: "ave a drink, ave a drink (.) ave a drink". ·shih
			(2)
10.	→	IE:	and I thought well what harm can it do it's my [family member] it's like family. ·shih

The IR's negative WH- question in line 8 implies some degree of surprise or conflict with the proposition on the part of the interviewer (Ehrlich, 2001) – i.e. that "go[ing] on the coke" would be the *expected* course of action, given that drinking alcohol leads her to "get drunk very easily", thereby reducing her ability to protect herself. The so-prefacing of this question is also significant – as Johnson (2002) demonstrates, so-prefacing is often used by police IRs to evaluate and label the previous answer. Combined with the question function, this constitutes a challenge to the appropriateness of the reported behaviour. Thus, the IE is forced to provide an explanation for her behaviour on the night in question. How she does so is also highly revealing of cultural assumptions about sexual violence. In line 10 she relies first on the suspect's insistence that she "ave a drink" to justify her continuing to drink alcohol. In the absence of a take-up from the IR in the two-second gap after the TRP the IE self-selects, continuing with her justification for taking the decision to drink more alcohol by referring to her familial relationship with the man in question. It is worth questioning here what assumptions feed into her emphasis on this familial relationship. Cultural understandings of rape and responsibility dictate that women should avoid putting themselves in vulnerable situations around men, such as being too intoxicated to withhold sexual consent – the implication in the extract is that if the man in question is a relative, the risk of rape is mitigated.

The IE displays a reliance on particular assumptions – namely that drinking a lot of alcohol puts one in a vulnerable position, but that members of one's family are to be trusted when one is in a vulnerable position – distinct, presumably, from less intimate acquaintances and strangers. This interpretation is supported by the question she reports having asked herself in line 12 "what harm can it do", suggesting that while drinking large amounts of alcohol in the company of another man might be easily interpretable as dangerous behaviour, in the company of her family member it is "common sense" to assume that she would be safe.

Although, as in Extract 1, we might expect excuses and justifications in the sequential position following a potentially blame-allocating turn, it has been demonstrated that in fact participants often anticipate that a question or sequence of questions are *leading to* blame allocation (Atkinson and Drew, 1979). On inspection of the data it becomes apparent that the interviewees display these patterns, pre-empting potential blame attribution by producing qualifying defences for the reported behaviours. These occasions are discussed in depth in MacLeod (2016), so I concern myself here with interactional moments in which interviewees appear to be constrained in the ways they characterise their experiences in more general terms.

Grice's (1975) maxim of relevance becomes significant here, since we must assume some connection between the information provided in IEs' responses and the events they are being asked to describe. Thus, implicature is a key aspect of the ongoing process of negotiation between IR and IE to tell the story, and the drawing of inference usually relies to some extent on culturally derived expectations. When an IE provides a description of events in line with these culturally derived expectations, she simultaneously displays a familiarity with, and in some cases acceptance of, dominant assumptions about rape. This is arguably "power by consent" in action: with the dominant assumptions presented as "natural" and "commonsensical" according to accepted standards – in this case patriarchal ones – it follows that the victims themselves also accept these attitudes.

For example, in Extract 2, taken from a different case, the interactants have been discussing a conversation the IE had with a male friend in a nightclub shortly prior to being attacked. The friend had been told that if he left the nightclub to walk her to a taxi then he would be required to pay for re-entry. The extract begins with the IR asking about who may have overheard the conversation.

Extract 2

1.   IR: right okay •hh was there anybody <u>stood</u> in the lobby hearing that conversation that you can remember
    IE: hmm hmm no (.6) not that I can remember
    (.5)
5.   IR: no
    IE: just <u>boun</u>cers probably=
    IR: =there's <u>no</u>body: hanging about
    IE: no- <u>prob</u>ably but (.2) ((coughs)) (.) I can't remember

The extract shows both participants displaying an understanding of "bouncers" (i.e. doormen at a nightclub) as being a category of person not included under the IR's description "anybody". Evidently the IE has understood the implicature of the IR's question in lines 1–2 to be that "anybody" refers to *anybody who may have posed a threat*, and her response is to answer in the negative, with the additional information in line 8 that in fact there were people there, but they were "just" bouncers. This understanding is confirmed by the IR in line 10, and reiterated by the IE in line 12.

This is a culturally rooted assumption that has been observed since the earliest feminist scholarship on rape. Sexual violence serves to "maintain the status quo … women have some level of consciousness about the fear of sexual assault [and] this serves to restrict and constrain their behaviours" (Griffin, 1971 cited in Ward, 1995: 22). It forces women to look to the "trustworthy" "non-raping" men in their lives for protection: "all the sane men must protect 'their' women from the few insane ones, and women without men must watch out" (Russell, 1975: 260). The construction of rapists as outside recognisable categories of person such as "bouncer" functions to perpetuate the myth that rape is a crime committed by a small minority of men who exist outside the boundaries of normality (see Clark, 1992). The shared understanding is thus highly ideologically charged, perpetuating this aspect of rape mythology and serving the interests of the dominant group – men.

In the following extract, another IE is describing what happened after she awoke from sleepwalking to find herself naked in her partner's lodger's bed. Charlie is her partner, and Michael is the lodger.

Extract 3

1. IE: Charlie was downstairs talking to Michael (.8) asking him what had happened. (2.2) e:rm and he was saying nothing had happened. (1.2)
   → e:rm (.4) and I <u>asked</u> him I said "have we had sex Michael just tell me
   → have y- have you had sex with me because I think we have I think
5. → you've had sex with me I can- I- it <u>feels</u> different I <u>feel</u> like- I (.) just
   → somebody's had sex ~with me~' •HHHH (.6) and he was saying "no no no hh no hh no'. hhh (.4) but I'm positive that he had (.7) absolutely positive he had.
   (.7)
10. IR: → right. (.6) and (.) what makes you <u>feel</u> like you had sex is is a mental thing or a physi[cal thing]

In Extract 3 the IE formulates what has happened to her as both "we had sex" once (line 3) and "you/somebody had sex with me" three times (lines 4, 5, and 6). As Ehrlich (2007: 132) points out, even when the attacker is grammatically represented as active, the predicate "have sex with" "is not one that conjures up images of coerced or forced sex". Evidence for this, she claims, comes from the fact that it can occur in reciprocal constructions, such as the "we had sex" in line 3. Note that this activeness on the part of the IE is foregrounded in the IR's question at line 10, "you had sex", even though her most recent and most frequent is the more passive "… had sex with me".

Of course, not all interviewees represent events in the ways detailed above. They do not all allow scope for themselves to be cast as active participants in the attacks. In the interview from which Extract 4 is taken, the IE unambiguously and repeatedly states that this was an action that was inflicted upon her. Importantly, the event being described is rape by a stranger – the IE is reporting having been dragged into an alleyway after a night out.

Extract 4

```
1.   →   IE:   he pulled my skirt down (2.9) pulled my underwear to one side (.5)
                undone his trousers (1.5) penetrated me (2.3) and he turn- turned me
                over so I was facing- I had my face to the wall? (1.9) and at that point I
                just (.7) found the courage to (.6) just run.
5.                 (.9)
     →   IR:   so th- the first time that he penetrated you (1) whereabouts did he
     →           penetrate?
```

As can be seen in Extract 4, in lines 6 and 7 the IR endorses the IE's line 2 description of the act as "[he] penetrated [me]". Such a representation does not allow for readings of the act as reciprocal or consensual in the way that the patterns observed in Extract 3 do. Arguably, the same restrictions are not exerted on the discursive resources available to this IE, owing to the fact that her experiences are more closely aligned with that of the "stranger rape", which as we have seen, is dealt with more straightforwardly as "real rape" than those involving an acquaintance.

Explicitly resisting implications

There are occasions when victims of non-stranger rapes can be heard explicitly resisting normalised ideologies around sexual violence. Extract 5 shows the IR referring back to the IE's account of the night in question, when she had woken to find the offender penetrating her while she and her partner slept.

Extract 5

```
1.         IR:   you said you were saying (1) don't hurt me or don't let him hurt me (.4) what
                  made you think (.6) that he was gonna hurt you ((or that he was hurting))
     →   IE:   cos he was having sex with me and I didn't want to.
                 (11)
5.   →   IE:   and that is hurting me.
                 (.4)
         IR:   yeah. mm (.5) •hhh I just wanted to get the: (.7) the way you were thinking and
                  obviously that is hurting you [but]
     →   IE:                                    [that] is hurting me [I wouldn't]=
10.      IR:                                                         [I was]
     →   IE:                                                                    =let him do
                that to me.
         IR:   I was (1.4) just exploring whether there'd been any physical threat [or]
         IE:                                                                        [no.]
15.      IR:   or anything like that.
         IE:   no.
                 (2.4)
         IE:   it was only me that hit him.
                 (.5)
20.      IE:   he didn't hit me back.
```

The IR produces a stretch of reported speech attributed to the IE, to the effect that she had, on waking to discover the suspect engaging in intercourse with her, attempted to wake her partner by "saying don't hurt me or don't let him hurt me". The IR's particularising question in lines 1–2, "what made you think…" suggests that the IE's reasons for reaching the conclusion "he was gonna hurt [me]" are not immediately obvious. The premise of the question appears even more anomalous when we consider that the IE has already provided the information that during this time, the suspect was engaging in intercourse with her without her consent. The IR has displayed an assumption that forced penetration is somehow distinct from "hurting" someone. The IE challenges this assumption quite convincingly in line 4 stating (again) "cos he was having sex with me and I didn't want to", displaying a view diametrically opposed to the IR's. Syntactically and semantically complete, with falling intonation, the IE's turn is over, and she offers the floor back to the IR. However, an 11-second gap follows, without so much as a receipt token or hesitation marker from the IR. As well as indicating that he does not deem the IE's response to be sufficient, this failure by the IR to take the floor forces the IE to self-select. She categorically describes non-consensual sex as a form of "hurting" and in line 9 the IR displays acknowledgement of this response, before attempting to backtrack somewhat – using the hedge "just", he downplays the significance of the conflict, and attempts to justify his original question by explaining what his intention was, "I just wanted to get the way you were thinking". He indicates that he is in agreement with the IE's categorisation, "obviously that *is* hurting you" (emphasis added), and then in lines 10–15 the IE, in an overtly challenging move considering her relatively powerless position, talks over him, once more reiterating that "that *is* hurting me, I wouldn't let him do that to me" (emphasis added). She successfully completes the turn despite an attempt from the IR to reclaim the floor with further justification for his question (line 13). He attempts again in line 17, this time successfully, but still revealing the same assumption – that forced intercourse is somehow separate from "any phy̱sical threat" (line 18). The emphatic stress on "physical" further supports that this is "new" information (Brazil, 1992), somehow different from what has gone before, and functions to contrast "physical" with other types of "threat". The IE, perhaps unsurprisingly, finally acquiesces to this definition, responding in the negative in lines 19 and 23, and elaborating in lines 25–27, now supporting the IR's framing of "physical threat" as including only actions such as "hit" and apparently *not* including forced penetration of the vagina.

Another example of competing assumptions is apparent in Extract 6. The participants have been discussing the attack itself and, despite having just been told about her actions of trying to push the offender off, the IR enquires about the actions the IE took to indicate the attack was unwanted.

Extract 6

```
1.    IR:  °°right°° (1.8) and (.8) whilst all this (.5) was happening (1.3) you said
           you had your hands on his chest (.8) was there anything else that you did
           (1) that you felt (.8) woul- °dunno what I'm trying to say here° (3.8) y-
           you're saying that- you obviously reported this to the police that you
5.         didn't want this to happen.
           (1)
      IE:  ((shaking head)) ((°°unclear°°))
      IR:  okay (1) how do you think that h- th- that you portrayed that to him?
           (2.8)
10.   IE:  e:rm (3.9) °don't know° (1.6) a l- when um- a lot of people (1) take
           advantage that I wear a short skirt when I go out that I'm- (.5) I'm (.)
           easy? (1.7) but I've never (1.7) I've never given anybody the come-on.
```

According to the Sexual Offences Act (2003: s. 1(1)c), not only must the victim not consent to the penetration, but it must be established that the perpetrator did not reasonably believe that the victim consented. This is somewhat at odds with our understanding of consent as a communicative act – that its expression brings it into being, and therefore that lack of communication of consent equals lack of consent.

In Extract 6 the IR's question about the IE's resistance during the attack proves problematic for the IR to construct, as flagged by the noticeably quieter aside in line 3. The content of the aside suggests that the IR is attempting to avoid betraying an expectation of more resistance – an expectation he nevertheless does eventually betray. He changes tack, and uses a reflexive statement in lines 4–5, "you obviously reported this to the police that you didn't want this to happen" which is produced as a basis for the question that follows in line 8, "how do you think that … you portrayed that to him?" This question implies first that it would conventionally be expected for a woman in this position to give some more indication that she did not want intercourse; and second, that there are set ways of portraying an unwillingness to have intercourse (including having one's hands on his chest, as is evident from the first attempt at formulating the question in line 2, "was there anything *else*").

Of further interest is the emphatic stress on "him", suggesting that, while the IR understands the meaning of the reported action of trying to push him away, the attacker himself cannot necessarily be expected to have interpreted this in the same way. The gap, filler, and pause before the IE's non-committal reply in line 10 could be an indication that these assumptions do not correspond with her own, or that she is having trouble understanding exactly what kind of answer the IR expects. She finally gives a more detailed answer, and once again we see an IE finding it necessary to justify her behaviour in line 12, "I've never given anyone the come-on". In effect, she is forced into denying the opposite behaviour from where the sequence started. For the IE, not having given "the come-on" is evidence enough for her lack of consent. From the IR's line of questioning on the other hand, it appears that he subscribes to a viewpoint whereby the IE would be expected to take some kind of affirmative action to communicate her lack of consent – rather, as we might expect given the communicative nature of consent, that in fact we would expect its presence, not its absence, to be explicitly signalled.

Concluding remarks

The extracts discussed in this chapter have given an insight into two seemingly opposing processes. On the one hand, some interactions demonstrate victims themselves articulating events in ways that downplay their violent nature. These patterns have been described elsewhere as being the "result of the absence of a well-developed sense-making framework … for the conceptualisation and description of non-stranger rape" (Ehrlich, 2007: 135). On the other, some show women resisting the implications of these same patterns. Thus, as well as experiencing constraints imposed by the patriarchal backdrop of their complaints, they can be seen to be taking up a more agentive position, describing their experiences in terms that do not conform to what is expected of them given the interactional context and the cultural backdrop.

We have also observed a range of articulations from IRs, and these are perhaps more easily explained. We have seen interviewers sometimes mirroring victims' narratives of victimhood, such as "he penetrated me", but the data also abound with examples of interviewers mirroring or even upgrading reciprocal descriptions of rape "you had sex", or themselves introducing ideologically problematic themes, "what made you think he was gonna hurt you?"

Descriptions of sexual violence do tend to be mediated through a highly restricted set of discourses for describing non-stranger rape (see Ehrlich, 2007). We have seen how patriarchal constructions of gendered violence are manifested through discursive choices of IRs. However, what we are also seeing here is the agentive nature of the women, who seek to describe their experiences in ways which, though novel in terms of the context in which they are produced, nevertheless seem a better fit for conceptualising their experiences of sexual violence. In so doing, they challenge the status quo by introducing re-readings of their experiences which are contrary to conventional representations of rape.

Note

1 www.theguardian.com/commentisfree/2017/oct/11/acquitted-rape-accuser-lying-prosecute

References

Anderson, I. and Doherty, K. (2008) *Accounting for rape: psychology, feminism and discourse analysis in the study of sexual violence.* Abingdon: Routledge.

Atkinson, J.M. and Drew, P. (1979) *Order in court.* Basingstoke: Palgrave Macmillan.

Auburn, T. and Lea, S. (2003) "Doing cognitive distortions: a discursive psychology analysis of sex offender treatment talk", *British Journal of Social Psychology*, 42(2), pp. 281–298.
Brazil, D. (1992) "The communicative value of intonation", *Discourse analysis monograph*, 2nd ed. University of Birmingham ELR.
Burt, M. and Estep, R. (1981) "Who is victim? Definitional problems in sexual victimisation", *Victimology*, 6, pp. 15–28.
Chiang, E. and Grant, T. (2018) "Deceptive identity performance: offender moves and multiple identities in online child abuse conversations", *Applied Linguistics*, 2018, pp. 1–25.
Clark, K. (1992) "The linguistics of blame: representations of women in the Sun's reporting of crimes of sexual violence", in Cameron, D. (ed.) *The Feminist Critique of Language*. London: Routledge, pp. 183–197.
Coates, L., Bavelas, J. and Gibson, J. (1994) "Anomalous language in sexual assault trial judgments", *Discourse & Society*, 5(2), pp. 189–206.
Coates, L. and Wade, A. (2004) "Telling it like it isn't: obscuring perpetrator responsibility for violent crime", *Discourse & Society*, 15(5), pp. 499–526.
CPS, Crown Prosecution Service (2018) *Violence against women and girls report 2017–2018*, www.cps.gov.uk/sites/default/files/documents/publications/cps-vawg-report-2018.pdf.
Drew, P. and Heritage, J. (eds) (1992) *Talk at work: social interaction in institutional settings*. Cambridge: Cambridge University Press.
Ehrlich, S. (2001) *Representing rape: language and sexual consent*. London: Routledge.
Ehrlich, S. (2007) "Normative discourses and representations of coerced sex", in Cotterill, J. (ed.) *The language of sexual crime*. Basingstoke: Palgrave, pp. 126–138.
Estrich, S. (1987) *Real rape*. Cambridge, MA: Harvard University Press.
Fairclough, N. (1989) *Language and power*. Harlow: Longman.
Gavey, N. (2005) *Just sex? The cultural scaffolding of rape*. Abingdon: Routledge.
Goffman, E. (1981) *Forms of talk*. Philadelphia, PA: University of Pennsylvania Press.
Grant, T. and MacLeod, N. (2016) "Assuming identities online: linguistics applied to the policing of online paedophile activity", *Applied Linguistics*, 37(1), pp. 50–70.
Grant, T. and Spaul, K. (2015) "Felicitous consent", in L. Solan, J. Ainsworth and R. Shuy (eds) *Speaking of language and law: Conversations on the work of Peter Tiersma*. Oxford: Oxford University Press.
Gregory, J. and Lees, S. (1999) *Policing sexual assault*. London: Routledge.
Grice, P. (1975) "Logic and conversation", in Cole, P. and Morgan, J. (eds) *Syntax and semantics, 3: Speech act*. New York: Academic Press, pp. 41–58.
Haworth, K. (2013) "Audience design in the police interview: the interactional and judicial consequences of audience orientation", *Language in Society*, 42(1), pp. 45–69.
Haworth, K. (2015) "The discursive construction of evidence in police interviews: Case study of a rape suspect", *Applied Linguistics* 38(2), pp. 194–214.
Heritage, J. (1985) "Analyzing news interviews: aspects of the production of talk for an overhearing audience", in van Dijk, T. (ed.) *Handbook of discourse analysis, Vol. 3: Discourse and dialogue*. London: Academic Press, pp. 95–117.
Heydon, G. (2005) *The language of police interviewing: a critical analysis*. Basingstoke: Palgrave.
Johnson, A. (2002) "'So…?': Pragmatic implications of *so*-prefaced questions in formal police interviews", in Cotterill, J. (ed.) *Language in the legal process*. Basingstoke: Palgrave, pp. 91–110.
Jordan, J. (2004) *The word of a woman? Police, rape and belief*. Basingstoke: Palgrave.

Lea, S.J. (2007) "A discursive investigation into victim responsibility in rape", *Feminism and Psychology*, 17(4), pp. 495–514.

Lees, S. (1993) "Judicial rape", *Women's Studies International Forum*, 16(1), pp. 11–36.

MacLeod, N. (2010) *Police interviews with women reporting rape: a critical discourse analysis.* Unpublished Ph.D. thesis, Aston University, UK.

MacLeod, N. (2016) "'I thought I'd be safe there': pre-empting blame in the talk of women reporting rape", *Journal of Pragmatics*, 96, pp. 96–109.

MacLeod, N. (2019) "'Tell me in your own words…': reconciling institutional salience and witness-compatible language in police interviews with women reporting rape", in Mason, M. and Rock, F. (eds) *The discourse of police interviewing*. Chicago, IL: University of Chicago Press.

MacLeod, N. and Grant, T. (2017) "'Go on cam but dnt be dirty': linguistic levels of identity assumption in undercover online operations against child sex abusers", *Language and Law/Linguagem e direito*, 4(2), pp. 157–175.

Matoesian, G. (1993) *Reproducing rape: domination through talk in the courtroom*. Chicago, IL: University of Chicago Press.

ONS, Office for National Statistics (2018) *Sexual offences in England and Wales: year ending March 2017*, www.ons.gov.uk/peoplepopulationandcommunity/crimeandjustice/articles/sexualoffencesinenglandandwales/yearendingmarch2017/previous/v1.

Russell, D.E.H. (1975) *The Politics of Rape: The Victim's Perspective*, New York: Stein & Day.

Thornborrow, J. (2002) *Power talk: language and interaction in institutional discourse*. London: Longman.

Tiersma, P. (2007) "The language of consent in rape law", in Cotterill, J. (ed.) *The language of sexual crime*. Basingstoke: Palgrave, pp. 83–103.

Ward, C.A. (1995) *Attitudes toward rape: feminist and social psychological perspectives*. London: SAGE.

9
LANGUAGE-BASED DISCRIMINATION IN SCHOOLS

Intersections of gender and sexuality

Helen Sauntson
YORK ST JOHN UNIVERSITY, UK

Introduction

Historically, feminist struggles have been focused on challenging forms of male domination. Whilst this continues, feminist activism has increasingly incorporated broader objectives around increasing acceptance of gender and sexual diversity and challenging hetero-normative practices. Schools have been identified as places where gender variant and LGBT+-identifying young people report routinely experiencing discrimination through discursive practices in schools. They are a key site for the enactment of the linguistically mediated violence explored throughout various chapters of this book. In the UK, research over the past few years has consistently shown that homophobia, biphobia, and heterosexism are prevalent in UK schools (Bradlow et al., 2017; Sauntson, 2018). This has also been found to be the case in a range of international contexts such as Poland (Pakula et al., 2015), Australia (Nelson, 2012), the United States (Bryan, 2012), Brazil (Moita-Lopes, 2006), and South Africa (Francis and Msibi, 2011). There is much evidence to suggest that when students feel excluded from lessons because of their sexual orientation, this can have a negative impact on their school engagement and levels of attainment (Pearson et al., 2007; Bradlow et al., 2017).

However, most of this existing research does not question how gender and sexuality-based discriminatory discourse operates in differing ways for young women and men, and tends to implicitly assume that homophobia is the only manifestation of sexuality-based discrimination and is experienced in a similar way. More attention has also generally been paid to the experiences of gay men and boys (McCormack and Anderson, 2010). Given the particularly detrimental effects of bi/homophobic discourse on girls (Bradlow et al., 2017), a more nuanced analysis of the gendered aspects of sexuality-based discriminatory discourse in schools is needed. Sauntson (2019) goes some way to redressing this balance by exploring young gay and bisexual women's experiences.

Formby (2015) is also critical of school-based research which places too much emphasis on sexuality in terms of "bullying" and which consequently emphasises suffering and the portrayal of LGBT+ young people as "victims". Glazzard (2018) also notes that the casting of LGBT+ young people as victims can have a pathologising effect, which subsequently neglects the roles that wider structural forces play in reinforcing marginalised and stigmatised identities. In previous research (Sauntson, 2018), I have argued that gender and sexuality-based discrimination often does not happen through overt bullying, but operates at a more discursive level which is difficult to challenge.

To explore these issues further, this chapter examines some of the ways that language can play a role in constructions of gender and sexual identities in school contexts. It focuses on exploring linguistic representations of sexism, homophobia, and heteronormativity in extracts of classroom interaction. In a development of an earlier study which examined discursive constructions of gender and sexuality in RSE (Relationships and Sex Education) guidance documents and in focus group interviews with young women (Sundaram and Sauntson, 2015), the current chapter focuses on the analysis of spoken interactional data taken from RSE lessons in two UK secondary schools.[1] The interactional classroom data consist of transcribed recordings of RSE lessons where the topic of the lesson is expected to address issues around gender and sexuality to varying degrees. A further reason for focusing on this aspect of school experience is that, in previous research (Sauntson, 2018), in which LGBT+-identified young people were interviewed about their school experiences, RSE featured highly among the phenomena which are negatively valued by the young people.

Such negative valuations were often realised as students commenting on their experience of RSE as irrelevant and meaningless due to its exclusive focus on binary gender and heterosexuality. Even within the discourses of heterosexuality, the students perceived these to be restrictive in only focusing on physiology, pregnancy, and contraception and not on topics such as pleasure and consent. They also commented on how these discourses are seen to be particularly detrimental to girls, an issue which is explored further throughout this chapter.

My analysis mainly focuses on uncovering manifestations of the interrelated concepts of sexism, homophobia, and heteronormativity in language. A key premise of queer theory-informed approaches to any form of linguistic analysis is that "heteronormativity" is the main object of critical investigation. Heteronormativity is defined by Cameron (2005: 489) as "the system which prescribes, enjoins, rewards, and naturalises a particular kind of heterosexuality – monogamous, reproductive, and based on conventionally complementary gender roles – as the norm on which social arrangements should be based". In this definition, gender and sexuality are interrelated, meaning that sexism and homophobia are also interrelated. Cameron and Kulick (2003) assert, importantly, that linguistic analysis can focus on the critical investigation of heterosexual identities and desires as well as those that are sexually marginalised. They note that research on language and sexual minorities tends to focus on analysing linguistic manifestations of homophobia and other kinds of sexuality-based discrimination, whilst queer linguistics more broadly encompasses an analysis of discursive formations of all sexual identities, including heterosexualities. Part of this analysis involves exploring the linguistic means by which heterosexuality comes to be seen as the assumed default sexuality, whilst other sexualities are marked as "non-normative". Furthermore, it is certain kinds of heterosexualities that are privileged and this is also a concern of queer linguistics so that heteronormativity can be problematic for some heterosexual-identified women and men, as well as for LGBT+ populations. Arguably, the perpetuation of heteronormativity can be particularly problematic for some women/girls in school contexts and these are key issues which are explored throughout this chapter.

Because the analysis focuses on the discourses of both gender and sexuality, the research is also informed by elements of intersectionality theory (Crenshaw, 1989) in which language, gender, sexuality, race, age, class, nationality, and a range of other facets of "identity" intersect to produce particular identifications and linguistic practices. In fact, much gender theory beyond the discipline of linguistics holds this view of gender intersecting with other aspects of a person's identity. The concept of intersectionality, then, disrupts the notion of a singular and coherent "identity" in relation to gender and sexuality. It recognises that there is no one way to be a woman, man, gay, straight, and so on. Furthermore, intersectionality theory does not simply view other identity categories as "add-ons" to gender. Rather, as Levon (2015: 298) explains, categories not only intersect, but they mutually constitute each other. Lazar (2017) highlights that this concept of intersectionality is particularly important in contemporary language, gender, and sexuality research because it encourages researchers to view identities as plural, intersecting, and mutually constitutive, rather than as isolated categories. Levon (2015) also points out that another crucial principle of intersectionality theory is that intersecting and mutually constituted identities are dynamic in nature, that is, they emerge in specific social and interactional configurations and therefore are not stable over time or context.

Some studies cited earlier reveal important intersectional dimensions of gender- and sexuality-related violence and discrimination. For example, the 2017 Stonewall survey (Bradlow et al., 2017) of LGBT hate crime and discrimination in Britain found that young people are at greater risk with 33% of LGB young people (aged 18 to 24) and 56% of trans young people having experienced a hate crime or incident in the 12 months preceding the survey. The study also found that Black, Asian, and ethnic minority LGBT people, LGBT people who belong to non-Christian faiths, and disabled LGBT people were all more likely to have experienced gender and/or sexuality-based hate crimes or incidents.

It is this approach to intersectionality which is adopted in this chapter as a means of making sense of how people use language to mutually constitute multiple identities which include gender and sexuality. Within this approach, I deploy the specific linguistic analytical framework of critical discourse analysis (CDA) which is explained in the next section.

Data and analytical frameworks

Three "Relationships and Sex Education" lessons – RSE (each 1 hour and 10 minutes in length) were recorded and transcribed in full. Two lessons were recorded in "School A" and one in "School B". Both schools were located in the York area of the UK over a period of three months. School B is located in York itself and has an intake of predominantly white, middle-class students from the urban area of York. School A is located outside York and has a more diverse intake of students from a wider range of urban/rural locations, and ethnic and social class backgrounds. These schools were chosen because of these different locations and student populations, even though they are located in the same part of the UK. Teachers and students at the schools were all used to having observers, in the form of parents, inspectors, and researchers, and the schools as a whole had a positive attitude towards educational research being carried out. This meant that neither the teachers nor the students felt uncomfortable about having a researcher present during their lessons. Consent was gained from the students' parents, via their teacher, to use the recordings in this research. Names of all participants involved in this part of the research have been changed or removed in all transcriptions.

The topics covered in the lessons are shown in Table 9.1. In School A, the two lessons were part of a series of four RSE lessons. The other topics covered were an introduction to relationships and a "summing up" lesson in which students designed a poster explaining what they had learnt about RSE and what other topics they still wanted to learn more about. This final lesson was observed and recorded but, as it yielded very little interactional data (as students were mostly working in silence), it is not included in the data-set. In School B, the recorded lesson was one in a series of three. The other two were focused on building relationships and I was not able to gain access to record them.

To analyse the data, I use some tools of CDA to investigate how the classroom is a site for the negotiation and enactment of intersectional gender and sexuality identities and power relations. The application of CDA to specific sequences of classroom dialogue can reveal how discursive features contribute to the construction and/or subversion of gender and sexuality ideologies. CDA is concerned with social injustice, power struggles, and in/equalities and with examining the role that discourse plays in constructing, reifying, and contesting these issues. This makes it a

TABLE 9.1 Data-set information

	Year/age of students	*Topic of lesson*	*Lesson duration*
School A lesson 1	Year 9 (age 13–14)	"Choices that affect your future" (delivered by class teacher)	70 minutes
School A lesson 2	Year 9 (age 13–14)	"Future goals" (delivered by class teacher)	70 minutes
School B lesson 1	Year 9 (age 13–14)	"Safer sex" (delivered by school nurse)	70 minutes

particularly relevant approach for investigating gender and sexuality in relation to language.

In Fairclough's (2001) often cited CDA framework, the analysis focuses on the realisation of three kinds of value in texts. These values, drawn from systemic functional linguistics, are *experiential*, *relational*, and *expressive*. Fairclough defines experiential values as being concerned with the content of a text, and the kind of knowledge and beliefs that are subsequently presented as an effect of a text's (selective) content. Relational values refer to social relationships and the ways in which those relationships are inscribed in the text. Finally, expressive values refer to textual enactments of particular kinds of social subjects and social identities. These values are realised through three sets of formal features in any text – vocabulary, grammar, and textual structures. In this chapter, I mainly focus on the linguistic realisation of experiential and relational values in the vocabulary of the classroom interaction data.

Various types of linguistic analysis are used, and there are various formal linguistic features which can be focused on in applying CDA, such as (but not limited to): lexical items; metaphors; evaluative language (e.g. semantic fields and adjectives); intertextual references; grammatical and syntactic structures. Fairclough (2001) offers a detailed and lengthy list of the specific linguistic features which may be examined, but the analysis in this chapter mainly focuses on the way ideologies are conveyed through *lexical* choices. More specifically, in the present study, I focus mainly on lexical items which Pakula et al. (2015) have identified as "gender triggered points".

Pakula et al.'s (2015) notion of identifying "gender triggered points" (GTPs) in classroom interaction to examine the discursive construction of gender and sexuality is based on an earlier CDA approach to analysing gender developed by Sunderland et al. (2002). In developing a CDA framework specifically designed for investigating how gender discourses manifest in language, Sunderland et al. propose that particular lexical items and phrases can function as "gender critical points" in classroom interaction in which explicit reference is made to male and female humans as a way of drawing attention to gender and making it relevant in some way to the lesson. A "gender triggered point", according to Pakula et al.'s development of this concept, happens when gender is negotiated into relevance through the spoken interaction that takes place around a particular text being used for teaching.

> Extending Sunderland et al.'s (2002) concept of the "gender critical point" to the notion of the "gender triggered point" we believe enriches the analytical apparatus by highlighting the dynamic character of classroom interaction and in particular the central role of teachers.
>
> *Pakula et al., (2015: 58)*

In other words, GTPs occur when teachers "gender" the texts they are using in the classroom. GTPs therefore do not reside in teaching materials themselves, but in interactional elaborations of them. Typical examples identified by the authors might include: gender roles being ascribed to characters or social actors; explicit linguistic instantiations of heterosexuality or heteronormativity; stereotypical or non-stereotypical representations of femininity and masculinity. In the studies by both Sunderland et al. and Pakula et al., the focus of analysis is on written textbooks used for language teaching, and the classroom interaction which takes place around the teaching of these texts. I added "sexuality" into this framework so that GTPs become GSTPs ("gender and sexuality triggered points") in the current analysis. In this chapter, I develop the concept of GTPs by proposing that they do not have to be triggered by written material (as is the focus of Pakula et al.'s work), but by any stimulus used in the classroom, including student- or teacher-initiated talk. GSTPs can occur, therefore, as soon as any participant in the interaction makes gender and/or sexuality "relevant" through the use of a particular word, phrase, or other discursive meaning-making practice. These GSTP words and phrases, then, are the focus of linguistic analysis within the CDA framework used throughout the chapter.

Analysis and findings

By focusing on GSTPs, this aspect of the analysis critically examines the ideologies which are constructed in sections of the discourse where gender and sexuality are "made relevant". Given that the subject is RSE, this does occur frequently. What is interesting for this chapter is that the predominant ideologies which are identified through critical analysis of the GSTPs are both sexist and heterosexist. Other discourses do sometimes emerge (discussed below) but these are rarer and therefore more marginal.

A first key finding is that there are in fact many tensions between the ideological assumptions regarding gender and sexuality in the interaction. For example, on the one hand, allusions are made to non-heterosexual relationships and identities by the teachers through the use of gender-neutral terms such as *partner*, as in the following example:

1. T: being put under pressure by partners boys and girls
2. not having planned or discussed it and feeling the lack
3. of control

This suggests the possibility of RSE being framed in terms of sexual diversity. But, more frequently, there are ideological assumptions made about normative gender and (hetero)sexuality which marginalise sexual diversity and function to uphold normative heterosexuality. In the example below, explicit reference is made by the teacher to "mum and dad", thus inferring that a heterosexual two-parent family structure is the expected norm:

1. T: you've got your mum and dad there and you're like
2. [singing noise] or your gran is even worse isn't it

In other examples, the teacher makes reference to "the guy" and "the girl" when discussing "relationships" in a general sense, thus reinforcing heterosexuality as the expected norm:

1. T: when we watched that "A to Z of Love and Sex" there
2. was <u>a guy</u> on there that talked about his first intimate
3. relationship was with <u>a girl</u> it was her first time

1. T: glide it out don't just pull your penis out
2. because what happens is the condom will stay inside <u>the</u>
3. <u>girl</u>

The fact that there are numerous unquestioned implied references to heterosexuality produces a normative discourse which has the effect of excluding non-heterosexual identities, relationships, and practices.

Another key finding is that restricted discourses of heterosexuality are (re)produced through the interaction as well as through the content of the lesson. This is again indicated through the occurrence of GSTPs in the interaction. In the examples above, GSTP references to "the girl" and "the guy" in their singular forms implies that a heterosexual relationship involving only two people is the assumed norm. Monogamous heterosexual relationships are ideologically afforded a high status and sexual activity which takes place within such relationships is prioritised. Other possible relationship and sexual activity options are notably absent from the discourse. This supports Motschenbacher's (2010, 2011) argument that heteronormativity is "ubiquitous" and continually thriving in everyday talk. But there is also no diversity represented *within* heterosexuality – it is almost always constructed as two-person, monogamous, and involving no physical sexual activity other than vaginal intercourse. Note how in the example below there is an implied focus on intercourse through focusing only on condom use as protection against sexually transmitted infections (STIs). This effectively precludes other forms of sexual activity (such as oral and manual sex) from the discussion and presents limited possibilities to the young people in the class. There is no discussion, for example, of how dental dams may be used to prevent STI transmission between girls engaging in oral sex.

1. T: we're going to use a condom that's the only thing the other
2. forms of contraception won't prevent an STI

Arguably, this unquestioned presentation of a hegemonic version of heterosexuality functions to marginalise any identities, relationships, and practices which sit outside of that normative discourse. And there is no scope for gender diversity within this restricted discourse of heterosexuality as it is manifested in the experientially focused GSTPs.

RSE provision in England and Wales has recently been reviewed and modified following heavy criticism in recent years, as well as the need for RSE teaching to incorporate relevant legal changes in the UK such as the Same-Sex Marriage Act (2013) and the Equality Act (2010). RSE is also scheduled to be made compulsory in all secondary schools in England from 2020. Relationships education will also be statutory in all primary schools in England from this date. However, despite the introduction of statutory provision, individual schools can still decide on their own curriculum and how they practically teach RSE as long as their plans are approved by the school's governing body. This means that, although there is government-produced guidance for teaching statutory RSE in secondary schools, there is no set curriculum for teachers to follow, resulting in a high degree of variability of interpretation of the guidance as it is put into practice in classrooms. The guidance itself contains some welcome changes, particularly the inclusion of LGBT identities and relationships. Although much has been made of this in the media at the time of writing, it is actually a very small sub-section which focuses on LGBT inclusion. Much of the rest of the guidance is very similar to the guidance which has been available to schools since 2000. When the research was conducted, it may therefore be that the absence of explicit references to LGBT inclusion in the guidance was a factor in the representations of restricted discourses of heterosexuality and heteronormativity in the lessons. The 2000 guidance and the updated 2019 version still emphasise teaching about the health risks and "dangers" of engaging in sexual activity which is another discourse which emerges in the classroom interaction analysed for this research.

In the interaction analysed, sex is constructed as risky and dangerous, even the vaginal intercourse that is presented as the primary activity taking place within heterosexual relationships. This supports findings from other studies (Allen and Carmody, 2012). In the examples cited through the rest of this section, words such as *emergency*, *dilemma*, *unwanted*, *unfortunately*, and *pressure* help to construct sex in negative terms, and always focusing on "unwanted" outcomes, such as pregnancy and the transmission of STIs. In the first example below, it is also interesting to note in line 2, an implicit gender construction of girls and women as the givers and exchangers of advice, thus placing responsibility for any negative outcomes of heterosexual activity with them.

1. T: right two things there
2. one was obviously giving advice to her mate
3. about the morning after remember we did that quick quiz
4. we did all about so we know that it's up to 72 hours
5. afterwards that the morning after pill can be used it's
6. now called the emergency contraceptive for that reason
7. because it's not just the morning after and then
8. obviously she went through that dilemma of obviously her
9. periods were late that can be caused by anything but if
10. it's coincided with her having intercourse with somebody
11. then obviously she wants to get it tested

1. T: a girl that I taught in my early teaching career who
2. mistakenly took sex okay as feeling loved and feeling wanted
3. and unfortunately she fell pregnant

These extracts echo findings presented elsewhere in this book (see Chapter 5 by Ribeiro and Bastos and Chapter 8 by MacLeod in this volume), which report that a common "message" received by girls is that they have to look after themselves – taking responsibility for problems within heterosexual relationships is women's/girls' responsibility rather than being a collaborative endeavour. In the data analysed in this chapter, the words and phrases used in the interaction indicate an implicit assumption that pregnancy is a "problem for girls" but not for boys. Similar gender discourses, which are evidently sexist in their differential treatment of girls and boys, have been found by Dobson and Ringrose (2016) in their analysis of campaigns to protect young people from sexual exploitation. Dobson and Ringrose highlight the emphasis on girls to manage their behaviour so as not to become victimised, rather than focusing on teaching boys to take responsibility for their behaviour (i.e. not engaging in any sexually exploitative behaviour). Related to this is the persistent notion that girls and women are ultimately responsible for consent in sexual relationships and encounters. If consent is not communicated effectively, it is implied that this is the responsibility of girls and women.

Cameron (2007) and Ehrlich (2001) draw attention to problems associated with framing consent as being solely about communication. They all argue that a focus on consent as communication implies that sexual violence can be avoided by communicating differently, with an implication in many legal cases that it is the victim's responsibility for communicating consent effectively and unambiguously. This is problematic first, because it places responsibility for consent on the victim (usually the woman) rather than the perpetrator and, second, because it fails to recognise the role that coercion often plays in sexual violence cases (see Chapter 8 by MacLeod in this volume).

This unequal treatment of boys and girls contributes towards the discriminatory/sexist discourses around gender which are reinforced throughout the lessons. And, again, the examples only focus on girls giving advice to each other in relation to heterosexual encounters. It seems then that restrictive binary gender discourses and normative heterosexuality are mutually constituting and, therefore, have an intersectional relationship with each other that is particularly salient in this context. These sexist and heterosexist discourses could be challenged by incorporating other kinds of advice-giving into the lesson which are available to all genders and not just implicitly directed at girls. This might include advice on coming out and expressing gender and sexual diversity as well as advice focusing on intimate relationships.

The ideological sexist gendering of heterosexual activity also occurs in relation to constructions of boys and men as always wanting sex and putting pressure on girls and young women to engage in sexual activity with them. The possibility of girls putting pressure on boys is never raised, neither is the possibility that boys may want to engage in sexual activity for positive reasons such as being in love.

This creates an ideological expectation that, within heterosexual encounters and relationships, boys will always put pressure on girls to have sex with them.

1. T: I've had girls coming to me and talking about
2. they've been with older boyfriends they feel that
3. pressure

1. T: some of the things we've just talked about
2. curiosity opportunity a real or imagined pressure you know she
3. talked about well she thought if she asked it would she would
4. he wouldn't put a condom on

Heterosexual activity is almost always discussed in relation to negative reasons for starting to engage in it, such as pressure (from partners and peers) and being under the influence of drugs and/or alcohol. Again, the possibility of sexual activity occurring because of positive reasons is notably marginalised. An emerging subtext involves giving greater agency to the adults who teach and define the subject area (in that they can decide when it is best for young people to start engaging in sexual activity), rather than bestowing agency on young people themselves.

Another key finding which emerged from the application of CDA to the data in terms of focusing on GSTPs was that "gender" was frequently conflated with biological sex especially in sequences of interaction where physicality was being discussed. GSTPs which referenced "girls", "boys", and any other gender-related lexical items were examined as evidence of this discourse. "Gender" is also constructed in binary terms and transgender and gender variance issues are ignored. For example, there were frequent references to lexical items such as "penis" (biological male) in relation to "boys" (gender). References to male genitalia were also much more prevalent than references to female genitalia. In the whole dataset, there were only three references to female genitalia – *vulva, vagina, where you put your tampon* – and one reference to *periods* as signifying biological femaleness. There were no references to the clitoris and no references to female orgasm or the idea that girls could derive any sort of physical pleasure from sexual activity. This contrasts with a total of 19 references to male genitals – 14 occurrences of *penis* and five occurrences of *semen/sperm*. The reduction of gender to biological sex, and in turn, to biological body parts as shown through this lexical analysis, entirely removes the possibility of trans and gender variant bodies from the context.

Furthermore, talk about biological body parts in relation to sex almost always occurred in relation to the negative consequences of engaging in sexual activity, such as the transmission of STIs, as illustrated in these GSTP examples (indicated through the lexical item "girl" in each case):

1. T: this is thrush so this is what a discharge would look
2. like boys the one below is what a thrush discharge would
3. look like for a girl

154 Helen Sauntson

1. T: genital warts and you can see warts on a boy's
2. penis and warts on a girl's vulval area

In examples such as these in which the teacher is discussing the negative consequences of engaging in heterosexual activity, there are more serious consequences for girls than for boys. The negative consequences include infertility, pregnancy, STIs (there are more examples discussed of girls having STIs than boys), being labelled, and having regrets. Thus, this constitutes a further gendered dimension to discursive constructions of (hetero)sexual activity.

In all of the classroom interaction observed, the talk of the students is highly restricted. Talk is dominated by the teacher in each lesson and students say very little. However, there were a small number of GSTPs when the students do raise issues around gender and sexuality which challenge normative discourses in a positive way. It is interesting to focus on these sections of interaction to examine how the teacher and other students respond and negotiate their way through such exchanges.

In the first example below, it is a student (S1) who introduces the possibility that not all young people are heterosexual. In doing so, this signals the possibility of a more inclusive discourse around sexuality. The class are being shown some statistics about the numbers of young people who report being sexually active before the age of 16. The numbers are higher for boys than for girls. In lines 6 and 8, the student suggests this difference may occur because some boys are engaging in sexual activity with each other ("they're gay").

1. T: 67 percent of young people are not sexually active before
2. the age of 16
3. S1: how does that work out it says a quarter of girls and a
4. third of boys so who are boys meant to have sex with I don't
5. get that
6. S4: they're gay
7. S1: if there's more boys
8. S3: they're gay
9. S1: all right yeah
10. T: do you get it now

This is, in fact, the only time that non-heterosexual identities were referred to in the data and so is particularly salient and "sexuality-triggering". Notably, in what follows this extract, the teacher does not take up the topic of sexual diversity but steers the dialogue back towards the risks associated with early (hetero)sexual activity.

In the next example, another student (S2) challenges the gendered notion that boys put pressure on girls to engage in sexual activity. The student objects to the way the boy in the video they have been watching is "demonised" in a way that the girl is not. The student raises an important critical point about gender here – boys are repeatedly constructed as coercive and their reasons for wanting to engage girls in sex is to do with power and dominance, rather than any positive feelings such as love. This is arguably another discriminatory discourse constructed around boys and heterosexual relationships.

1. S2: don't you think they were being like a bit unfair
2. on that video thing like that group of kids that like
3. talked about it like they were saying like the guy the
4. guy should do it but it should be the girl as well they
5. were being really like thought about the guy but it
6. should be the girl as well
7. T: oh absolutely yeah you have a responsibility that it's
8. two to tango as they used to say
9. S2: yeah
10. T: right yeah you have an ultimate it doesn't matter what
11. relationship or stage in the relationship
12. S2: like they were always talking about the guys
13. being the ones to form the relationship they weren't
14. talking about girls
15. T: yeah you're right

Again, the teacher is supportive of the challenge (lines 7 and 15) to the gender discourse previously constructed during the lesson, but does not pursue the topic any further, thus closing down the possibility of the class continuing to explore a more inclusive and diverse discourse around gender and sexuality.

All of these contributions by students to the interaction raise important issues. They show a great deal of awareness on the part of the students and perhaps a desire to know and understand more about these issues. The examples show that students are aware of same-sex relationships, gender and power issues, and the possibility of manipulation and coercion into sexual activity. But these issues are not explored much beyond the sections of interaction in which they are initiated by the students. These, I argue, are lost opportunities for educating the students about gender and sexuality in ways which are framed by pro-diversity and inclusive approaches.

Discussion

The analysis presented in this chapter shows how linguistic choices in the data work as a form of social practice which can include and exclude certain gender and sexual identities in classroom settings. It highlights how important it is for educational practitioners to think carefully and critically about how language use in lessons may exclude certain groups and may discourage thinking about diversity. These findings are particularly timely given the recent protests which took place in Birmingham against the revised RSE guidance for England which now includes a section on positively teaching about LGBT+ relationships and identities.[2] The protests suggest that although there is support for the new guidance, including its section on LGBT+ identities, there are still groups in society who are opposed to teaching about this dimension of equality. Given these conflicting reactions to changes in RSE, it is particularly important that the language used in the RSE guidance is as positive and inclusive as possible – this chapter has shown that more can still be done to make the language of the guidance more effective in terms of advancing gender and sexuality equality in schools.

There are a number of discriminatory discourses of gender and sexuality that emerge from the analysis presented in this chapter. First, a discourse of gender emerges that presents differential values for girls and boys which are usually negative and potentially harmful to both. Girls are responsible for their own behaviour and are more heavily judged (negatively) for their sexual behaviour. It is discursively implied that girls have a greater responsibility for safer sex than boys. Girls are also discursively constructed as having less sexual agency than boys. In fact, the only agency they are afforded is to do with ensuring that any sex that takes places is "safe". Unlike boys, girls have no agency in terms of initiating sexual activity or relationships. Boys, on the other hand, are discursively constructed as predatory (putting pressure on) and always "ready for sex". In these discursive formations, gender itself is presented as binary, static, and conflated with biological sex. These inequities emphasise the importance of including a gender dimension to research on language and sexuality in schools.

Second, sex itself emerges as a practice that is risky, dangerous, and something to be avoided and "delayed". Sex often has "unwanted" outcomes and, in all of the lessons observed, there are no explicit mentions of any positive outcomes of sex. Boys are more active in terms of initiating sexual activity, whereas girls are presented as reflecting and talking about it, often in negative terms (indicated through words occurring in GSTPs such as *worry, pressure, concern, dilemma*, and so on). Sex is presented as happening more often for negative, rather than positive, reasons such as being drunk, peer pressure, and as a result of pressure from partners.

The student-initiated interaction in the lessons observed indicates a potential mismatch between what is taught in RSE and what students actually want to know. This supports the work of Hilton (2007) who notes a well-established gap between the content of RSE delivered in schools and what young people want to know. There are significant absences revealed through the analysis. In the GSTPs, there are, for example, hardly any references to sexual and gender diversity, coercion and consent, gender issues, and positive aspects of sexual relationships such as love and pleasure.

Finally, the main focus of all of the classes is on heterosexual reproduction and there is a continual reinforcement of heteronormativity. There is often an implicit, taken-for-granted assumption of heterosexuality, including in families as well as in the future sexual orientation of the students themselves. Furthermore, heterosexuality itself is represented in a very restricted way. It is constructed as always monogamous and, in terms of sexual activity, enacted through vaginal intercourse only. Other possibilities for heterosexual desire, activity, and identity are absent. This supports Allen and Carmody's (2012) argument that there is a need for an extended "discourse of erotics" in RSE which acknowledges different forms of desire (and pleasure). This would not only be beneficial to LGBT+ students and teachers, but also to heterosexual-identifying individuals. Furthermore, the intersectional lens enables us to see how restrictive binary gender discourses and restrictive discourses of normative heterosexuality are mutually constituting. I would therefore add that an intersectional approach to gender and sexuality diversity would also enhance RSE provision in schools and would help to challenge discrimination and promote inclusion.

Notes

1 Some of these data also appear in Sauntson (2018).
2 See, for example, www.thetimes.co.uk/article/mayor-andy-street-demands-stop-to-birmingham-protests-over-gay-rights-lessons-xhr58bm9c and www.dailymail.co.uk/news/article-6854329/Dozens-parents-children-protest-outside-second-Birmingham-primary-school.html

References

Allen, L. and Carmody, M. (2012) "'Pleasure has no passport': re-visiting the potential of pleasure in sexuality education", *Sex Education*, 12(4), pp. 455–468.

Bradlow, J., Bartram, F., Guasp, A. and Jadva, V. (2017) *School report: the experiences of lesbian, gay, bi and trans young people in Britain's schools in 2017*. London: Stonewall.

Brook (2013) *Brook and FPA briefing on sex and relationships education*. At: www.fpa.org.uk/sites/default/files/sre-briefing-brook-fpa-september-2013.pdf

Bryan, J. (2012) *From the dress-up corner to the senior prom*. Plymouth: Rowman and Littlefield.

Cameron, D. (2005) "Language, gender and sexuality: Current issues and new directions", *Applied Linguistics* 26 (4): 482–502.

Cameron, D. (2007) *The myth of Mars and Venus: Do men and women really speak different languages?* Oxford: Oxford University Press.

Cameron, D. and Kulick, D. (2003) *Language and sexuality*. Cambridge: Cambridge University Press.

Crenshaw, K. (1989) "Demarginalizing the intersection of race and sex: a black feminist critique of antidiscrimination doctrine, feminist theory and antiracist politics", *University of Chicago Legal Forum*, 1, Article 8.

Dobson, A. and Ringrose, J. (2016) "Sext education: pedagogies of sex, gender and shame in the schoolyards of Tagged and Exposed", *Sex Education*, 16(1), pp. 8–21.

European Union Agency for Fundamental Rights (FRA) (2013) *European Union lesbian, gay, bisexual and transgender survey*. Vienna: FRA.

Fairclough, N. (2001) *Language and power*, 2nd ed. London: Longman.

Formby, E. (2015) "Limitations of focussing on homophobic, biphobic and transphobic 'bullying' to understand and address LGBT young people's experiences within and beyond school", *Sex Education*, 15(6), pp. 626–640.

Francis, D. and Msibi, T. (2011) "Teaching about heterosexism: challenging homophobia in South Africa", *Journal of LGBT Youth*, 8(2), pp. 157–173.

Glazzard, J. (2018) LGBT+ inclusion in schools. *BERA blog*. At: www.bera.ac.uk/blog/lgbt-inclusion-in-schools (accessed 27 September 2018).

Hilton, G. (2007) "Listening to the boys again: an exploration of what boys want to learn in sex education classes and how they want to be taught", *Sex Education*, 7(2), pp. 161–174.

Lazar, M. (2017) "Sociolinguistics of gender/sexual stereotyping: a transnational perspective", *Gender and Language*, 11(4), pp. 575–585.

Levon, E. (2015) "Integrating intersectionality in language, gender, and sexuality research", *Language and Linguistics Compass*, 9(7), pp. 295–308.

McCormack, M. and Anderson, E. (2010) "'It's just not acceptable any more': the erosion of homophobia and the softening of masculinity at an English sixth form", *Sociology*, 44(5), pp. 843–859.

Moita-Lopes, L.P. (2006) "Storytelling as action: constructing masculinities in a school context", *Pedagogy, Culture and Society*, 11(1), pp. 31–47.

Motschenbacher, H. (2011) "Taking queer linguistics further: sociolinguistics and critical heteronormativity research", *International Journal of the Sociology of Language*, 212, pp. 149–179.

Motschenbacher, H. (2010) *Language, gender and sexual identity: poststructuralist perspectives*. Amsterdam: John Benjamins.

Motschenbacher, H. and Stegu, M. (2013) "Queer linguistic approaches to discourse: introduction", *Discourse & Society*, 24(5), pp. 519–535.

Nelson, C. (2012) "Emerging queer epistemologies in studies of 'gay'-student discourses", *Journal of Language and Sexuality*, 1(1), pp. 79–105.

Pakula, L., Pawelczyk, J. and Sunderland, J. (2015) *Gender and sexuality in English language education: focus on Poland*. London: British Council.

Pearson, J., Muller, C. and Wilkinson, L. (2007) "Adolescent same-sex attraction and academic outcomes: the role of school attachment and engagement", *Social Problems*, 54(4), pp. 523–542.

Sauntson, H. (2018) *Language, sexuality and education*. Cambridge: Cambridge University Press.

Sauntson, H. (2019) "Challenging gender- and sexuality-based discrimination in UK schools: young women's experiences of illegitimation and resistance", in Kjaran, J. and Sauntson, H. (eds) *Schools as queer transformative spaces: global narratives on sexualities and genders in schools*. London: Routledge.

Sundaram, V. and Sauntson, H. (2015) "Discursive silences: using critical linguistic and qualitative analysis to explore the continued absence of pleasure in sex and relationships education in England", *Sex Education*, 16(3), pp. 240–254.

Sunderland, J., Cowley, M., Abdul Rahim, F., Leontzakou, C. and Shattuck, J. (2002) "From representation towards discursive practices: gender in the foreign language textbook revisited", in Litosseliti, L. and Sunderland, J. (eds) *Gender identity and discourse analysis*. Amsterdam: John Benjamins, pp. 223–255.

INDEX

#ImmodestWomen 25
#MeToo 5, 20, 79–81, 86, 87, 88
#*meu primeiro assédio* ("my first harassment") 79
#*mexeu com uma mexeu com todas* ("messing with one, messes with all") 79

abortion 10, 79
abusive partner, murder of *see R v Craig* (2011)
Action Man 62
ageing 34–56; invisibility and 36–39; and sex 36, 39, 44, 45, 50, 53–54; stereotypes 34, 36, 37, 38, 39, 49–53, 55; transgressive 36, 44, 46, 53
All in the Family (television programme) 3
Allen, L. 157
American Dialect Society 7
Anderson, I. 133
apologising 13
appearance, female: and ageing 36–39; LEGO minifigures 69–71; male intrusion and 26; Trump on 10–11; in workplace 104
Ardern, J. 95
Armstrong, S.L. et al. (1983) 57n11
Atkin, A. 66
Attenborough, F. 116, 127, 128
attention, gendered 25–29
Auburn, T. 134
Auburn, T. et al. (1995) 116

Bacon, D. 28
Barbie 62
Battered Woman Syndrome 115, 119
Baxter, J. 98, 108–109
Bell, A. 116, 122
Bennis, W. 109
Billig, M. 20
Billions (television series) 7–8
binary language 7–8, 65, 145, 152, 153, 156–157
Bing, J.M. 77, 78, 80, 81
Blasey Ford, C. 12, 14
Blommaert, J. 89
Bonderman, D. 11
Bosco, F. 80–81
Bovy, P.M. 25
Bowater, D. 37
"boys' clubs" 99–100
Brazil, sexual harassment in media 77–90; frames 78; Leão on 78, 79, 82–89; *Lei do Femicídio* (Femicide Law) 90n2; *Maria da Penha* legislation 90n2; rape 79, 84, 85; street demonstrations 79
Britain 30, 95, 146
Bucholtz, M. 7, 66
bullying 11, 80, 145
Burke, T. 90n1
Burr, R. 12

Caldas-Coulthard, C.R. 38, 45, 61, 62
Cameron, D. 5, 6, 14–15, 97, 113, 114, 145, 152
Canada *see R v Craig* (2011)

160 Index

Carmody, M. 157
Castro, J.V. de 80–81
CDA (critical discourse analysis) 146, 147–149, 153
Chira, S. 11, 12
"citizen sociolinguistics" 30
Clark, H. 95
Clinton, H. 13–14, 37
co-leadership 109
Coates, L. 134
Coates, L. et al. (1994) 133
coercive control 115, 119, 127
colour: and portrayals of grandmothers 39, 44–45, 47, 51, 52–53; toys and 45, 61–62, 66, 67, 71
Connell, R. 96
content and discursive practice 9–11
Cook, B. 47, 49
Copper, B. 38
Corrêa, S. 80, 81
Craig, J. *see R v Craig* (2011)
Craig, T.C. *see R v Craig* (2011)
Criminal Code of Canada 1985 115
critical discourse analysis *see* CDA
Crosley, S. 13
culture order 99, 109
Curzan, A. 7

date-(acquaintance) rape 5
Delegacias da Mulher (Women's Police Stations), Brazil 90n2
Deneuve, C. 79, 87
Denmark 97
discursive practice and sexism: content and topic 9–11; covert 4–5; interrupting 11–12, 25, 28, 29, 30, 100; monitoring female speech 12–15; silencing 11–12, 25–29, 39
Dobson, A. 152
Doherty, K. 133
Dominion Post (newspaper) 95

Eades, D. 126, 129n3
Eckert, P. 35, 97
Edwards, D. 122, 128
Ehrlich, S. 4, 5, 8, 9, 85, 132, 133, 137, 141, 152
Estrich, S. 132

Fairclough, N. 36, 38–39, 148
Feinstein, D. 12
Femicide Law, Brazil *see Lei do Femicídio*
Files, J.A. et al. (2017) 22, 23
Fiorina, C. 10

Formby, E. 145
Forna, A. 27
France 79–83, 86–87, 89, 90n4
Freed, A. 15
Freeman, H. 37
Fuller, J. 9

Gangsta Granny (children's book) (Walliams) 46–47, 49
Gardner, C. B. 26–27
Gender and Language (journal) 35
gender and sexuality triggered points *see* GSTPs
gender order in workplace 95–110; concept of 96–97; gender stereotypes 97–98, 105–108, 110
gender stereotypes: grandmothers and 34, 36, 37, 38, 39, 49–53, 55; harassment and 83, 88; language and 6; and leadership discourse 97–98, 105–108, 110; silencing and 11; and toys 61, 62–63, 73–74; in workplace 97–98, 105–108, 110
gender triggered points *see* GTPs
Glazzard, J. 145
"global gag rule" 10
Globe & Mail (newspaper) 24
O Globo (newspaper) 79, 85, 86–87
Goffman, E. 26, 88
Golden Globe Awards 79, 82–83, 84
Goldenberg, M. 80
Goldenberg, S. 37
Google 13, 39–40, 121
Gorsuch, N. 10
"Grand Rounds" 22–23
grandmothers 34–56; Bank of English corpus data 49–53; derogation of 54–55; image banks 39–44; and sex 36, 39, 44, 45, 50, 53–54; stereotypes 34, 36, 37, 38, 39, 49–53, 55; texts about 44–49; traditional 36, 39, 41, 43, 44, 49, 51–54; transgressive 36, 44, 46, 53
Gransnet 50, 55–56
Grant, T. 132
Grassley, C. 12
Greer, G. 36, 38–39
Gregory, J. 133
Grice, P. 136
GSTPs (gender and sexuality triggered points) 149–150, 153–154, 156
GTPs (gender triggered points) 148–149
Guardian (newspaper) 34, 37
Gudjonsson, G. 116
Gullette, M. 38
Gulliver, K. 23–24

Hamilton, H.E. 35, 38
Hansen, A. 40
Hareven, T.K. 38
Harris, K. 12
hate crimes 30, 146
Hawkins, D. 11
Heenan, D.A. 109
Heffer, C. 118
Hepworth, M. 38
heteronormativity 145–146, 150, 151, 156
Hibberd, J. 7–8
Hilton, G. 156
Huffington, A. 10, 11
Human Rights Commission Report 96
Huxford, J. 123

inclusive language 6
indexicality 66
"informalisation" 23
initiator frame 78, 81, 82
interactional sociolinguistics 98
interpreters, court 115
interrupting of female speech 11–12, 25, 28, 29, 30, 100
intersectionality theory 146
intimate partner homicide 114
invisibility 34, 36–39, 52, 55

Jackson, B. 98
James, B. 95
Jespersen, O. 11
Johnson, A. 118, 135
Johnson, C. 10
Johnstone, B. 66
Jönsson, L. 126
judicial frame 78

Karpowitz, C. 26
Kassin, S. 116
Kavanaugh, B. 10, 12, 14
Kiesling, S.F. 66
King, R. 5, 8, 9
Klobuchar, A. 12
Koller, V. 62
Kress, G. 35, 36, 40–43, 64
Kulick, D. 145

Lakoff, R. 3, 7
Language in the Workplace Project *see* LWP
Lazar, M. 146
Lea, S. 133, 134
leadership in workplace: co-leadership 109; gender stereotypes and 97–98, 105–108, 110; power relations and 101, 108

Leão, D. 78, 79, 82–89
Lees, S. 133
legal system, female victims in 131–141; interpreters 115; judicial "summing ups" 118; power relations 132, 136
LEGO minifigures 60–74; colour and gender 61–62, 66, 67, 71; functionalisation 71–72; gender stereotypes 61, 62–63, 73–74; identification 68–73; social actor framework 65–67
Lei do Femicídio (Femicide Law), Brazil 90n2
Lessing, D. 38
Levon, E. 146
lexical (morphological) forms of sexism: ageing 35, 40, 49, 50; gender and sexuality triggered points (GSTPs) 153; gender triggered points (GTPs) 148; new words and occupational terms 5–6; overt 4–5; pronominal usage 6–8; titles 8–9
LGBT+ 144–157; discrimination 144–146, 152, 155–157; hate crimes 146; heteronormativity and 145–146, 150, 151, 156; transgender language reform 8
Lillian, D. 9
Linell, P. 126
Lombardo, L.X. 77, 78, 80, 81
LWP (Language in the Workplace Project) 96, 98–99
Lyft 8

Machin, D. 36, 40
MacLeod, N. 134
Macron, B. 10
male intrusion and female speech 26, 27–28, 29
male-marked terms 5–6
Manjoo, F. 8
"manosphere" 20, 28
mansplaining, first use of term 5
Maria da Penha legislation, Brazil 90n2
Martin, J.R. 36, 45–46
Matos, M. 80
Mayer, J. 84, 85
McCain, J. 12
McConnell, M. 11–12
McConnell-Ginet, S. 35, 97
media: and *R v Craig* 114–128; sexism in 9–10, 13, 14, 113; on sexual harassment 77–90; 116, 121–127
Mendelberg, T. 26
Michaels, S. 9
Millet, C. 79
Mitchell, R. 12
Moita Lopes, L.P. 88
Le Monde (newspaper) 79, 90n4

monitoring of female speech 12–15; self-monitoring 109
Moon, A. 10
Moon, R. 67
morphological forms of sexism *see* lexical forms
Motschenbacher, H. 150
Ms. Magazine 9
multi-tasking in workplace 101–102, 109
My Granny (children's book) (Newman) 47–49

Narloch, L. 81
New York Times 8, 9, 13, 90n1, 90n4
New Zealand, gender order and workplace 95–110; "boys' clubs" 99–100; clients' sexism 102–104, 108; co-leadership 109; female appearance and 104; female ministers 95; gender stereotypes 97–98, 105–108, 110; multi-tasking 101–102, 109; "old boys' networks" 100–101, 108; Pākehā (European-based) culture order 109; power relations and 101, 108; side-lining of women 98, 104–106
Newman, N. 47–49
Nicolson, D. 114
Nicolson, H. 23
Nielsen, M.F. 97
Noh, M. et al. (2010) 114, 127

occupational terms 5–6
Ochs, E. 66
O'Donnell, R. 10
"old boys' networks" 100–101, 108
Ostermann, A.C. 88
Ottawa Citizen (newspaper) 121–122, 124–126
Ottawa Sun (newspaper) 126–127

Pakula, L. et al. (2015) 148–149
Parry, K. 98
patriarchy 28, 80, 88, 136, 141
Peirce, C.S. 66
Pereio, P.C. 81
Phillips, S. U. 19
Planned Parenthood 10
Plester, B.A. 97–98
Polanski, R. 87
police: attitude in rape cases 132, 133; and hate crimes 30; *R v Craig* (2011) 116–127
power relations: ageing and 36, 37, 38; black women and 27; culture order 109; gender order 96–97; gender respect and 19–20; leadership in workplace 101, 108; legal system 136; police 132; sexual harassment and 80, 81, 82, 86, 89; sexuality and 147, 155
prestige and occupational terms 5–6
pronominal usage 6–8

R v Craig (2011), media recontextualisations 114–127; of police interviews 116–127
racism 3, 8, 27
rape: Brazil 79, 84, 85; female speech and 28; legal system 131–141; media recontextualisation 113; new terms 5; online threats 20; police attitude 132, 133
rape-culture, first use of term 5
Rappeport, A. 10
Relationships and Sex Education *see* RSE
respect and gender 19–30; female speech and 25–29; female status and 21–25; sexual harassment and 26–27, 30
Riddell, F. 24–25
Rigg, J. 26
Ringrose, J. 152
Romaniuk, T. 13–14
Ross, T. 46–47, 49
Rousseff, D. 37
RSE (Relationships and Sex Education) 145, 149, 150–151, 155–157
Russell, D. 137

Sainsbury's 60, 63
Sauntson, H. 145
Saville-Smith, K. 95
Sayers, J. 97–98
scarcity and occupational terms 5–6
Schulz, M.R. 55
Schuman, R. 24
Sessions, J. 12
sexism, clients' in workplace 102–104, 108
sexism, first use of word 5
sexual consent 152
sexual harassment: Brazil 77–90; first use of term 5; frame analysis approach 77, 78; gender respect and 26–27, 30; social media 79; structural sexism 25
Sexual Offences Act *see* SOA
sexuality *see* LGBT+
Shear, M. 30
Shipley, J. 95
side-lining in workplace 98, 104–106
silencing of female speech 11–12, 25–29, 39
Slinkard, S. 117, 129n3
SOA (Sexual Offences Act) 131–132, 140
social actor framework 65–67
social constructionist framework 98
social realist approach 96

Index

social science frame 78, 80, 81, 82, 87
Southern Illinois University 9
Spaul, K. 132
speech, female: interrupting 11–12, 25, 28, 29, 30, 100; male intrusion and 26, 27–28, 29; monitoring 12–15; self-monitoring 109; silencing 11–12, 25–29, 39
"Spencer paradox" 81
Stark, E. 129n5
status 5–6, 8–9, 21–25
Stokoe, E. 128
Stonewall survey 146
street remarks 26–28
Sunday Republican (newspaper) 8–9
Sunderland, J. et al. (2002) 148–149

Tahmaseb-McConatha, J. 37
Teo, P. 123
Thompson, M. 37
Tiersma, P. 132–133
Times Colonist (newspaper) 122–123
Time's Up 80
titles and status 8–9, 21–25
topic and discursive practice 9–11
toys and gender 61–63; colour 45, 61–62, 66, 67, 71; LEGO minifigures 60–74
transgender language reform 8
Trump, D. 10–11, 38

Uber 8, 11
urban spaces 26–27
US, social upheaval 3
US Supreme Court 10, 14

Valentine, J. 9
van Leeuwen, T. 35, 36, 40–45, 61, 62, 64, 66–67, 68

Veja (magazine) 84, 86–87
Vera-Gray, F. 27–28
victim frame 78, 80, 81
violence against women 113–128; consent and 152; intersectional 146; judicial "summing ups" 118; language and 6; legal system 131–141; *pseudo-direct speech* or *pseudo-quotes* 122–123; *R v Craig* (2011) 114–127; recontextualisations by media 116–127; sexual harassment and 79, 80, 85, 89; street remarks and 27; *see also* rape
Violence Against Women Act 10

Wade, A. 134
Walliams, D. 46–47, 49
Walsh, D. 37
Ward, C. A. 137
Warren, E. 11–12
Washington Post (newspaper) 90n4
Watts, J. 37
West, C. 29
White, P. R. R. 36, 45, 46
Women's Police Stations, Brazil *see* Delegacias da Mulher
words, new 5–6
workplace: "boys' clubs" 99–100; clients' sexism 102–104, 108; co-leadership 109; female appearance and 104; gender order 95–110; gender stereotypes 97–98, 105–108, 110; multi-tasking 101–102, 109; "old boys' networks" 100–101, 108; power relations and 101, 108; side-lining 98, 104–106
Wouters, C. 23

Zimman, L. 8
Zimmer, B. 8–9
Zimmerman, D. 29